Beowulf

Twayne's English Authors Series

George D. Economou, Editor

University of Oklahoma

TEAS 477

When placed in the great Sutton Hoo ship burial, this bronze stag was
fixed to the whetstone-scepter as a symbol of royal authority. The red deer (*cervus
elaphus*) has been highly prized by huntsmen since antiquity. Female red deer
are hinds, the males harts (from Anglo-Saxon *heorot*, the name of Hrothgar's
royal hall in *Beowulf* and *Widsith*). Adult males, also called stags, may stand five feet
high at the shoulder and weigh as much as 550 pounds.
Reproduced by courtesy of the Trustees of the British Museum.

Beowulf

By George Clark

Queen's University

Twayne Publishers
A Division of G. K. Hall & Co. • *Boston*

Beowulf
George Clark

Copyright 1990 by G. K. Hall & Co.
All rights reserved.
Published by Twayne Publishers
A division of G. K. Hall & Co.
70 Lincoln Street
Boston, Massachusetts 02111

Copyediting supervised by Barbara Sutton.
Book production by Janet Z. Reynolds.
Book design by Barbara Anderson.
Typeset in Garamond by Huron Valley Graphics, Inc. Ann Arbor, Michigan.

Printed on permanent/durable acid-free paper
and bound in the United States of America.

First published 1990.
10 9 8 7 6 5 4

Library of Congress Cataloging-in-Publication Data

Clark, George, 1932–
    Beowulf / by George Clark.
        p.   cm.—(Twayne's English authors series ; TEAS 477)
    Includes bibliographical references.
    ISBN 0-8057-6996-X (alk. paper)
    1. Beowulf.   2. Epic poetry, English (Old)—History and criticism.
I. Title.   II. Series.
PR1585.C55   1990
829′.3—dc20   89-77340
                                                              CIP

For Elizabeth

Contents

About the Author

George Clark received his M.A. from the University of California at Berkeley in 1958 and his Ph.D. from Harvard University in 1961. From 1961 to 1963 he taught at the University of Wisconsin (Madison); from 1963 to 1965 at the University of Texas (Austin); and since 1965 he has taught at Queen's University in Kingston, Ontario, focusing on the history of the English language, Anglo-Saxon and *Beowulf*, Old Norse including the Icelandic sagas and the Eddas, Chaucer, the Scottish Chaucerians, and Shakespeare.

Clark studied Icelandic in Reykjavík during the summers from 1968 to 1972 and was Professor E. O. G. Turville-Petre's tutee in Old Norse poetry in 1972–73. He has published articles on *Beowulf*, *The Battle of Maldon*, *Njáls Saga*, the alliterative *Morte Arthur*, Chaucer, Robert Henryson, and William Golding.

Clark is married to Elizabeth Greene; he has two sons, Erec, a dancer, and Alan, who asks hard questions like "Why does luke mean half in lukewarm?"

Preface

Beowulf may be called a heroic and philosophical epic in a traditional verse form, an exploration of the possibilities of meaning in a finite life bounded by darkness. The poem's powerful story gives its vision of the human condition substance and authority; a reading of *Beowulf* must come to terms with its story and its stories, its characters and their world. This is a royalist's poem, its great hero is born a prince and dies a king still serving the memory of the beloved king of his youth. The characters of the poem are royals, courtiers, court poets, and aristocratic warriors; the poem's vision of history is dynastic and cyclical; royal families prove as mortal as royals themselves. The poem's brilliant world is seen as transitory from the first and at the last the poem proposes in a world of uncertainty a value not subject to the injury of time, the fame that survives the hero.

Beowulf is a traditional poem, an oft-told tale quite possibly preserved as a legacy of their past by an Anglo-Saxon dynasty (perhaps the East Anglian) with real or fabled connections to some of the poem's chief peoples and figures. Traditionally composed and transmitted stories continually renew themselves, are reshaped to find their place in a new cultural and political setting, hence *Beowulf* does not reflect the society and the hopes of fifth- and sixth-century Denmark and southern Sweden or the world of earliest Anglo-Saxon England. The poem represents a world like the one its earlier audiences knew and reflects the ideals or aspirations as well as the realities of the world it springs from. As we have it, *Beowulf* expresses the ideals and depicts the institutions of a secular society that is heroic, hierarchical, and royalist. But though both traditional and secular, *Beowulf* may be regarded as a philosophical poem deeply engaged in the contemplation of the existential questions. The poem does not passively reflect but tests both the values of the heroic world and those of Christianity—in the form of a monotheism that assumes God's universal power and benevolence—against a vision of the reality of the human condition.

The poem's story pits its hero against three monstrous enemies in three battles, but places the first two monsters and battles in part I, the last in part II of an asymmetrical structure. The monsters differ from each

other and the battles and their narration vary continuously and significantly. The differences between the three great battles and the three great
enemies are central to the poem's artistry and its significance.

In style and spirit, the first great battle and part I generally are
expansive and optimistic, buoyant and suggestive of the high spirits of
Beowulf's youth. The expansiveness and buoyancy of part I give way to
concentration and melancholy in part II and a striking stylistic difference marks this change. In part I the poem's digressions reach out to
capture narrative matter from what seems the whole of the ancient
Germanic world; at the same time the poem furnishes its present world
with a domestic, social, and political reality, a sense of place and things
from swords and ships to beds and pillows. In part II the digressions
focus on the wars of the Swedes and the Geats; the past holds the
present and the foreseen future captive. The social and domestic reality
of part I survives in a few remembered images; the main action of the
narrative present in part II is set in a wasteland dominated by a great
grave mound or barrow; the principle actions of the narrative past take
place on desolated fields of battle, in unredeemed nature, the image of
chaos.

The poem's language suggests that Grendel represents evil according
to a Christian view of reality and suggests that Beowulf is part of God's
benevolent plan encompassing mankind and enveloping Grendel in
irony. But even in part I no explicit signals encourage the audience to
identify Grendel's mother as a symbol of evil. She comes as a surprise
and her story remains full of suspense until and even beyond the hero's
victory. Though beaten, Grendel's mother challenges the optimistic
interpretation her son's destruction seemed to establish for the action.

The last enemy, the most completely characterized of all, is nowhere
described as evil or traced back to Cain or Lucifer or otherwise explicitly
drawn into a Christian framework of understanding. The poem leaves
the dragon's origins, unlike Grendel's, out of the narrator's and the
audience's vision. Even the wise Hrothgar did not know Grendel's
origins and could not explain the cause of the monster's coming, but
these mysteries were transparent to the audience. Beowulf correctly
deduces what the narrator reports, and what the audience knows of the
dragon and the beginning of his raids. For us, as for Beowulf, the
dragon remains inexplicable.

The poem begins with Grendel in whom the old Germanic world's
vision of archetypal disorder joins with a Christian myth of evil. But
the representation of Grendel's mother and of the dragon insistently

challenges and finally rebuts the interpretation of the poem Grendel seemed to create. The movement of the story through the three great battles leads from a clear moral vision in which evil is definable and can be seen to have a unique and explicable origin and a subordinate place in a well-ordered world to a sense of darkness, obscurity, and doubt. Grendel's mother surprises the audience by challenging its view of Grendel's meaning and thus of a well-ordered world. The dragon terrifies. His coming means Beowulf's death and the devastation of the Geats, and it raises the problem of evil in all its intractability. The dragon has no separate origin or explanation; he acts according to his own nature, which is not separable from nature. What we might like to call evil and attribute to a special origin not of the Creator's doing seems in the dragon part of the eternal and inevitable nature of things.

The poem ends where it began, contemplating the death of a great hero, representing the ceremonies of his funeral, and leaving its audience with a mystery and a certainty: whatever lies beyond, the hero's fame remains behind, a monument as enduring as earth.

Queen's University   George Clark

A Note on the
Text and Translations

Unless otherwise noted I have cited the third edition (with the first and second supplements) of Fr. Klaeber's still unrivaled edition of *Beowulf* (Boston: D. C. Heath, 1922, 1928, 1936, 1941, 1950) by line numbers in the text. The translations are my own unless otherwise noted. Assertions about the meanings of the words rest on Joseph Bosworth, *An Anglo-Saxon Dictionary*, edited and enlarged by T. Northcote Toller (Oxford: Clarendon Press, 1882–98); T. Northcote Toller, *An Anglo-Saxon Dictionary: Supplement* (Oxford: Clarendon Press, 1921); and the fourth edition of John R. Clark Hall, *A Concise Anglo-Saxon Dictionary*, with a supplement by Herbert D. Merritt (Cambridge: Cambridge University Press, 1960).

Acknowledgments

This work, much delayed and much changed in form from my original design, was begun in the academic year 1972–73 during a sabbatical made possible by a fellowship granted by the American Council of Learned Societies. A travel grant from the same generous foundation and a subsistance grant from the Canada Council in 1971 helped me to complete a study of the saga analogues to *Beowulf,* read to the First International Saga Conference in 1971 and published in the *Proceedings of the First International Saga Conference* (London: Viking Society, 1973).

I have discussed life, love, literature, and *Beowulf* with my wife and colleague, Elizabeth Greene, for almost twenty years; her view of the poem has deeply influenced mine and her comments on successive drafts of the present manuscript have kept me writing.

I owe many debts of gratitude, some old, some new, to my teachers, students, friends, and colleagues in medieval studies.

My mentors at Berkeley were Professors James R. Caldwell, Joseph Fontenrose, Arthur Hutson, Assar Janzén, Charles W. Jones, and Alain Renoir; at Harvard, Professors William Alfred, Albert B. Friedman, Karl-Ivar Hildeman, F. P. Magoun, Jr., Louis Solano, and B. J. Whiting.

I had the good luck to be a student in a great age of graduate teaching. The questions, curiosity, challenges, and companionship of students in Anglo-Saxon, Old Norse, and Chaucer classes have enlarged my view of medieval literature and literary studies. My thesis students—Donna Barne, Susan Blackall, Virginia Evans, Janis Peterson, William Schipper, Alexandra Smith, Kelvin Smith, Anna Smol, and James Weldon—led me into books I might have missed without them.

In the years since I began studying Anglo-Saxon, the books, articles, conference papers, and conversations with friends and colleagues have renewed my spirits and work. Frederic Amory, Larry D. Benson, Jess. B. Bessinger, Paul Bibire, F. G. Cassidy, Howell D. Chickering, George Economou, Roberta Frank, R. D. Fulk, Walter Goffart, Elizabeth Greene, Stanley B. Greenfield, Edward B. Irving, Robert Kellogg, Simon Keynes, Michael Lapidge, Bruce Mitchell, Richard N. Ringler, Fred C. Robinson, T. A. Shippey, and Rudolph Willard come especially to mind, and I remember them gratefully.

Chronologies

Major Persons and Events of the Poem

The dates given in this first section are legendary, conjectural, or even fictitious except for the one marked with an asterisk which, though perhaps a few years off either way, my be regarded as historical.[1]

495   Beowulf born to Ecgtheow and a daughter of the Geatish king, Hrethel.

502   Beowulf sent, at seven, to Hrethel's court for his upbringing.

503   Hrethel dies of sorrow because his second son, Hæthcyn, killed his first-born son, Herebeald. Hæthcyn succeeds to the Geatish throne. Hrothgar, the Danish king, builds a great hall, Heorot, and Grendel begins his nightly raids on it.

503   The sons of the Swedish king, Ongentheow, raid the Geats.

510   Hæthcyn and his brother Hygelac raid the Swedes. King Ongentheow and Hæthcyn die in battle. The victorious Hygelac succeeds to the Geatish throne.

511–514   Beowulf's youthful adventures, first (?) the seafaring contest with Breca and battle with some sea-monsters, and later (?) battles with giants and sea-monsters.

515   Beowulf kills Grendel and Grendel's mother, thus relieving Hrothgar and the Danes of an affliction that had gone on for twelve years.

524*   Hygelac is killed while raiding in the Netherlands (apparently a datable event). According to the poem, Hygelac is avenged by Beowulf, who becomes the Geatish regent during the minority of Heardred, Hygelac's son.

525   Hrothgar dies; his nephew Hrothwulf (rather than a son of Hrothgar) succeeds to the Danish throne.

532   Ohthere, the Swedish king, dies; his brother Onela succeeds him. Ohthere's sons, Onela's nephews, seek refuge with the Geats. Onela attacks the Geats and kills his nephew Eanmund and the Geatish king, Heardred. Beowulf becomes king of the Geats.

535   Beowulf assists Ohthere's surviving son, Eadgils, to invade Sweden; Onela killed, Eadgils succeeds him.

582   Beowulf dies in battle with the fiery dragon after ruling for fifty years (perhaps meaning only "for a long time").

The Poem

700–800?   The poem, in something like its present form, first committed to writing, probably after a long circulation in oral tradition.

ca. 1000   Our unique Anglo-Saxon text of the poem copied from an older manuscript now lost.

1563   Lawrence Nowell acquires the only copy of the poem.

1705   The poem first catalogued and described (inaccurately) by Humfrey Wanley.

1807   Excerpts from the poem first printed and translated (very inaccurately) by Sharon Turner.

1815   First edition of the poem, with Latin translation, introduction, and indexes, published in Copenhagen by Thorkelin. Text and translation very inaccurate.

1820   First translation of the poem into a modern language (in Danish ballad-meter, by Grundtvig).

1833,
1835–1837   First and second editions of Kemble's edition and English translation of the poem, the first modern, scholarly text of *Beowulf*.

Chapter One
Beowulf to Our Time

Recovering the Text

Beowulf is a once-lost poem rediscovered and deciphered by a series of modern researchers. In Chaucer's lifetime no one could have read *Beowulf;* in Shakespeare's lifetime a handful of learned antiquaries could read Anglo-Saxon prose, but the greatest of them could not comprehend *Beowulf,* the most important text preserved in the language. When T. S. Eliot published *The Waste Land, Beowulf* was the nearly exclusive property of those who studied English literature at an elite university, a text read in pursuit of an honors degree at Oxford or Cambridge or a graduate degree at Harvard or Yale. Fr. Klaeber published the still definitive students'—and scholars'—edition of the poem in 1922, the year of *The Waste Land* and of James Joyce's *Ulysses.* But as the twenty-first century approaches, *Beowulf* has become a part of the current tradition of English literature, a work better known than any of Chaucer's poems and one known, like *Hamlet,* to many persons who have not read the text. *Beowulf* is an anomaly in English literature, an ancient work without a long reading history. Chaucer's poetry has been known and deeply loved by every generation of English poets down to the present, but *Beowulf* as an acknowledged, read, and studied work of English literature is hardly older than Conrad's *Lord Jim.*

Although *Beowulf* did not begin to reach a wide literary audience until after World War I, the poem has been increasingly recognized as a great literary masterpiece and as an extraordinarily powerful story. Since the end of World War II, *Beowulf* has become an influence on modern literature and even a kind of cult book. A popular modern writer, John Gardner, published a philosophical novel retelling the story from Grendel's point of view. The poem has also inspired other novels, various comic books, a musical, and a stage play. The poem may have influenced both William Golding and Ingmar Bergman.[1] *Beowulf* has an immediate and direct appeal to our age. The late eighteenth and nineteenth centuries rediscovered the poem and began to recognize its greatness, but found it somehow uncomfortable: neither the form nor the matter of *Beowulf* suited the aesthetic and moral tastes of the Enlightenment or of the Victorian period.

A few uncertain clues hint that *Beowulf* did have an appreciative audience in the Anglo-Saxon period: around the year 1000,[2] two monastic scribes set out to produce a new copy of the poem, which meant that a significant investment, in human and material terms, was committed to the task of duplicating a secular poem. A number of Anglo-Saxon charters refer to places known as "Grendel's mere"[3] (or mire or stream), one of the *Blickling Homilies* (a collection of sermons usually dated about 1000) describes hell in terms that may be borrowed from the poem's description of Grendel's mere,[4] and a man named Biuuulf appears in an eighth-century list of Northumbrian monks.[5] These scraps of evidence may attest to the poem's general circulation, and so may the frequently suggested influence of *Beowulf* on *Andreas,* a life of Saint Andrew in Anglo-Saxon verse, but the parallels between the two poems may arise from their joint inheritance of a traditional poetic language. In any event, *Beowulf* survived to our time in a single manuscript copy saved (slightly scorched) from the fire of 1731 that destroyed many ancient books belonging to the Cottonian Library.[6]

In the Middle English period various learned monks or clerics were able to read some Anglo-Saxon, but a poem as difficult as Beowulf probably went without readers from about 1200 until the revival of Anglo-Saxon studies that began in the sixteenth century, and may not have been read through until the early 1800s. Early Anglo-Saxonists generally neglected the poetry of the period because it seemed both difficult and not generally useful in constructing a revisionist history of the English church. Daniel G. Calder claims that "early Renaissance interest in matters Anglo-Saxon was in part antiquarian, but mainly politico-religious. The sermons of Ælfric and the *Anglo-Saxon Chronicle* became weapons in the successive battles fought during the century of Protestant reformation."[7] An interest in local history led some antiquarians to the oldest surviving records and their language. Legal history and a search for the original laws and constitution of England drew still others into the field, and some scholars like Laurence Nowell were motivated by an unbiased love of historical truth. Whether led by bias or curiosity, the early scholars chiefly studied the prose texts, the chronicles, the laws, other legal documents, such as wills, charters, and collections of sermons.

After the Anglo-Saxon age, the manuscript containing the only copy of *Beowulf* survived (though damaged by rainwater and bookworms) unread and unreadable in the comfortable, secure neglect of a monastic library. The Protestant Reformation endangered the manuscript but, paradoxically, also encouraged the movement that regained our knowledge of the language and restored *Beowulf* to English literature. The *Beowulf* manuscript was in the gravest danger following Henry VIII's 1535–39 dissolution of the monasteries, and we do not know how it survived to 1563. Most of the poetry of the Anglo-Saxon period and much else besides perished in a riot of looting led by the King's favorites; many ancient manuscripts were torn up, some to wrap fish, some for bookbinding materials. The plain and slightly undersized manuscript containing *Beowulf* might have perished, but fortunately it fell into the hands of a learned antiquarian, Laurence Nowell.

Nowell (active in Anglo-Saxon studies from about 1561, disappeared after 1569) somehow acquired the *Beowulf* manuscript, wrote his name and the date 1563 at the top of the first page,[8] and possibly wrote an English definition of a word in line 4 of the poem.[9] Nowell's book, now frequently called the "Nowell codex," probably contained three texts in Anglo-Saxon prose, *Beowulf,* and all that survives of the Anglo-Saxon poem *Judith.*[10] Nowell, "the first restorer of the Saxon language,"[11] was thus the first modern owner of *Beowulf.* Nowell read very widely in Anglo-Saxon prose and collaborated with William Lambarde in producing a text and Latin translation of the Anglo-Saxon laws (*Archaionomia,* published under Lambarde's name in 1568).[12] Nowell seems to have read little of the poetry and possibly never guessed the value of the codex that now bears his name. Some years after his disappearance, his book appeared in the possession of Sir Robert Cotton (1571–1631), a collector of manuscripts, whose son (Sir Thomas) and grandson (Sir John) succeeded to the ownership of the Cottonian Library, a center for intellectuals and antiquarians for three generations.[13] Sir Robert had the Nowell codex bound together with some quite unrelated manuscripts; this composite volume is still known as Cotton Vitellius A xv, its identification in the Cottonian Library.[14]

While it was still part of the Cottonian Library, Vitellius A xv (including the Nowell codex) was examined three times. In 1628 or 1629 Cotton's librarian, Richard James, wrote a useful list of the book's contents, but his numbered entry for *Beowulf* consists of four blank lines. James could not make enough sense of the text to guess about its matter. In 1696 Thomas Smith compiled a catalog of the Cottonian collection working from James's accounts of the contents of individual books but did not list *Beowulf* among the contents of the manuscript.[15] In 1705 the first great scholar of Anglo-Saxon manuscripts, Humfrey Wanley, described the contents of the *Beowulf* book in his catalog of the surviving manuscripts containing Anglo-Saxon texts. Wanley quotes the first nineteen lines of the poem and the beginning of the first numbered section or *fitt* (that is, lines 52–73), and adds that the poem seems to report the wars a Dane of royal blood named Beowulf waged against the Swedish kings.[16] We may guess that Wanley, who had a great many manuscripts to go through, read little further than line 73 at the beginning of the poem, and then turned toward the end where the name Beowulf and lines referring to the wars of the Swedes and the Geats caught his eye. Even at that, Wanley's comprehension of what he read was imperfect.

Despite the inaccuracy of Wanley's admitted guess at the narrative matter of *Beowulf,* his catalog alerted philologists and antiquarians in Britain and Europe to the poem's existence. The next steps in the recovery of the poem came slowly. In 1805 Sharon Turner published a broad survey of the Anglo-Saxon period that includes a number of illustrative citations (and very inaccurate translations) from the text of *Beowulf.*[17] The second (1807) and third (1820) editions revise and enlarge the selections from the poem. The description of *Beowulf* in Wanley's catalog attracted the attention of Jacob Langebek, a Danish antiquarian, who in 1772 cited Wanley's description of the poem and wondered that no English scholar had edited a source so valuable for the study of Danish history and English poetry.[18] Apparently Langebek did not know that the Cottonian collection had been transferred to the British Museum. In 1786 Grímur Jónsson Thorkelin, a native Icelander (and, therefore, a Danish subject) received a royal grant for research in England, Scotland, and Ireland. Two months into his work at the British Museum, Thorkelin had the only surviving copy of *Beowulf* in his hands. His notebook entry for the manuscript refers to Wanley's catalog, but we cannot be sure whether Langebek's remarks inspired Thorkelin's search. At some point, Thorkelin had a professional copyist transcribe *Beowulf;* after studying the transcript, he recopied the poem himself.[19]

Following his return to Denmark in 1791, Thorkelin prepared an edition and Latin translation of *Beowulf* that was tragically destroyed in the great Copenhagen fire of 1807 (started by an English naval bombardment). Thorkelin began again and published an edition and Latin translation of *Beowulf* in 1815.[20] The inadequacy of Thorkelin's Anglo-

Saxon scholarship was noticed at once. His text and translation have no value now, but his transcripts, made before the crumbling of the manuscript was far advanced, preserve hundreds of readings that otherwise would have been lost. Moreover, the appearance of his edition marked a giant step in the poem's rediscovery, since Nikolai S. F. Grundtvig, one of the leading Danish intellectuals of his day and perhaps the greatest *Beowulf* scholar of all time, began his study of the poem with his severe review of Thorkelin's edition.[21]

Wanley's catalog, Thorkelin's transcripts (lent to various others and indeed recopied), Turner's excerpts, and Thorkelin's edition and translation brought *Beowulf* into the center of Anglo-Saxon studies where the poem remains to the present day. The early students of *Beowulf* found themselves face to face with a text that combined the difficulties of ancient and contemporary literature: they inherited no critical or exegetical tradition from the poem's own time, yet they had to place the text in a distant historical context and in an archaic literary tradition that they knew very imperfectly. At the end of the eighteenth and beginning of the nineteenth centuries, *Beowulf* challenged antiquarians, philologists, and scholars to unravel its literal sense, fathom its artistic design, discover its place in literary history, and assess its merit as a work of art.

Early Appreciation and Criticism

Grundtvig considered *Beowulf* an imperfect masterpiece and identified three major faults in the poem: its mixture of history and folktale, its lack of organic unity in the main plot, and its many episodes or digressions.[22] Grundtvig's long reflections (1815 to 1861) on *Beowulf* create a dialectic of admiration and doubt: he views that faulty mixture of folklore and history as an essential part of the poet's moral vision, arguing that the poet represents the hero's struggles against Grendel and the dragon as "a continuation of the devil's and the old giants' fight against God" and that these episodes give the poem's historical elements "a higher meaning."[23] This moral vision or "higher meaning" unifies the poem when Grundtvig reflects that if there really are two parts in the great war with evil, and if those two parts are appropriately assigned to Denmark and the land of the Geats, "then the monster stories become temporary shadows, representations of that epic tale which the history of the North, seen in the light of truth, really makes, and then the poem as a whole receives a true mythical meaning."[24]

Grundtvig saw clearly that the kind of moral meaning or "higher truth"
he sometimes understood as a principle of unity in the poem required
that the dragon, like Grendel, be construed as one of the forces of
darkness or evil, yet at times Grundtvig doubted the "poetical connection"[25] between the stories of Beowulf's battles with the two trolls and
the dragon and perceived a logical difficulty in creating that link by a
symbolic interpretation: the poet had erred in "putting the dragon to
some extent in the right."[26]

Grundtvig's struggles to reconcile his ideas of artistic excellence with
his response to the poem's power led him to conclude in 1861 that
Beowulf should not be compared to classical but rather to Gothic art,
"for it is high and bold . . . although the parts by no means blend as
beautifully as in the works of the Greeks, each part in itself has far
greater worth, and the whole is far more pregnant with meaning."[27] As
a student of *Beowulf* Grundtvig has been remembered chiefly for his
scholarly contributions to the study of the poem—he first proposed
many of the emendations to the text now generally accepted, and he
first made the identifications that locate the action of the poem in the
history and legendary history of the North—but he also aimed at
achieving a literary analysis and literary evaluation of *Beowulf* taken as a
serious, and indeed a great, work of art. Grundtvig's criticism may
seem quaint in phrasing, but it goes to the heart of the problem of the
narrative and thematic unity of the poem and anticipates the major
topics of *Beowulf* criticism to the present day.

Grundtvig responded generously to *Beowulf;* he taught himself
Anglo-Saxon and reviewed Thorkelin's edition in 1815; he translated
the poem in 1820; he published his own edition in 1861; and he wrote
studies on it between these dates. In the nineteenth century no other
critic struggled so persistently with the variety of challenges that the
rediscovery of *Beowulf* posed. Grundtvig intended to see the poem
whole and steadily. The scholarship of the succeeding age was largely
expended in a useful and laudable attempt to solve the poem's minor
mysteries: to elucidate words, lines, episodes; to bring ancillary
studies—history, archaeology, folklore—to bear on the poem. Other
and now more controversial objects of later nineteenth-century scholarship were to mine the poem for survivals of Germanic paganism; to
dissect the received text into the older poems that a late poet or editor
had fitted together; and to discover a nature myth (or allegory) that
would explain the action of the poem (Grendel was variously identified
as the North Sea and as malaria).[28]

Around the turn of the century, William Paton Ker articulated the most comprehensive critical statement on *Beowulf* since Grundtvig's.[29] Ker faulted the poet's execution, not so much protesting the fusion of folktale and history as censuring the very inclusion of folktale. Grundtvig saw the poem's greatness in the poet's moral vision, while Ker praised its dignity of style. "[T]he poem is a spiritual whole the construction of which might have been more skillful. The eye saw true, but the hand made mistakes. . . . The poet's gaze was deep and wide" writes Grundtvig. Ker claims that "It is too simple. Yet the three chief episodes are well wrought and well diversified. . . . [T]he great beauty, the real value, of *Beowulf* is in its dignity of style. . . . The thing itself is cheap, the moral and the spirit of it can only be matched among the noblest authors. It is not in the operations against Grendel, but in the humanities of the more leisurely interludes, the conversation of Beowulf and Hrothgar, and such things, that the poet truly asserts his power."[30]

Tolkien and *Beowulf*: The Critical Canon

Despite Ker's brilliance, vast erudition, and popular success as a literary arbiter, his criticism of *Beowulf* did not reawaken interest in the literary study of a poem that continued to be explored chiefly for its value as a linguistic, cultural, and historical source. Since the poem was treated as a quarry rather than a work of art, its literary value was denigrated or simply ignored. In D. H. Lawrence's novel *The Rainbow* Ursula Brangwen enters a teachers' college where, after a term of euphoria, she comes to detest the meaninglessness of conventional education. Anglo-Saxon and *Beowulf* become metaphors for the aridity and emptiness of the college: "At the Anglo-Saxon lecture in the afternoon, she sat looking down, out of the window, hearing no word of Beowulf or of anything else."[31] The novel was published in 1915, so Ursula's fictional lecture predates Robert Graves's actual encounter with the poem at Oxford by about four years: "The Anglo-Saxon lecturer was candid about his subject. He said that it was of purely linguistic interest, that there was hardly a line of Anglo-Saxon extant of the slightest literary merit. I disagreed; *Beowulf* and *Judith* seemed good poems to me. Beowulf lying wrapped in a blanket among his platoon of drunken thanes . . . —all this was closer to most of us at the time than the drawing-room and deer-park atmosphere of the eighteenth century."[32]

The work of J. R. R. Tolkien, successively Rawlinson and Bosworth

Professor of Anglo-Saxon (1936–45) and Merton Professor of English
Language (1945–1959) in the University of Oxford, and author of *The
Hobbit* and *The Lord of the Rings,* marks the turning point in the history
of *Beowulf* in the modern age. His lecture to the British Academy in
1936 dramatically set a new agenda for *Beowulf* scholarship: Tolkien
proposed criticism, the interpretation and appreciation of the work as a
poem.[33] Not all *Beowulf* criticism since 1936 can be fairly described as a
footnote to Tolkien, but in 1968 R. E. Kaske remarked that Tolkien's
main contentions had won general acceptance and that his essay maps
out the general direction that comprehensive interpretation of the poem
must take.[34] In 1983 Michael Alexander's popular introduction to
Anglo-Saxon literature claimed that "Only since J. R. R. Tolkien's
1936 British Academy Lecture . . . has an intelligible general view of
the poem prevailed."[35] John Niles's book-length study observed that
when Tolkien "admitted *Beowulf* fully into the ranks of English literature with his eloquent address to the British Academy, he took the
monsters as his main point of reference. . . . Since Tolkien's address,
the monsters of *Beowulf* have come into their own."[36] In 1984 Jess
Bessinger and Robert Yeager's indispensible handbook for *Beowulf* teachers judged Tolkien's essay "perhaps the most influential modern article
on the poem."[37]

In 1936 academic criticism, as always lagging behind the literary
avant-garde, was ready for the powerful impetus of Tolkien's essay.
Tolkien, a creative artist and a scholar, spoke for both communities in
addressing the state of *Beowulf* studies and the poem's place in English
literature; he noted that students of poetry (not just students of "origins") were attending to *Beowulf* and that the dragon had inspired more
than one recent poem.[38] Tolkien also noted that Professor Archibald
Strong in 1921 had claimed that the poem is mainly of interest as a
historical source but in 1925 had translated it into verse, and that R.
W. Chambers's preface to the translation, "*Beowulf* and the Heroic
Age," was the most important single essay on the poem.[39] Though
Tolkien maintained that *Beowulf* studies were weak in criticism, he
correctly judged that the scholarly world was ready for a general critical
interpretation of the poem. The subsequent vast success of Tolkien's
literary medievalism apparently took him quite by surprise,[40] as the
influence of his critical essay almost surely did not, but the same forces
made Tolkien's interpretation of *Beowulf* and his fictions irresistible.

Tolkien's paradigmatic interpretation of the poem appears in "*Beowulf:*
The Monsters and the Critics," in appendices A, B, and C to that essay,

and in "The Homecoming of Beorhtnoth, Beorhthelm's Son," a combination of an original literary work, a verse drama, and a critical essay mainly treating the Anglo-Saxon poem *The Battle of Maldon.*[41] The "Homecoming" silently modifies the view of heroism and the hero developed in the essay of 1936, but the revisions of 1953 arise from ambivalences already present in the lecture of 1936. Tolkien's interpretation was less original than it seemed; his account of the poem was extremely selective and ultimately limiting, but his poetic gift, his rhetorical power, and his deftness in argument carried the day and his reading of *Beowulf* has entered the critical canon. Tolkien successfully defended *Beowulf* as a literary masterpiece and maintained that the poem's supposed defect—the large role assigned to the monsters—expressed a profound moral vision that establishes the poem's serious artistic merit. In a sense, Tolkien gave Grundtvig's most positive vision of the poem a rhetorically powerful and consistent expression in English.

Tolkien's critical paradigm precisely fitted the literary, moral, and political convictions of the postwar period. In the age of a New Criticism absorbed with lyric poetry, he first redefines *Beowulf* as "heroic-elegiac,"[42] "a balance, an opposition of ends and beginnings." Hence the poem's structure is "*static*" (emphasis Tolkien's), and its genre elegy rather than epic, or lyric rather than narrative.[43] Second, Tolkien maintains that the monsters in *Beowulf* are presented as God's enemies and symbolize evil though they remain mortal beings, inhabitants of the real world rather than allegorical personifications.[44] Postwar modernism was enormously sympathetic to Christian interpretations of literature and particularly those that found a Christian meaning beneath an apparently secular surface. Third, Tolkien's essay creates an extremely persuasive myth of the *Beowulf* poet that becomes central to his reading of the poem. Since the text of *Beowulf* taken literally offers little support for a specifically Christian reading, one strategy for authenticating such a reading would be to argue from authorial intention.

Tolkien gave *Beowulf* a lyric structure balancing youth and age, beginnings and endings, and a symbolic, Christian meaning in which the monsters represent the forces of evil as both pagan mythology and Christian truth would understand it. That two-part claim satisfied both the aesthetic and moral assumptions of postwar modernism but required straining the text. To re-create *Beowulf* as a static, elegiac balance and as a symbolic representation of the eternal conflict against the forces of darkness, Tolkien had to exclude Grendel's mother and assimilate the inescapable dragon to Grendel. Thus Tolkien announced his subject was primarily "the *monsters*—Grendel and the Dragon."[45] Grendel's mother spoils the lyric balance of ends and beginnings, and critical reflection on her place in the poem emphasizes its narrative. Worse still, the poet's explicit representation of Grendel's mother (and of the dragon) seems morally neutral. Her sole appearance in "Monsters" comes in a parenthetical paragraph closing Appendix A, "Grendel's Titles." Appendix A argues that the poem's vocabulary for Grendel makes him a figure and symbol of evil, but the poem's explicit description of Grendel as an enemy of God, object of God's anger, and one doomed to hell, give the monster his symbolic meaning, not his more mundane titles. In the penultimate sentence of the paragraph and appendix, Tolkien claims that "Grendel's mother is naturally described, when separately treated, in precisely similar terms." Grendel's mother thus becomes a marginalized woman. At the high point of her career, she was sitting astraddle the poem's hero drawing her broadbladed knife to finish him off, but in Tolkien's one sentence on her she becomes an appendage to her son ("when separately treated"). The claim that Grendel's mother is described "in precisely similar terms" suggests that her mundane titles (as human and as water-dwelling monster) prove her symbolic status in the poem.[46] They do not. Having marginalized Grendel's mother, Tolkien trivializes the dragon into an emblem of malice, blaming the monster for being too symbolic, for not being "dragon enough," then graciously relenting with the comment "But for *Beowulf,* the poem, that is as it should be."[47] But it is not so. The poem creates the dragon in concrete details only and in a description wonderfully free of explicit abstraction or exegesis.

Tolkien's major critical statements on *Beowulf* and on *The Battle of Maldon* gain much of their rhetorical force from a compelling myth of the poet, an evocation of the personality that must have created the work as Tolkien read it. In "Homecoming" the myth of the poet becomes an independent fiction, a verse drama juxtaposing a heroic and a wise understanding of the events of 10 August 991, the Battle of Maldon. The wise understanding is that of an old and deeply Christian follower of Byrhtnoth, the heroic that of a young poet, a minstrel's son full of epic tales and heroic notions from a bygone and even pagan past. As the two companions search for Byrhtnoth's body, their conversation recreates the events of a battle in which Byrhtnoth's pride allowed the Viking invaders combat on even terms and so brought about the defeat at Maldon. We are to guess that after Byrhtnoth's Christian burial the young poet, grown sadder and wiser, will compose the *Battle of Maldon.*

Tolkien's myth of the *Beowulf* poet also makes that artist an heir to an ancient poetic tradition who lived at a seemingly unique moment of transition from which he could contemplate both the pagan and Christian worlds and worldviews. According to Tolkien's dating of the two poems, some two hundred and fifty years separate the poets of *Beowulf* and *Maldon,* yet both occupy this "pregnant moment of poise."[48] Tolkien's *Beowulf* poet, a learned Christian antiquarian armed *"first"* with his mastery of Christian poetry and "[*s*]*econdly*" with "considerable learning" in the old poetic traditions, set out to *"write* a poem . . . unlike a minstrel's lay" (Tolkien's emphases)[49] that would capture the heroism and the despair, the nobility and the hopelessness, of that disappearing past. This poem would represent the "old dogma: despair of the event, combined with faith in the value of doomed resistance"[50] (Tolkien's essence of heroic paganism) as a Christian would understand it in that particular postpagan, premedieval moment.

Tolkien identified his model for Anglo-Saxon paganism, its mythology and its heroic ideal of perfect courage in a lost cause, as Scandinavian and Icelandic without explicitly naming texts. This common Northern mythology and ethos set gods and heroes alike in mortal conflict with the monsters, forces of "Chaos and Unreason" who were destined to win the last battle and unmake the world of men and gods.[51] The *Beowulf* poet fused this heroic doctrine with the Christian vision when he linked the monsters of his poem with giants who warred with God and their progenitor, Cain. "At this point," writes Tolkien, "new Scripture and old tradition touched and ignited"—perhaps Tolkien had particularly in mind the point at which the sound of the harp celebrating God's creation of the world set off Grendel's rage against the light.[52] Tolkien makes the monsters of *Beowulf* symbols of evil by an argument parallel to Grundtvig's. Indeed, Klaeber's review of the 1936 essay includes just one footnote that remarks that one looks in vain for Grundtvig's name in Tolkien's footnotes.[53] Moreover, Tolkien's conception of the *Beowulf* poet as a man strategically placed at the turning point of a great cultural transition, a man blessed with the power to look into a dark past and yet to see a new world, suggests Sigurður Nordal's reading of the greatest of the Old Norse Eddaic poems, *Völuspá,* an important source for Tolkien's idea of the worldview of the pagan Anglo-Saxons.[54]

Nordal, an Icelandic scholar, intellectual, and diplomat, claimed that *Völuspá* was composed in Iceland just at the time of the conversion of Iceland (by parliamentary decision), and composed by a deep-minded philosophical poet. Nordal's key to the *Völuspá* is the unique and fortunate coincidence of a poet and a historical moment: "The poet was at once a man of profound vision and a great artist, and must have lived in an age which forced him to exert all his powers in this creative effort."[55] Nordal's reconstruction of the poet's spiritual biography becomes a hermeneutical myth dramatizing the poem's meaning. When the poet composed *Völuspá* paganism was becoming less harsh, yet "Over the minds of men still hung the old pessimism, the fear of an evil, hidden fate, the conviction that all would perish."[56] Nordal called the time a "temporal crossroads" (123) and argued that at this time "exceptional men in the van of spiritual progress" could no longer "be happy at the bidding of the will."[57] The result of the Icelandic poet's struggle with his own and the age's spiritual crises was a great poem, the expression of a personal religion neither pagan nor Christian but unique.

The membrane separating Tolkien's critical and creative faculties was permeable in both directions. As John Pope acutely observed, the "Homecoming" essay manifested Tolkien's "abiding sympathy for the heroism of the little man,"[58] but that sympathy includes a rejection of the traditional hero and heroic ideal. Tolkien's major fiction like his criticism redefines heroism: the desire for honor and pursuit of fame are imperfections, the true heroism proves to be a selfless acceptance of duty in the face of the worst. Thus "Homecoming" made Byrhtnoth's followers heroic, their lord chivalric, flawed, and tragic. In Tolkien's major fiction the vast archetypal struggle against immensely powerful forces of evil depends on the moral heroism of Frodo Baggins, a hobbit, the "little man" writ large, but at last Frodo fails the moral test and yields to the temptation of power, the possibility of becoming a hero. Only a providential stroke delivers the ring of power to the fires of Mount Doom and breaks the power of evil. Frodo's faithful servant, Sam Gamgee, in temporary possession of the ring, feels the same temptation of fame and sees himself as a hero winning lasting fame: "Wild fantasies arose in his mind: and he saw Samwise the Strong, Hero of the Age, striding with a flaming sword across the darkened land, and armies flocking to his call as he marched to the overthrow of Bharad-dur."[59] The passage reveals Sam's full name (not from Samuel but Anglo-Saxon *Sam*, "half," plus "wise"). Being half-wise Sam rejects heroism and the lure of fame to do his duty and thus becomes Tolkien's hero as a "little man."

In "Homecoming" Tolkien concluded that the poet of the *Battle of*

Maldon meant to visit "*severe* criticism" upon Byrhtnoth, for the decision (prompted by his "chivalry") to allow the Viking battle on equal terms. Tolkien then asserted that Beowulf had similarly erred in fighting the dragon single-handedly, and was at fault for leaving his people undefended against their traditional enemies at his death. Tolkien's distinction between chivalry and heroism in "Homecoming" makes the heroic action one enforced by necessity and duty, the chivalric inspired by a desire for praise: "this element of pride, in the form of the desire for honor and glory, in life and after death, tends to grow, to become a chief motive, driving a man beyond the bleak heroic necessity to excess—to chivalry." Beowulf's decision to fight Grendel on even terms, without arms and armor, is, Tolkien intimates, legitimate since the hero has no obligations to the Danes and any glory he gains will also honor his nation, but Beowulf is at fault when, as an old king, he does not "rid himself of his chivalry" even though his people depend upon his survival.[60] How deeply Tolkien had modified his earlier judgment on Beowulf appears in his changing treatment of the meaning of the poem's last word, also the last on the hero, "lofgeornost" ("most eager for fame"). In "Monsters" this superlative was "the summit of the praise of the dead hero," but in "Homecoming" the word struck an "ominous note."[61]

In "Monsters" Tolkien raises a still more ominous note when he asserts that the poem was inspired by the long debate regarding the damnation or possible salvation of "heathen ancestors." Tolkien's equivocal answer claims that the poet demonstrates the value of the impulse to remember "man's struggles in the dark past,"[62] but leaves the value of the struggle itself in doubt. Tolkien seems convinced—almost, at any rate—of Hrothgar's salvation and, amid illustrations that neither Beowulf nor his people held any hope of salvation, suggests that the poet's ambiguous statement that Beowulf's soul departed to seek "either the glory that belongs (in eternity) to the just, or the judgement of God upon the just" indicates that Beowulf's soul was not condemned to "the fiery hell of punishment]"[63]

Tolkien's Legacy

Varieties of Christian Meaning   Tolkien's theses that *Beowulf* is a written poem, an artistically unified work expressing the intention of a Christian author learned both in Christian poetry and in traditional Anglo-Saxon poetics, underlie many modern studies of the poem. Later criticism has commonly adopted Tolkien's unitarianism more strictly than the master himself since he suggested that two moralizing passages (lines 181–88 and 1740–60) were interpolations, not the work of the author who shaped the whole.[64] Early in the postwar period Charles Donahue remarked that the old view of a patchwork *Beowulf*, the product of a pagan poet and Christian editors, was "generally abandoned," but a more recent dualism survived in the notion of an internal struggle of a Christian poet contending with his own pagan spirit, or with essentially pagan material he could not master. Given either dualism, Donahue observed, *Beowulf* "is still felt to lack complete integrity of tone," but considered as the work of a Christian poet reflecting on the pagan past of his own people, a poet whose "appreciation of the tragic beauty of that world sprang precisely from his Christianity," *Beowulf* "acquires a unity of tone."[65] Donahue begins with the conviction that Tolkien had shown that *Beowulf* meets the artistic criteria the New Criticism demanded and demonstrates the moral seriousness and religious depths postwar culture, especially in America, longed for. Not coincidentally, postwar criticism awarded *Beowulf* a higher place in the canon of English and indeed world literature than Tolkien claimed for it in 1936. That criticism has been able to confirm its ideas of artistic excellence and moral vision from the text of *Beowulf* is better proof of the poem's power than of the eternal validity of the artistic assumptions or finality of the moral interpretation.

Tolkien's reading of the poem makes the monsters symbolize evil, but does not make Beowulf into a Christian knight, or a symbol of the good. The *Beowulf* poet Tolkien imagined contemplated the hero and the heroic world from a deeply Christian stance that mixed respect and regret for that bygone world. Tolkien's ambivalence about the poem's hero and his world reflected and reinforced the antiheroic bias of modernist criticism. The possibility that the poem takes a disapproving view of Beowulf or of the heroic world (or both) has been a recurring theme of modern *Beowulf* criticism. An article from the early 1980s illustrates the disturbing possibilities Tolkien's essentially critical view of Beowulf and the heroic world set loose. Martin Camargo argues that the poet's didactic aim was to persuade his audience to "abhor the lingering vestiges of paganism in their hearts." His rhetorical method to achieve this aim? "By skillfully revealing the traces of Grendel in Beowulf, the poet held up to his audience a mirror in which they might view the traces of Beowulf in themselves."[66]

Although he detested overtly Christian allegorizing, Tolkien's reading of *Beowulf* was philosophically Christian and in harmony with the critical zeitgeist of the new, postwar age. Classical paganism, Tolkien claimed, led inevitably to philosophy (or anarchy) because it had evaded "the problem" by banishing the monsters from "the centre." Tolkien insisted that these "horrors" could not forever be left out of account and, worst of all, "under suspicion of being connected with the Government."[67] Thus obliquely and metaphorically Tolkien asserts that *Beowulf* addresses the problem of evil and attempts to justify God's rule ("the Government") to a Christian audience by recalling the answer Germanic paganism made to the same overwhelming question. The metaphorical veil seems slight, but *Beowulf* critics and Tolkien's literary audience have alike overlooked his nearly explicit claim that the poem and the pagan tradition it draws on anticipate *Paradise Lost.* For Tolkien the mythology of Germanic paganism met the problem of evil by allowing the monsters the dreadful victory of Ragnarök ("the doom of the gods") and awarding the honor of the battle to the defeated. Thus the pagan Germanic world made individual heroism, "naked will and courage," its answer to the problem, but the Christian poet of *Beowulf* saw that "the wages of heroism is death" even as he recognized the moral virtue of the heroic age.[68]

Despite efforts in the nineteenth and early twentieth centuries to read *Beowulf* as a pagan work to which monastic copyists had added a few Christian passages, specifically Christian views of the poem were warmly advanced before Tolkien's lecture. These readings usually idealized Beowulf. In 1912 Klaeber presented a massive body of material in support of his contention that the language and thought of *Beowulf* are essentially, not superficially, Christian; he summarizes the evidence and his conclusions in "The Christian Coloring" section of his great edition where he finds Beowulf "a truly ideal character" and concludes "We might even feel inclined to recognize features of the Christian Savior in the destroyer of hellish fiends, the warrior brave and gentle, blameless in thought and deed, the king that dies for his people. . . . It would indeed be hard to explain why the poet contented himself with a plot of mere fabulous adventures so much inferior to the splendid heroic setting, unless the narrative derived a superior dignity from suggesting the most exalted hero-life known to Christians."[69] Despite postwar modernism's general hostility to heroes, some modern scholars have followed Klaeber's rather than Tolkien's lead. Father M. B. McNamee claimed that all three of Beowulf's great fights against the poem's monsters strongly suggested the struggle of good against evil, the

process of conversion and salvation, and the life and death of Christ.[70]
That the link between Grendel and Cain makes the poem figuratively
represent the struggle against evil is, of course, Tolkien's interpretative
centerpiece, but McNamee's idealization of Beowulf as an example of
the "Christian concept of magnanimity" and his reading of Beowulf's
death as an allegory of the Crucifixion follows Klaeber rather than
Tolkien.[71]

Klaeber's research was widely accepted as having demonstrated that
Christianity permeates the language and texture of *Beowulf,* but his case
depended on recognizing allusions and parallels to the Psalms, the
liturgy, and the Gospels in the poem. Both the suggested parallels and
their implications raise many doubts. William Whallon reexamined
the evidence and urged, against Klaeber, that "the religious elements
[of *Beowulf*] are actually those of a barely reformed Germanic heathen-
ism."[72] Taken literally, the text of *Beowulf* contains no references to
Christ, the New Testament, or ordinary Christian doctrine. From the
vast store of sacred history, the poem's Christian author refers only to
(1) the creation; (2) Cain's murder of Abel and his banishment; (3) the
Flood (without Noah, the ark, or the rainbow); and probably (4) the
Last Judgment. The evidence suggests that the poet and his audience
had absorbed rather little from the constellations of story that might be
said to constitute Christianity. Dorothy Whitelock argues, in agreement with Klaeber, that the language of the poem has been reformed
by Christianity. She dismisses the text's silences with the argument
that the faith would have been taught beginning with the "major
doctrines," the Passion and the Redemption, with the Old Testament
coming later, hence the poem's seemingly sparse biblical material actually attests to the audience's Christian sophistication.[73] Kenneth Sisam,
however, adduces a variety of evidence to show that Anglo-Saxon Christians may well have learned the exciting stories of the Old Testament
before mastering the doctrines of the New Testament and suggests that
"the poet was not much concerned with Christianity and paganism."[74]

Most Christian interpretations of *Beowulf* tacitly assume that Tolkien's poet wrote the poem for Whitelock's audience. We can be sure
that Anglo-Saxon England could have assembled Whitelock's audience
whether or not the poem was composed or written for it, but we have
no evidence for an Anglo-Saxon poet like Tolkien's, indeed like Tolkien
himself, a nostalgic re-creator of lost worlds, of pastiche. Though
Whitelock accepts and illustrates Tolkien's assertion that the poet
"repaganized" the poem's language, she demonstrates that in several

surprising ways *Beowulf* reflects the social and cultural realities of Anglo-Saxon England after the conversion. Without Whitelock's sophisticated Christian audience, readings of *Beowulf* like Margaret Goldsmith's, or even R. E. Kaske's, could hardly be considered possible. Whitelock's little book may be taken as a cornerstone of the cathedral of Christian interpretation of *Beowulf* as well as an examination of the poem's cultural and historical situation.

Tolkien's second thoughts on the poem's last word made his ambivalent attitude toward Beowulf explicit and inspired a series of basically negative readings of the hero or of the culture and values he represents. This critical theme concentrates sometimes on Beowulf's possible moral failure, sometimes on the failings of heroic society. The hero appears not as a figure of Christ but as the child of an unstable social system, or as a member of a hopeless pagandom. E. G. Stanley argues strongly and disturbingly that the poet deliberately suggests that possibility of Beowulf's damnation: "Doubts of Beowulf's salvation come with each rereading of the poem: the poet meant them to come."[75] In his treatment of the poem's last word, that "lofgeornost" Tolkien regarded (though without explanation) as "ominous,"[76] Stanley tilts those doubts toward a dark conviction: he asserts that Anglo-Saxon "lofgeorn" has a meaning like "vainglorious" and adds that the dying Beowulf could think only of the gold his last victory won and the barrow that would perpetuate his honor—"avarice and vainglory" in this severe view.[77] Though Stanley seems to begin with a hint from "Homecoming," he differs with Tolkien on one important point: Stanley sees Beowulf, not Hrothgar, as the poem's ideal king. Hence his reading of the poem presents us an image of "the ideal ruler of a society held together by bonds of love and service" who may be eternally lost, a tragic and powerful idea.[78]

Stanley's argument that *Beowulf* deliberately suggests doubts about the hero's salvation, or indeed represents Beowulf as a lost soul, makes the poem a Christian tragedy and rather brilliantly supplies the hopelessness, darkness, and bleakness Tolkien so often promised.[79] Stanley's case rests on (1) a negative understanding of the poem's last word; (2) an extratextual premise that since most Christian writers had held that there is no salvation outside of the Church, the poet must have considered Beowulf lost among the other pagans; and (3) an interpretation of lines 3062–75 as indicating, in the context of the dragon fight and Beowulf's death, that an ancient curse on the dragon's treasure dooms the hero to perdition.[80] All these arguments have encountered vigorous rebuttals. First among several others, Stanley B. Greenfield challenged the philological argument that the poem's last word, "lofgeornost," must have a negative meaning and thus indicate Beowulf's moral fault. Roberta Frank cited Old Norse evidence for a positive meaning of "lofgeorn" in heroic contexts[81], and A. D. Horgan neatly turned the argument around, claiming that the poem's last word deliberately recalls Saint Paul on the way to salvation in Romans 2: 6–7: "For he will render to every man according to his works: to those who by patience in well-doing seek for glory and honor and immortality, he will give eternal life."[82] Since seeking for "glory and honor and immortality" sums up Beowulf's career reasonably well, the poem's last word might hint at the hero's salvation to a Christian audience familiar with the Latin New Testament.

The poet's supposed syllogism—(all pagans are damned, Beowulf was a pagan, therefore Beowulf . . . runs into various difficulties. Whallon's position that the poet anachronistically saw Beowulf and Hrothgar as his older contemporaries and Christians like himself[83] opposes the minor premise (Beowulf was a pagan). Against the major premise (all pagans . . .), Charles Donahue maintains that the poet's view of his characters was not shaped by the harsh attitude of continental Christianity but by the "singularly sweet, warm-hearted, and tolerant spirit of Irish Christianity" to borrow the words from Klaeber who previously hinted at this solution to the problems raised by idealizing a pagan hero.[84] In a later article, Donahue argues that the poet had meditated deeply on the "spiritual and moral life of men under the natural law" and in presenting the poem's action contrasted the "limited hope of his protagonists against the fuller Christian knowledge of his audience. . . . One might almost describe the poem as a Christian's meditation on hope as he looks back on a pre-Christian heroic age."[85] Donahue reads the poem's main action as a history of Beowulf's spiritual growth and finds that the hero dies in a state of grace of which he is unconscious. Indeed, having lain down his life for the defense of his people and having thanked God for winning the dragon's treasure for their use, Beowulf suggests the figure of Christ: "Our poet . . . liked diptychs, and he left his audience with a pair of images, Beowulf at the dragon's barrow on one side of the diptych, Jesus on Calvary on the other." The spirit and qualities Klaeber saw in early Irish Christianity also characterize Donahue's reading of Beowulf.[86]

Margaret Goldsmith develops a consistent and impressive argument that the three great fights in Beowulf allegorically represent mankind's universal battle against the sins of cupidity and pride and that the poem reveals the transience and worthlessness of earthly wealth and honor. In his fatal encounter with the dragon, Goldsmith argues, Beowulf was guilty of an excessive desire for the dragon's gold and an excessive reliance upon his own strength (rather than God's favor), but Goldsmith regards Beowulf as one of the just though an example of fallen (and pagan) mankind.[87] At first Goldsmith declines to state the destination of Beowulf's soul, but she seems rather sanguine about the hero's prospects though she declares he was not a Christ figure.[88] As she closes her study, Goldsmith finds Beowulf something of a Christ figure in his victories over Grendel and his mother and a kind of Adam in his defeat by the dragon. That end is, she insists, "melancholy . . . but by no means despairing. . . . because Adam's fatal contest with the Serpent-Dragon had a typological significance. . . . The second Adam [Christ], the divine warrior, is shadowily foreseen when the Dragon is struck down, as the Lord piercing Leviathan with his sword in the day of ultimate victory."[89] Beowulf has, at this point, nearly reached the elevated status Goldsmith initially denied him. Her conclusion that the poem's end is "melancholy" but not "despairing" implicitly rejects Tolkien's recurring judgment on the hero and his world and explicitly rejects Stanley's dark reading of Beowulf's eternal prospects. Goldsmith's interpretation of the poem as a moral allegory fits the story of Beowulf's three great battles better than any explicitly Christian reading yet proposed, but accommodates only that part of the poem. Goldsmith's argument seems enormously learned, clearly stated, fairly argued, yet implausible.

In Robert Kaske's reading of *Beowulf,* an ethical ideal summed up in the ancient word pair *sapientia et fortitudo,* "wisdom and strength," becomes the "controlling theme" of *Beowulf.*[90] The hero himself combines the two qualities in youth and age in contrast to Hrothgar whose declining strength has effectually impaired his wisdom: he cannot comprehend a solution to the problem of Grendel and vainly trusts, as Beowulf sees, that diplomacy will resolve his conflict with the hostile Heathobards.[91] Beowulf's strength and wisdom similarly contrast the undoubted strength (courage, or spirit) of his youthful king and uncle. King Hygelac proves deficient in wisdom or prudence and falls in a Viking raid on the Franks, a victim of his own folly and his enemies' warlike prowess.[92] From the pattern of contrasting deficiencies of *sapientia* or *fortitudo* in other characters (and the perversion of those qualities respectively in Grendel and the dragon), Kaske urges that Beowulf's possession of almost mutually exclusive virtues makes him an ideal king and hero. Kaske concludes that Beowulf's death in battle with the dragon does not symbolize the hero's guilt or imperfection or failure but reflects the inescapable tragedy of man's mortality, the impermanence of any human perfection.[93] Kaske often seems to be forcing the categories of *sapientia* or *fortitudo* upon recalcitrant materials, but his final view of the poem as a meditation on human transience carries more conviction than his theory.

Social Transformations of Christian Readings

Tolkien's "Homecoming" links the words "lofgeornost" and "ofermod" which in *Beowulf* and the *Battle of Maldon* respectively describe the heroic spirits (or flaws) of the poems' heroes. Tolkien examines Beorhtnoth's "ofermod," tracing that hero's fatal error back to "a defect of character . . . but a character, we may surmise, not only formed by nature, but moulded also by 'aristocratic tradition.' "[94] Though Tolkien did not make the suggestion, we might suppose that a similar tradition also formed Beowulf's character. John Leyerle grasped the opening: in his development of Tolkien's hint, Beowulf's "defect" reveals "a fatal contradiction at the core of heroic society," and the poem's criticism seems shared between a society that demanded contradictory qualities of the hero and the king, valor in the first, but prudence in the second. Thus Beowulf erred by remaining a hero even after acquiring the responsibilities of a king.[95] Like Tolkien, Leyerle identifies the prudent Hrothgar rather than the heroic Beowulf as the poem's ideal king, but Beowulf's fault in Leyerle's account seems less a personal moral failing than the expression of a tragic flaw in the heroic society itself. Leyerle seems undecided whether to take "lofgeornost" as indicating a moral fault, a sin, or a dysfunctional social ideal, but his effort to locate the poem's principle of "unity" in the "fatal contradiction" at the heart of the heroic world leaves the monsters unexplained. John Halverson seems less ambiguous in finding the origins of Beowulf's flaw or fatal error in the mistaken values of the heroic society; the hero was "molded gloriously and inflexibly by his world."[96]

Leyerle and Halverson especially see the poet examining a weakness in the heroic world from a point of view not necessarily and uniquely Christian. E. G. Stanley treats Beowulf as an individual moral agent, but indicates the poet's critical view of the heroic world in a specifically Christian context: "By the standards of asceticism the Germanic heroic ideals are ultimately insufficient. The poet depicts the ideal of secular Germanic society in such a way that it seems glorious, with the emphasis for the most part on the glory, but sometimes on the seeming."[97] David Williams sees a Christian twist in the poem's critique of Beowulf's world: the Geats are doomed "because of the inability of pagan social institutions to guarantee peace and order." This "ideological" vision includes admiration for the people of the pagan past but is "uncompromisingly Christian in perceiving the failure of the pagan society as inevitable and complete."[98] Harry Berger and Marshall Leicester take social analysis of the heroic world further and find in *Beowulf* a powerful image of the heroic society as self-destructing, caught in a series of economic and social double binds that the poem's characters can neither understand nor survive. In this view, the characters within the poem see virtuous actions (in a secular and heroic context) as requisite for social stability, but the poem represents those virtues as leading to destruction. Thus, Berger and Leicester claim, the defects of society, as the poet represents them, cannot be traced back to the ethical or moral failures of the individual: the heroic world destroys itself.[99] Clearly enough, Leyerle's idea of a "fatal contradiction" and Halvorsen's conception of individualism as a fundamental weakness of the heroic society anticipate the elaborated theory of Berger and Leicester. The validity of these social-literary critiques depends on a specific historical reality that the critics have not documented. If it existed, the heroic world did not self-destruct. Eventually conquest produced large nation-states, and larger, more destructive wars that have finally impressed upon most of us the necessity of an end to wars. The poem sees an endless cycle of heroic worlds with mortal kings and passing dynasties.

Discovering the Poem's Form   Between Grundtvig and Tolkien a whole school of criticism took the poem's apparent or real lack of unity of action to indicate its composite origin, its beginning in a number of "lays" or short narrative poems (songs) composed by traditional bards and later compiled into a single story. F. A. Wolf first articulated this, the *Liedertheorie,* in his *Prolegomena ad Homerum* (1795), an epochal study of the Homeric poems. Karl Lachmann extended the theory to the *Niblungenlied* and his student, Karl Müllenhof, became the most famous of a number of scholars who applied the theory to *Beowulf.* Müllenhof turned the composition of the poem into a drama: the cast included two original poets, two continuators, and two interpolators (A and B). The poem began as separate lays (the Grendel fight, the dragon fight) by the original poets; Grendel's mother was added by one continuator, the poem's opening to line 193 by another;

interpolator A added Beowulf's return to his native country, interpolator B joined the Grendel and dragon stories and added the Christian coloring.[100] Ultimately conjectures like Müllenhof's fell out of favor, but the problems the *Liedertheorie* was intended to solve remain unresolved.

Eventually the proponents of the *Liedertheorie* were maligned as the "dissectionists," but they made contributions of lasting value to the study of *Beowulf:* they analyzed the structure of the poem carefully and indicated the vastness of the realm of stories from which *Beowulf* arose, or one might say, they mapped the intertextuality of which the poem is part. Klaeber's view of the structure and origins of the poem owes something to the dissectionists; he suggests that parts I and II of the poem (the Danish adventure, the dragon story) are mutually independent, being joined only in the person of the hero, and adds that part I includes two actions that have been closely related and become one story (the fights with Grendel and his mother) and a third action, Beowulf's return home.[101] In another section of his introduction, Klaeber traces the "development of the story-material into our epic poem"; his conjecture rather resembles Müllenhof's except that Klaeber imagines an English poet creating *Beowulf* from a knowledge of originally Scandinavian lays—"a lay or two on the slaying of Grendel and his mother, another one on the dragon adventure, besides, at any rate, two Danish (originally Geatish) poems on the warlike encounters between Geats and Swedes leading up to the fall of Ongentheow and Onela respectively."[102] This author "combined the Grendel stories with the dragon narrative and added . . . the account of Beowulf's return, in short, conceived the plan of an extensive epic poem with a great and noble hero as the central figure."[103]

F. P. Magoun, Jr., pondering the poem's narrative structure and reconsidering especially Beowulf's version of the story of his battles with Grendel and Grendel's mother (told to the hero's king and uncle Hygelac), divided the poem into three separate stories designated as *A, A prime,* and *B.* Magoun's *A* corresponds to the usual part I up to Beowulf's return to the Geats; *B,* the dragon fight, is part II, but *A prime* includes a variant or alternative version of the Grendel story that an Anglo-Saxon editor of the poem wished to preserve and fitted into his anthology of Beowulf poems. This Anglo-Saxon editor put the extra version of Beowulf's Danish adventures into the hero's mouth as his report to King Hygelac. Rather like Müllenhof's interpolator B, Magoun's conjectured Anglo-Saxon antiquarian composed the verses necessary to fit *A prime* into "Beowulf's return" and to link the composite Danish adventure with *B,* the dragon story. Magoun's model for this, the most convincing of the theories of a composite *Beowulf,* was Elias Lönnrot's practice of creating composite versions of Finnish traditional lays he knew in several versions and his subsequent compilation of the *Kalevala* from originally independent poems in which the same persons, for example Väinämöinen and Lemminkäinen, often appear.[104]

The anatomy of *Beowulf,* no matter how skillfully laid bare, does not reveal the dynamics, the movement, and the power of its story as apprehended by an audience. Tolkien solved the problem of narrative unity and narrative movement in *Beowulf* at a stroke. He insisted the poem was not a narrative at all, but a "contrasted description of two moments in a great life," called its structure "*static*" (Tolkien's emphasis), compared Anglo-Saxon poetry to "sculpture or painting," and in his allegory of the author and text transformed *Beowulf* into a stone tower.[105] His solution diminished the poem. John Leyerle applied the ambiguous term "interlace" to the structure of *Beowulf* and at once likened the poem to art objects like the "carpet pages" of the Lindisfarne Gospels and the interwoven serpents of the Sutton Hoo belt buckle, and to narratives like the late French romances of Arthur, the Vulgate Cycle, to which Eugene Vinaver applied the term "interlace."[106] In this sense, an interlaced narrative (the Vulgate Cycle, parts of Spenser's *Faerie Queen*) tells several stories usually interrupting A to continue B from the point the last interruption left it, but such an "interlace" can hardly be compared to the visual arts.

The attempt to describe *Beowulf* adequately has led some critics to dynamic rather than static metaphors. The poem's movement has been called circular or recursive, powerful and irresistible yet not direct. Joan Blomfield (Joan Turville-Petre) professes herself completely persuaded by Tolkien's remarks on the poem's structure, but approves Klaeber's recurring references to the "circuitous" movement of *Beowulf* and finds the hero at the center of a force field that draws the poem's diverse elements into a "static unity."[107] Clare Kinney nicely observes that the "career of [the poem's] rather isolated hero undeniably supplies the work with a powerful linear thrust, but even as it advances chronologically, Beowulf's story also continually attracts unto itself other stories, other times, and other places," and thereby suggests larger patterns of "circularity" in the whole. That "powerful linear thrust" ultimately makes *Beowulf* a whole, yet the poem "is full of potential tensions between the ultimately linear nature of the heroic poem and its tendency to generate spontaneous realities . . . which temporarily take over the narrative foreground."[108]

The critics' present task still remains (1) to discover a unifying principle in the telling of the story of Beowulf's three great fights, two in Denmark during his youth, one at home in his age; and (2) to describe or analyze the movement of a story often interrupted by digressions, halted by moral reflections, and delayed by repetitions. These two separate searches require a consistent, unified solution.

New Directions In 1936 Tolkien began with the observation that the study of *Beowulf* was weak in criticism though rich in many other departments. Since Tolkien's lecture scholarship has developed his paradigm extensively and some students have begun to find new approaches to the interpretation of the poem and to reflect on the aesthetic implications of older scholarly initiatives. The poem's sources in folktale, wondertale, legend, or myth now seem likely to stimulate new approaches to *Beowulf* as a narrative. Mircea Eliade's comparative studies of myth and Joseph Fontenrose's theory of a "combat myth" offer new contexts for the study of *Beowulf*. Inquiries into the contemporary historical background of the poem (despite the nearly insoluble problem of its date) seems a possible source for renewing our reading of the poem. Reawakened interest in reading the narrative literally seems promising. Klaeber thought the story ("a plot of mere fabulous adventures") required an allegorical gloss or Christian interpretation to match the "dignity" of its setting, but a compound of fantasy and realism has a positive appeal to postmoderns.

The new age of *Beowulf* criticism might be said to have begun with the publication of Edward B. Irving's book, a study of *Beowulf* as a secular and indeed heroic poem. In this notably undogmatic work, the hero and the ideal of heroism become central, the figure of Beowulf the poem's real subject. Irving reads the poem as a New Critic or "close reader" and with a remarkable sensitivity and perceptiveness, but reads the poem more as a series of scenes than a narrative. Irving must be among the first critics of *Beowulf* to apply Eliade's idea of sacred time and space to the story of Heorot. The book has stimulated some extremely interesting writing, notably Berger and Leicester's article on the vision of heroic society in the poem. Gwyn Jones puts *Beowulf* in the context of North European heroic literature and of myth (he draws on Fontenrose's identification of the poem as an example of the "combat myth") and reads the poem as a narrative with an eye to its variety and vigor as well as its moral seriousness and humanity.[109] T. A. Shippey also reads the text of *Beowulf* as a literal narrative rather than an invitation to an allegorical interpretation; he examines ironies most earlier interpretations ignored and gritty realities (deep drinking, socially approved violence) rarely treated in criticism.[110] The current age of *Beowulf* criticism seems determined to examine the poem's surface more deeply and from more critical perspectives than the last generation that looked beyond the surface for the text's meaning.

Chapter Two
Traditions and the Poem
The Stories in *Beowulf*

The study of *Beowulf* may begin with its stories rather than a myth of
the poet or author whose identity, dates, and relationship with the oral
tradition from which the poem ultimately descends cannot now be
discovered. An inventory and ordering of the stories might seem the
simplest and best beginning for the study of the poem, but retelling,
summarizing, and clarifying the stories into a story is not simple and
may distort our perception of the poem. *Beowulf* seems quite a different
work in longer and shorter summaries and descriptions, as W. W.
Lawrence pointed out: "The 'plot' of the epic, stated briefly, reads like a
wonder-tale. . . . A more elaborate outline of the epic quickly assumes
a very different character, however; it becomes historical and realistic,
with long episodes, shorter digressions, passing allusions to legend,
scenes of court life and genealogizing."[1] A short summary of *Beowulf*
(Lawrence's "wonder-tale") could report that the hero fights and kills a
monster, then the monster's monstrous mother, and at last is mortally
wounded as he fights and kills a dragon.

Different retellings or outlines of the poem may cumulatively give a
less misshapen reflection of *Beowulf* as a narrative. A "more elaborate
outline" of the story of Beowulf's three great fights, sometimes called
the main or central story of the poem, could report that the hero, at
home in the land of the Geats (in southern Sweden), hears that a
monster has been raiding the great hall of the Danish king, Hrothgar.
Beowulf at once commands a ship to be fitted out and sails swiftly and
easily to Denmark. On the first night of his Danish visit, Beowulf waits
up in Hrothgar's hall; the monster, Grendel, comes as usual, but finds
himself in the grip of an enemy stronger than himself and escapes only
by leaving his arm behind. In the morning the Danes rejoice at the
evidence of Grendel's defeat; that night they celebrate Beowulf's victory and reward the hero richly for his deed; but after the celebration
Grendel's mother comes to the hall and avenges her son by killing a

great nobleman. The next day a company of Danes and Geats tracks the female monster to her home, a haunted pool. Beowulf plunges in, and, after a difficult struggle, kills Grendel's mother and decapitates Grendel's corpse. Beowulf and the Geats return to Heorot with Grendel's head; at their parting the next morning, Hrothgar gives Beowulf twelve great treasures. Beowulf sails smoothly and swiftly home where he reports on his trip to his king and uncle, Hygelac.

The second part of the poem begins with ten lines that report that after Hygelac died in battle, and after his son Heardred was killed in a Swedish attack, and after Beowulf had succeeded to the throne and ruled well for fifty years, a dragon began to attack the Geats at night. Beowulf has a great iron shield made for protection against the dragon's fire, and proceeds to its lair with a small company of Geats and the unwilling thief who aroused the dragon by stealing a precious cup from its hoard. Beowulf challenges the dragon; in the fight his sword breaks on its invulnerable head, but just as the battle seems lost, Wiglaf, Beowulf's young kinsman, comes to his aid. Together they kill the dragon, but Beowulf dies from its poison. The poem ends with Beowulf's cremation and funeral eulogy.

Though this summary omits most of the matter that makes *Beowulf* "realistic" and much that makes it "historical," the poem seems different; the "wonder-tale" has acquired a setting in legendary history and its human characters have assumed places in a social order. Indeed they uniformly belong to a ruling class. From its opening to its close, the poem alludes to, sketches, or retells a number of stories from the legendary history of the Germanic peoples. Before Grendel's appearance, the poem briefly traces a golden age of Danish history from Scyld Scefing to his great-grandson Hrothgar and notices without detail that the Danes endured a time of lordless hardship before Scyld. After Beowulf's fight with Grendel, a group of Danes tracks the wounded monster to his blood-stained mere; as they ride back, a Danish poet tells the story of Beowulf's victory (but this story is not reported), of Sigemund and Fitela's exile, and of Sigemund's winning an immense treasure by killing a dragon. At the feast celebrating Beowulf's victory, a Danish poet retells a version of the story of the Danish-Frisian conflict at Finnsburg. The narrator of *Beowulf* then adds a brief prophetic account of the death of Hygelac, Beowulf's uncle and king of the Geats. On his return home, Beowulf reports to Hygelac, foretells the future failure of Hrothgar's attempt to cement peace with the Heathobards in a vivid and moving narrative realized in a single scene, and summarizes the story of his battles with Grendel and his mother. Part I ends with a magnificent gift exchange between Beowulf and Hygelac that leaves the two noble kinsmen living in harmony.

The multitudinous stories of part 1 come from various heroic legends of the old Germanic world, usually told or referred to just once and frequently given in compressed and allusive forms. In part II one set of stories cumulatively constructs a history, told mostly in antichronological order, of the wars between the Swedes and the Geats. After Beowulf's death and the final and fullest retelling of King Ongentheow's death in battle, the historical narrative in which the dragon's story is embedded becomes clear. The other set of stories relates the dragon's taking possession of the hoard, its origins, and the theft that provoked the monster's attack on the Geats.

The rich and varied texture of *Beowulf* includes more than its stories; powerful descriptive passages, speeches, and dialogues make a significant part of the experience of hearing or reading the poem. The conversations and speeches in the poem have generally a formal or a rhetorical appearance as parts of the poem's art, or the poem's appreciation of the art and decorum of conducting a noble life in a finite and passing world, but the speeches in *Beowulf* also spring from the inner reality of the speakers themselves and their relationships with the other members of their world. No speech in *Beowulf* needs to be taken as a poet's interpretation or guide to interpretation of the poem. Even at the poem's end, the final praise is not quite a poet's summation on the real, essential Beowulf; at the end the Geats praise the hero as they saw him, not quite as the poem presented him.

Backgrounds of the Story

Folktale and Myth   Students of *Beowulf* have generally believed that the hero's first two adventures, the fights with Grendel and Grendel's mother, derive from a folktale or märchen like the one studied (in 202 variant versions) by Friedrich Panzer.[2] This tale-type was called "The bear's son" tale and though these stories are now classed under two folktale types, 301 and 650A, respectively entitled "Strong John" and "The three stolen princesses," the old name remains current.[3] In 1921 R. W. Chambers concluded that "Panzer has . . . proved that the struggle of Beowulf in the hall, and his plunging down into the deep, is simply an epic glorification of a folk-tale motive," and in 1980 Douglas D. Short asserted that "whatever other materials the poet brought to the composition of the poem, *Beowulf* is fundamentally a folktale, albeit one that has been embellished and modified by a sophisticated artist."[4] Beowulf is more readily identified as folktale hero from his first great adventure rather than a mythical figure from his last. Moreover his name must mean "bear" (the "wolf," or enemy, of the bee), does not appear elsewhere in the legendary history of the North, and does not alliterate with the name of his father Ecgtheow or his kinsman Wiglaf. In the fight with the dragon, however, Beowulf does not resemble a folk hero and the origin of his story seems doubtful. The closest parallels to that story are the Old Norse accounts of Thor's fatal battle with the world serpent at Ragnarrök, the end of the world, and the story of Sigurðr's victory over the dragon Fáfnir. In his treatise on poetic language, Snorri Sturluson indicates the kennings poets may use (and have used) for Thor: we may call him "verjandi Asgarðs, Miðgarðs, dólgr ok bani jötna ok trollkvinna, vegandi Hrungis, Geirröðr, þrivalda, . . . dólgr Miðgarðsorms" (the defender of Asgard, of Midgard, enemy and slayer of giants and trollwomen, slayer of Hrungir, Geirröðr, and þrivaldi . . . the opponent of the world serpent). Hrungnir, Geirröðr, and þrivaldi are three of Thor's slain giants.[5] From giants to trollwomen to the great dragon makes Thor's story parallel Beowulf's whom we could call the defender of the Danes and Geats.

／ If we take *Beowulf* as a myth transformed into a heroic story (rather than as a folktale raised to heroic status), Thor might seem a reasonable model for Beowulf. Thor will fight his great enemy at the end of the world, still defending mankind from the forces of chaos and old night, and, like Beowulf, will kill his dragon and die dragon-poisoned. The parallel between Beowulf and Sigurðr seems less convincing. Sigurðr kills Fáfnir, thus winning the dragon's immense treasure and his mortal curse, but this exploit comes early in the hero's career, not at its close. In *Beowulf,* a Danish poet attributes a variant of this story to Sigemund (Sigurðr's father), but this allusively sketched dragon fight is probably another youthful adventure.

A narrative bearing considerable resemblance to the Grendel story appears in a Sanskrit text, the *Vishnu Purana,* and Joseph Fontenrose has pointed out a rather convincing parallel to the story of Grendel and Grendel's mother in an Akkadian creation myth, *Enuma Elish;* both of these are mythical rather than folktale parallels to the *Beowulf* story.[6] The hero of *Enuma Elish* is the young god Marduk; of the Sanksrit story, Krishna. In *Enuma Elish,* the monsters of chaos of the deep are first angered by the young gods' noisy merriment:

> The divine brothers banded together,
> They disturbed Tiamat as they surged back and forth,
> Yea, they troubled the mood of Tiamat
> By their hilarity in the Abode of Heaven
> Apsu could not lessen their clamor
> And Tiamat was speechless at their ways.[7]

Later Tiamat makes war against the gods to avenge Apsu, her consort. The grievance of these embodiments of the primeval sea suggest Grendel's outrage at the rejoicing and the song celebrating the creation itself in Heorot; in the event, the young god Marduk defends the world of the young gods against the force of chaos.

Beowulf as Three-Part Theme   The closest parallels to *Beowulf* are neither Panzer's folktales nor Fontenrose's myths but the various recreations of a traditional story that Nora K. Chadwick treated in a learned but knotty, and often neglected, article of 1959. In these stories, the adventure seems an inheritance to which various members of a noble family of the Gautar (the "Geatas," or Geats of *Beowulf*) or members of "the Hálogaland family of Ketill Hængr" succeed. The heroes carry on a feud with three great enemies who are frequently themselves related: "The *draugr* Agnarr and his variants; the dragon Hárekr; and an evil supernatural woman," a triad clearly paralleling Grendel, Grendel's mother, and the dragon. Though all the texts exemplifying this recurring story are later than *Beowulf*, it seems unlikely that the Anglo-Saxon poem is their source. A common tradition older than *Beowulf* must lie behind the Anglo-Saxon poem and the various versions of Chadwick's story of the noble hero and the three monsters, or, as she puts it, "The theme is an old one, of a high and ancient literary lineage."[8]

For a variety of reasons, Chadwick's paper has not much influenced the consensus of opinion on the origins of *Beowulf:* in 1959 her conclusions did not fit the dominant critical movements; her article makes hard reading; and in 1959 only two of the sagas she cites were readily available in English translation—even published editions of the Old Norse texts themselves were not widely available. Moreover Chadwick's case seems liable to some objections. The sagas she cites are much later than *Beowulf* (but earlier than most of the folktales cited by Panzer). The hero's feud with the triad of enemies paralleling Grendel, Grendel's mother, and the dragon frequently come as episodes in stories of lives filled with supernatural encounters—hence skeptical readers might have concluded that the combination was merely accidental, not a connected and recurring theme. Moreover, only two of the texts she cites include a treasure-guarding, tomb-dwelling dragon, and neither of those were available in English.

Chadwick's argument seems to have been anticipated in some sense by Snorri Sturluson (1179–1241) and the anonymous author of *Njál's Saga* (written around 1280), for both create brief sketches of heroic careers resembling Beowulf's and the author of *Njál's Saga* assumes that his audience would recognize a brief sketch of the adventure as a familiar literary motif subject to retelling, manipulation, or even parody. Both of these instances of the theme are probably earlier than any cited by Chadwick, though they are, like almost all Old Norse texts, later than *Beowulf*. Snorri, too, seems to have seen a plot like that of *Beowulf* as a recognizable literary form. In *Gylfaginning* (The deception of Gylfi), a delightfully duplicitous and equivocal narrative, Snorri creates a Trojan archetype for Thor and gives him a story that in part seems a compressed *Beowulf* analogue. Trór, a grandson of Priam, distinguished himself when he explored the world "ok sigraði einn saman alla berserki ok alla risa ok einn inn mesta dreka ok mörg dýr" (and singlehandedly defeated all berserks, giants, and the biggest dragon, and many wild animals). The anticlimatic final detail hardly spoils the triad and the emphasis—*all* berserks, giants, and *the* biggest dragon—gives this princely Trór adventures to match those of Chadwick's heroes. And indeed this Trór, "whom we call Thor," founds a line of descendants leading to "Voden whom we call Odin" and thus to Thor who, in the stories of the pagans at any rate, defends the citadel of the gods, the world of men, fights giants and trollwomen, and at the end of world will fight the world serpent, the greatest dragon.[9]

Chapters 119 and 120 of *Njáls Saga* create a dramatic episode in which two of the saga's characters, transformed into types of Grendel and Beowulf, confront one another and, to the audience's almost unwilling pleasure, the troll figure wins the battle of wills. The saga first makes a historical character, Thorkell "hákr" ("bully," so called because of his abusive words and deeds) into one of of Chadwick's heroes. In the process, the saga first traces Thorkell's ancestory back to Ketill Hængr, thus giving the ruffian one of the genealogies Chadwick noted as typical. Thorkell appears in two other sagas, but only here is he traced to "the Hálogaland family of Ketill Hængr" and only in *Njál's Saga* is he credited with having done great deeds in other lands. The saga's brief account of Thorkell's exploits abroad seems an abstract of Chadwick's pattern for Scandinavian parallels to *Beowulf:*

He had killed a robber east in Jamtland Forest, and then travelled east to Sweden, where he joined forces with Sorkvir the Old. Together they harried in the Baltic. One evening, on the coast of Finland, it was Thorkel's turn to fetch water for the crew; he encountered a fabulous monster and was only able to kill it after a long struggle. From there he travelled south to Estonia, where he killed a flying dragon. . . . [in] Iceland . . . he had these feats carved above his bed-closet and on a chair in front of his high-seat.[10]

Thorkell's first enemy, the robber, appears in the text as a *spellvirki,* an "evil-doer, brigand, outlaw"—a satisfactory variant of the *"draugr* Agnarr"; the second enemy, a fabulous monster met while drawing water and by implication probably resident in a pool of some sort, is a *finngálkn,* a monster partly human and partly animal.[11] In *Örvar-Odds Saga (Arrow-Odds Saga)* a *finngálkn* (a fantastic monster) is one of the hero's enemies and the mother of his chief adversary, Ögmundr (a variant of Agnarr).[12] Thorkel's third enemy, the flying dragon (*flug-dreki*), briefly completes the triad of familiar enemies. Thorkell's invented genealogy makes him a kinsman of Arrow-Odd and Grettir the Strong; that pedigree and his striking adventures, lent to him for this context, make Thorkel a type of Beowulf.

The narrator of *Njál's Saga* transmutes Thorkel into a traditional hero just as the sons of Njál and their closest kinsmen turn toward Thorkel in their search for supporters in a coming lawsuit. Their procession from one chieftain to another has not gained their unpopular cause many supporters, but in its progress Skarphedin Njálsson, the greatest of Njál's heroic sons, has been transformed into a type of Grendel. At one establishment after another, a leading Icelander asks who the fifth man in the line may be and remarks on his formidable appearance. The first explicitly describes the hero as *trollsligr,* "troll-like," and another observes that Skarphedin is as "grim-looking as if he had come from a sea-cliff," a normal dwelling place for a troll. Skarphedin and Thorkel, their transformations into archetypal enemies completed, confront one another in chapter 120 of the saga. The audience recognizes that the scene re-creates a familiar opposition but finds its sympathies diverted from the newly made hero to the freshly labeled troll. At the crucial moment, their weapons restate their roles as hero and monster, as types of Beowulf and Grendel. Thorkel half-draws his sword, announcing "[t]his is the sword I got in Sweden . . . I killed a great warrior to get it." The "great warrior" (*inn mesti kappi*) is presumably the *spellvirki,* or robber, of Thorkel's foreign adventures, the sword (*sax*) a prize several Beowulfian heroes (including Grettir, Thorkel's kinsman in this context) gain from the defeat of a monstrous enemy. In answer Skarphedin raises his axe *Rimmugȳgr,* "battle-troll," and offers Thorkel the choice of death or discomfiture. Thorkel, a man of violent words and deeds, and otherwise unblemished courage, slides his sword back into its sheath and sits down in defeat. [13]

Theme, Origins, and Context of Composition   Chadwick's

contribution to *Beowulf* studies brings new material and a new perspective to some of the oldest questions in the discussion of the poem. Traditional criticism has found the poem's "folkloristic" material (Grendel and his mother, and sometimes even the dragon) and its real geography, historical context, and historical or legendary matter an anomalous combination. A wonder tale should not give such seemingly definite answers to the usual questions, "who, when, and where," nor should an Anglo-Saxon poem give such thoroughly Scandinavian answers to those questions. The geographical setting seems appropriate to the story taken as a whole; Chadwick's thesis connects the setting and the essential plot as well as clearing away the problem of the separate origin of the dragon story. We do not have, after all, a mythical narrative grafted onto a folktale, and though we may not find an Aristotelian unity in the story, the genetic unity of *Beowulf* seems probable[14] and we may believe that successive audiences found the story artistically satisfying as a whole.

But why would an Anglo-Saxon poetic tradition adopt, sustain, and even perfect a story with widespread and ancient connections in a form so specifically localized in Scandinavia? The poem attests to direct English-Scandinavian connections prior to the Viking age; the forms of the place-names "Scedenig" and "Scedeland" (1686, 19) may have entered the language before the Anglo-Saxon conquest of Britain; and in general the Scandinavian names in *Beowulf* are "authentic inheritances from a much earlier time."[15] This does not prove that *Beowulf* goes back to that time but does indicate that the names and some discourse connecting them had a continuous history in spoken English or Anglo-Saxon from that "much earlier time" to the disputed date of the poem's composition. The most probable context for that tradition in the Anglo-Saxon period is in East Anglia where the evidence of the Sutton Hoo ship burial, and indeed other evidence continuing archaeological work is discovering and assessing, suggests an early connection with Scandinavia, as well as a social and material culture with remarkable parallels to the world of the poem.

Sutton Hoo was the ancestral burial ground of the East Anglian kings, called the "Wuffingas" (Wuffings) from Wuffa, whose father Wehha was said to be the first of the dynasty to rule the East Angles. The burial ground, on an escarpment overlooking the estuary of the Deben River, includes more than fifteen barrows or grave mounds. In 1939 Mound One was excavated and proved to contain a great ship burial, "the richest treasure ever dug from British soil, and the most important archaeological document yet found in Europe for the era of the migrations of the Germanic peoples (5th to 7th centuries A. D.) in which the settlement of England . . . was an episode."[16] The grave goods included thirty-seven gold coins of Frankish origin, probably the most reliably datable part of the find. Rædwald (d. 624 or 625) has been generally taken to be the East Anglian king honored in the ship burial since an important study of the coins concluded that the collection was completed about 625, but that date makes Rædwald a marginal candidate. A very recent paper by Alan M. Stahl suggests that the hoard (which he characterizes as a random collection) contained no coin earlier than 595 and none later than 613, a date to which four of the coins apparently belong. The coins, in short, were probably assembled well within Rædwald's probable reign (599?–624/5).[17] We may call the man in Mound One Rædwald, though the identification can never be certain.

Ship or boat burial was practiced in Scandinavia, in Denmark, Sweden, Norway, and in East Anglia (Sutton Hoo and Snape) at various times from the 400s to the Viking age, but the closest chronological and archaelogical connections seem to connect Sutton Hoo and Swedish Uppland. The Sutton Hoo helmet was made in Sweden (possibly a century before the burial) or in England by a Swedish workman, and so, too, was the shield.[18] It has been noted that archaeological finds at Sutton Hoo connect the Wuffings with the Swedes and not the Geats whose poem *Beowulf* seems to be, and that on the other hand the names in the royal genealogy of the Wuffings seem to associate them with the Geats,[19] not the Swedes, but these apparent paradoxes may rest on modern notions of nationality and family. In the second part of the poem, Beowulf's loyal follower and kinsman, Wiglaf, is the son of Weohstan who fought on the Swedish side during Onela's invasion of the Geats. Wiglaf is described as a "leod scylfinga" (260; a Swedish prince) whose rights and patrimony (among the Geats we may guess) Beowulf restored. As he dies, Beowulf calls Wiglaf the last of the Wægmundings, "our kindred," and that family seems to have both Geatish and Swedish affiliations.

The poem begins (nearly) and closes with funerals variously reminiscent of the royal burials at Sutton Hoo now that the site can be considered as a cultural document, a statement some generations of East Anglian royals made to their world, and not just as a single, astonishingly rich archaeological find. In the poem's opening, Scyld Scefing is honored with a variation on ship-burial which may be compared to the great burial in Mound One at Sutton Hoo. Scyld's body was placed beside the mast along with a supply of arms and armor; treasures were placed in his lap, and his golden standard set high over his head (36–48). At Sutton Hoo, the forty-oared ship in Mound One has no mast although the design of its hull suggests that it was capable of being sailed. Possibly the mast fittings were removed to lighten the ship which had to be moved some six hundred yards inland and uphill, and to make room amidships for the burial chamber.[20] The chamber contained the dead man's arms and armor, various household goods, cups, dishes, vessels for the dispensing of food and drink, artifacts and symbols of lordly or even royal status, and objects directly representing royal authority. These are a ceremonial whetstone (in effect, a barbaric scepter) surmounted with an elegantly wrought bronze stag and a tall iron object once regarded as a lampstand, but probably a royal standard.[21] The poem—as only poems can—gives us golden standards, one placed high over Scyld's head (47–48), one towering among the dragon's treasures and supernaturally illuminating the tomb (2767–71). At Sutton Hoo the burial mounds look out over the tidal waters of the Deben estuary; in the poem, Scyld's funeral ship is set out to sea, possibly a unique funeral appropriate for a hero who came mysteriously from the sea.

The bronze stag that completed the scepter is probably Celtic in origin and was old when it was included among the grave goods; the stag may have symbolized Rædwald's status as "bretwalda" or ruler of Britain and successor (in Anglo-Saxon eyes) to the Roman rulers of the province.[22] The stag was almost certainly joined with the whetstone as a sign of power and status. The stag or hart, a magnificent game animal, was held in great esteem by many peoples in the old Germanic era; great heroes were sometimes compared to harts and men were sometimes given the name "hart."[23] Rædwald may have given the ancient object a new meaning based on the Anglo-Saxon word for the stag and even claimed for himself another affinity with the world of the heroic North. In *Beowulf* the name of Hrothgar's new hall, the symbol of the Scyldings' power, is *Heorot,* "hart." The old king claims that a stag ("heorot") would be torn apart by the hounds on the bank rather than take refuge in Grendel's uncanny mere, an observation that makes antitheses of the Danes' great hall and Grendel's domain. The name of Hrothgar's hall is attested in English but not Scandinavian traditions.[24]

(Beowulf's funeral closes the poem and recalls the mystery of Scyld's ship burial, but the poem's hero is cremated and buried in a great barrow looking out over the sea.) Like Scyld and Rædwald, Beowulf is buried with rich grave goods (specified in ambiguous terms, perhaps rings, necklaces, and armor, perhaps valuable objects, jewels, and ornaments; 3163–64), but the gifts honoring Beowulf come from an ancient buried treasure that had become the dragon's hoard; those treasures seem also to have accompanied Beowulf on his funeral pyre where swords, shields, and coats of mail are mentioned (3139–40).) What the flames of the pyre left behind was "wealle beworhton" (3161; "enclosed by a wall") and the recently reexcavated Mound Two (partially excavated in 1939, excavated and largely emptied in the nineteenth century), originally included a ship buried in the mound above a chamber grave that enclosed the dead man's body and grave goods with a wall of overlapping upright (and sturdy) planks set in a narrow ditch and secured by a ringbeam.[25] The few fragments remaining from the treasures of Mound Two suggest its occupant was as richly buried as Rædwald. Mound Two, the largest at Sutton Hoo, is later than Mound One and its timber-built burial chamber resembles Beowulf's grave even as Mound One suggests Scyld's ship burial. Rædwald's thirty-seven Frankish coins (and three blanks) could have represented the wages of the forty oarsmen who would have formed the ship's crew. Scyld put to sea literally in the poem, while Rædwald was ready for a metaphorical or ghostly voyage.

East Anglia and the dynasty of the Wuffings potentially bridges the fissure between the poem's English origins, its Scandinavian setting, and the Scandinavian form of its central theme. *Beowulf* may have been composed, performed, and preserved in something like its present form among the Wuffings because they believed themselves to be Swedish, Geatish, or both in descent and perhaps even believed themselves to be descendents of Weohstan and Wiglaf and thus even of Beowulf.[26] Moreover the cultural background of East Anglia provides an appropriate setting for the origins of the poem which, at a literal reading, combines a benevolent monotheism, a few spectacular stories from the Old Testament, a reasonably accurate idea of pagan burial practices, a hint of something like Christian hope, and an older, durable attitude we might call heroic existentialism. Sutton Hoo may have been a late pagan burial ground beginning around A.D. 600 and in use until the ninth century,[27] mute evidence of a high culture not fully pagan or Christian and nicely represented by the great Rædwald who kept both Christian and pagan altars in his temple. In East Anglia Christianity and pagan practices seem to have lived together longer than our written records suggest. Tolkien anxiously attempted to keep the pagan past distant from the poem and the poet yet somehow recoverable (but only partly and inaccurately) by the Christian author's dutiful impulse to remember something of his ancestors' greatness. The poem now seems closer to the world it creates, a rich combination of realism and fantasy, but not of pastiche.

Archaeological and comparative studies offer a new synthesis in the study of the greatest poem in the English language before the *Canterbury Tales*. The next decade should be filled with learned debate centering on philology, archaeology, and the theory of reading traditional narratives. The next millennium should have a new paradigm for the reading of *Beowulf*.

Poetry in the Tradition and in *Beowulf*

The materials of *Beowulf*, the story of the hall-haunting monster and of the fight at Finn's stronghold alike, have their origins in the preliterate history of various Germanic peoples, in materials they shared with other cultures, and in materials older than the formation of the Germanic languages. The wide dispersal and varying antiquity of the surviving evidence for traditions behind the poem indicates that the matter of *Beowulf* circulated in an oral tradition before literacy became general in Northern Europe.[28] One medium for the transmission of this oral tradition was verse. The Germanic peoples shared a common verse form that appears in runic inscriptions of the third and fourth centuries[29] and may be older still. At the beginning of the *Germania*, an account of the Germanic peoples, the Roman historian Tacitus reports that "In their ancient songs, their only form of recorded history, the Germans celebrate the earth-born god, Tuisto. They assign to him a son, Mannus, the author of their race"; a few lines later Tacitus adds,

"Hercules, among others, is said to have visited them, and they chant his praises before those of other heroes on their way into battle."[30] Tacitus was writing about A.D. 98 his much challenged but inescapable testimony may attest to the antiquity and matter of very early Germanic poetry.

Only a few single lines of early Germanic poetry have survived, but Anglo-Saxon, Old Norse, Old Saxon, and Old High German poetry preserve the basic Germanic line and the survival of the verse form attests to a tradition of poets and audiences. The earliest Germanic poetry would have necessarily been oral, and oral poetry survived well into the Christian era. Non-Germanic oral poetries survived in some parts of Europe until the present century, and even until the present day. In Finland, for example, about one and a half million lines of traditional narrative poems (of the type Lönnrot reworked into the *Kalevala*) were collected by "lettered men . . . from the mouths of unlettered singers"[31] before widespread literacy marginalized and finally extinguished the ancient art. Vigorous traditions of oral narrative poetry flourished among the South Slavic peoples, both Christian and Muslim, until very recent times (and survive even now); modern collectors have recorded performances of traditional poems rather than having to take them down by dictation. Assuming that traditional poetry in the old Germanic world behaved (in social rather than metrical terms) like oral poetry in contemporary and near-contemporary settings, we may conjecture that the Germanic poets learned their art from their elders. The essence of becoming an oral singer of tales lies in mastering the art, not in memorizing a text or group of texts. Though the intricate poetry of the Icelandic skalds probably includes exceptions, traditional poetry generally exists in performance (that is, when being recited to an audience), and no two performances are exactly alike even though the singer himself may be deeply convinced that they are. The skalds probably polished at least some of their arcane poems to a textual gloss, a final, fixed form. Though some early students of traditional poetry thought of the singer's work as extempore and therefore artless (at least not verbally artful), one could as well say that every performance of a poem becomes a rehearsal for the next. Thus, the singer's craft is indeed an art.[32] The theory of oral composition and transmission implies that the singer never arrives at a final version of his tale—the work never becomes a text until fixed in writing by a scribe. Singers typically believe that they repeat their songs word for word and line for line, but they do not.[33]

The acquisition of some skill in poetic composition was probably a social necessity in Anglo-Saxon England. In his *Ecclesiastical History* Bede tells the story of a cowherd, Caedmon by name, who miraculously received the art in a vision in which he sang a hymn praising the Creator. The occasion of the miraculous dream was a drinking party from which Caedmon withdrew because the others were passing around a harp and taking turns singing a poem to its accompaniment. Unlike his fellows, presumably also agricultural laborers, Caedmon could not take up the harp and compose a poem. The Anglo-Saxon translators of Bede's history add that when the harp approached him, Caedmon rose up and left the party "for scome," out of a sense of his inadequacy, ashamed of his disability. Bede's story has been much discussed, but few commentators have attended to Caedmon's companions: they were not newsworthy in the age of Bede even though they could sing. Like Caedmon, we may assume, they could not read or write, but composing and listening to poetry were among their regular entertainments. Abbess Hild of Whitby and the monastic community accepted Caedmon's gift as miraculous and took him into the monastery. Interpreters taught him biblical narratives and Christian doctrine that he reflected upon and turned into excellent English poetry, but save for the first brief hymn composed in his dream none of it survives.[34]

Bede does not report that Caedmon's poems were transcribed but simply that they were heard and appreciated. The Anglo-Saxon translators of Bede add that those who taught him the biblical matter of his poetry copied and learned his poems. The translators may have conjectured that Caedmon's poetry was written down because they had a text purporting to be the hymn sung in the miraculous dream, but they also may have known a body of written poetry attributed to Caedmon, or they may have known other instances of oral poetry being preserved in writing. Although King Alfred did not learn to read until he was twelve or older, "he was a careful listener, by day and night, to English poems, most frequently hearing them recited by others, and he readily retained them in his memory." Still before he could read, Alfred learned the English poems contained in a book his mother offered as a reward to the first of her sons to master its contents. As king, and even when engaged in a deadly struggle with the Vikings, Alfred's activities included "reading aloud from books in English and above all learning English poems by heart."[35] What Asser describes as memorization may actually be an adept's act of adding a traditional poem to his repertoire, not repeating a text word by word. The recitations of English poems that so entranced the young Alfred may well have been performances by traditional poets, and the books from which Alfred read aloud may have been traditional poems taken down by scribes. We may fairly suspect that as a youth Alfred could sing even as Caedmon's fellow laborers could.

Whether *Beowulf* is essentially an oral poem preserved in writing by a scribe or the work of a lettered poet who had mastered the craft of traditional composition as well as the power of literacy cannot be ascertained. The only test for orality is observation, and the witnesses to the preservation of *Beowulf* have fallen silent. However, the poem has a dramatic role for the traditional, oral poet. After Beowulf's encounter with Grendel in Hrothgar's royal hall, a party of Danes and Geats track the defeated monster to his retreat, an uncanny pool in the depths of a swamp. The pool seethes with Grendel's blood and terrible surging waves, gratifying evidence that his wound was mortal and that the horror of twelve years of the monster's raids has ended in a single night. The Danes ride back to Hrothgar's hall in high spirits, praising Beowulf's glorious deed and observing—with no disrespect to Hrothgar— that the hero has demonstrated his worthiness to be a king. In the course of this joyful and spirited ride home, a poet, a man with an extensive repertory, composes a new poem on "sið Beowulfes" (872), that is, Beowulf's journey, arrival, course of action, conduct, and lot or fate, if we take the range of appropriate meanings common to "sið" as present in this context. The narrator of *Beowulf* thus summarizes the Danish poet's song about Beowulf in one half-line and spends five half-lines (872–74) reporting the song's composition with emphasis on the Danish poet's wisdom, prudence, and skill. The narrator's brief summary of the Danish poet's account of Beowulf's venture makes the Anglo-Saxon and the (fictional) Danish poem one since the audience's model for the Danish poem is what they have heard of the Anglo-Saxon *Beowulf,* and thus joins the poem's actors and its audience as sharers of a single poetic tradition.

The Danish poet's Beowulf story combines the hero's venture and two digressions, the first mythical, the second legendary: the stories of Sigemund the dragon killer and of Heremod, the Danish king who preceeded Scyld Scefing. The Danish poet's story of Sigemund concludes with the hero killing a dragon and loading his ship with its treasures. The Old Norse account of Sigemund's savage and heroic career in the *Völsunga Saga* brings him at length to his rightful throne: "Sigmundr gerisk nú ríkr konungr ok ágætr, vitr ok stórráðr" (Now

Sigmundr becomes a powerful and excellent king, wise and ambitious),[36] and the last adjective summing up Sigmundr's qualities seems a conspicuous parallel to the Anglo-Saxon poem's last word on Beowulf—that he was "lofgeornost," "most eager for fame." The digression on Sigemund within the implied Danish poem on Beowulf seems prophetic both in Danish and Anglo-Saxon terms: the Danish poet sees Sigemund's victory over the dragon as paralleling Beowulf's victory over Grendel. Since Sigemund's exploits ended in his kingship, his succession to the place of King Völsungr, the Danish poet confirms the opinion of the riders from the mere that Beowulf merits royal advancement. The Anglo-Saxon poet shares that view and also sees Sigemund's youthful victory over the dragon and acquisition of its treasure as prophetic of Beowulf's last, fatal victory.

The other digression in the Danish poet's Beowulf poem contrasts the Geatish hero with the Danes' once-promising Heremod, who became a menace to his own people and ended badly—in explicit contrast with Sigemund who became a good king and a model Beowulf eventually excels. The digressions in the Danish poet's version of Beowulf's story become digressions in the Anglo-Saxon poem and thus another link between the audience of *Beowulf* and the actors within the poem (themselves frequent auditors of poetry). The digression on Heremod is one of the repeated historical or legendary episodes within *Beowulf* since Hrothgar retells that tragic-exemplary tale before generalizing on the ways Germanic kings can go wrong for Beowulf's benefit. The repetition of Heremod's story illustrates the importance of traditional oral poetry as a cultural institution for the Danes of *Beowulf;* the story has been transmitted in song, as the Danish poet's work illustrates; thus preserved, the tale of Heremod becomes part of Hrothgar's rhetoric. A Danish court poet—whether or not the composer of the song about Beowulf, Sigemund, and Heremod—performs another poem in the course of the celebration of Beowulf's victory. The occasion is more formal than the ride back from the mere: Heorot is decorated, a feast served, Beowulf rewarded, and compensation paid for the Geat whom Grendel devoured. Then suddenly the poet's song is reported. It tells the story of the heroic and tragic affair at Finnsburg, the stronghold of the Frisian king, Finn.

The narrator of *Beowulf* imagines a Danish world peopled with singers and responsive to a variety of poetic expression. At the great drinking ceremony celebrating the completion of Hrothgar's royal hall, a poet sings a hymn of praise to God the Creator of mankind, the world, sun and moon, and all living things. The narrator's account of this poem begins with an audience Hrothgar's poet did not consciously address: a grim enemy resident in undisclosed darknesses listened in grief and anger to the sound of joy and the song of creation. The story then returns to the hall, its joys, and the beginning of its sorrows. Heorot's first poem retells a great myth and re-creates an archetypal opposition of creation and destruction. When Beowulf returns to his homeland and retells his adventures among the Danes, he reports still another poet and kind of poetry sung in Heorot. At the great celebration of Beowulf's victory over Grendel's mother, Hrothgar himself performed a number of poems, some of which were "soð ond sarlic", some "syllic" (2109), that is "true and sorrowful" and "rare, strange, marvellous" or "excellent." The most intriguing of Hrothgar's reported poems, however, must be his laments for his past youth and deeply emotional evocations of his memories of the past:

> hwilum eft ongan   eldo gebunden,
> gomel guðwiga   gioguðe cwiðan,
> hildestrengo;   hreðer inne weoll,
> þonne he wintrum frod   worn gemunde.
> (2111–14)

(and at times the old warrior bound by age lamented his youth and his warlike strength; when he, old in years, remembered so much his heart surged within him)

The first poem sung in Heorot recreated a cosmic myth of opposed forces, creation and destruction; the last laments the universal human condition of mortality. Between the cosmological myth and the personal elegy, Danish traditional poetry as created in *Beowulf* preserves the history of a people and parallels Germanic poetry as Tacitus describes it.

Chapter Three

The Heroic Age, Ideal, and Challenge

Past and Present in the Poem

From the opening lines the narrator places the action of *Beowulf* in another country and another, earlier, time, but an Anglo-Saxon audience learned in a vernacular poetic tradition could have deduced that the people and action of the poem belong to a familiar past, not deepest antiquity. The poem's action and actors seem to belong to an era of particular importance to the Anglo-Saxons, a period in which the legendary past and their almost definable history met. The poem's present action seems set in that historical moment defined by the coming of various Germanic groups traditionally identified as Angles, Saxons, and Jutes to Celtic Britain and their acquisition by conquest of a new homeland. That great event marked an epoch for the Anglo-Saxons, the beginning of their history in a new world. In 937, Alfred the Great's grandsons, King Æthelstan and Prince Eadmund, defeated a combined force of Scots and Vikings in a major pitched battle at "Brunanburh," a site not now known. The Anglo-Saxon poem celebrating the battle and exulting in the English victory compares this triumph to the Anglo-Saxon conquest of Celtic Britain. For the poet of *The Battle of Brunanburh,* that victory closed the Viking age and secured the original conquest, but his apt (though hyperbolic) comparison illustrates how deeply the migration and conquest were embedded in the Anglo-Saxon consciousness.

The sense that the action of the narrative present in *Beowulf* belongs to the great era of the conquest of Britain seems to be hinted by the probable inclusion in *Beowulf* of a recognizable allusion to a hero of the conquest. If the Finnsburg story has a hero, the victor and possessor of the spoils of war, Hengest, has best claim to the title. Anglo-Saxons could hardly fail to identify the bearer of this atypical name (*hengest* means "stallion") with that legendary Hengest who with his brother

Horsa ("mare") was one of the original conquerors of Britain. According to Bede and the *Anglo-Saxon Chronicle,* the legendary brothers accepted an invitation from the British ruler Vortigern to defend Romanized Britain from the Picts. After some early successes, Hengest and Horsa decided to conquer Britain for themselves, turned on their employers, and invited other Germanic warriors from the Continent to join them.[1] One could accuse the legendary Hengest of double-dealing with the Britons. In the "Finnsburg episode," the poem's Hengest chooses to honor his heroic obligation to avenge Hnæf his late lord rather than his oath to keep a truce with Finn, the Frisian king who was responsible for Hnæf's death. This Hengest, too, might be faulted for oath-breaking, but both Bede and the *Anglo-Saxon Chronicle* report the legendary Hengest's dealings with Vortigern without disapproval and *Beowulf* describes the other Hengest's revenge on Finn as the fulfillment of a universally acknowledged duty.[2] The names are the same, the lives have parallel ambiguities; an Anglo-Saxon audience would almost surely have taken the poem's Hengest for the hero of the conquest of Britain and seen the Finnsburg story as taking place in the generation that began the conquest. Indeed, the old story of Finnsburg would have held as much interest for the Anglo-Saxon audience of *Beowulf* as it did for the Danes and Geats who hear it as part of the celebration of Beowulf's victory over Grendel.

Since Grundtvig we have dated the events of the poem by the North Star of Hygelac's fatal raid on the Franks, a historical event (also reported in Gregory of Tours) which certainly falls within the period 515–30, but this precise dating is a work of modern scholarship[3] and requires a good knowledge of Latin and of Gregory, neither of which could be expected of a secular Anglo-Saxon audience for *Beowulf.* Hengest was widely known to the English before and after the Anglo-Saxon period and is more likely to have been a traditionally learned Anglo-Saxon's clue to the time of the action than Hygelac or Hrothgar. Marijane Osborn has developed this thesis as an entertaining specula-tion, and I suggest the speculation was available to the poem's early audiences.[4]

If the poem's action was, in the imagination of some of its Anglo-Saxon audiences, connected with the great hero Hengest and the con-quest of Britain, the past in *Beowulf* could be described as layered (and inconsistent—as traditional history is) with Beowulf, Hrothgar, and Wiglaf standing at the margins of legend and almost in reach of the audience's ancestry. Scyld defines another margin; behind that ancient figure lies a deeper past. In part II the search for the origins of the dragon's treasure attains a glimpse of time's abyssal deep in which every name has drowned and which challenges at least for a moment the poem's claim of a value not subject to the injury of time.

Beowulf seems older than the beginnings of the Anglo-Saxon conquest of Britain because the poem excludes any explicit reference to the migration or the conquest. These exclusions create the possibility of an indeterminate time scheme, one in which the poem's action might be placed in the era of the Anglo-Saxon conquest or in the deep past of the Continent, or of the world. Just as the poem excludes explicit references to the Germanic conquest of Britain or to the insular history of the Anglo-Saxons, it also excludes references to the conversion of the Anglo-Saxons or indeed to the Christian faith. The poem's unambiguous references to events specifically known to Christian history—the Creation, the story of Cain and Abel, the Flood,—belong to the Book of Genesis, the most ancient stratum of sacred history. The poem's actors seem to know only of the Creation; the narrator traces Grendel's descent back to Cain, but the wisest of the Danes, Hrothgar himself, cannot account for the monster's origins. Nor does Hrothgar know the story of the Flood which is somehow represented on the hilt of the ancient sword, the work of giants, with which Beowulf decapitates Grendel's mother and the monster's corpse. Christian doctrine has generally held that human reason unaided can discover the necessity of a god and a creation; Snorri Sturluson's prologue to the *Prose Edda* translates that belief into a delightful narrative of the rediscovery of God by the natural activity of the mind.[5] With the exception of one brief passage, the characters of *Beowulf* apparently believe that one benevolent god created and rules the world as reason supposedly teaches.

Dorothy Whitelock postulates a learned, Christian audience who would have known that *Beowulf* represents a relatively recent era of Germanic paganism, but the poem's silences could imply that its actions (though postdiluvian) belong to the oldest of the three eras of human history Ælfric distinguished: the time before the establishment of the old, Mosaic law; the time of the Mosaic law; and the time of the new law of Christ.[6] A traditionally learned Anglo-Saxon might have aligned the poem's historical setting with the conquest of Britain; a contemporary acquainted with some of the Old Testament might have

placed the action in the age of the patriarchs. To see the events of
Beowulf as part of history before the Mosaic law might have distinguished the poem's actors from the pagans of later ages, but Anglo-
Saxons with a deeper grounding in biblical history should have known
that all Cain's descendents perished in the flood as Ælfric explicitly
notes in his introduction to the Old and New Testaments.[7] Grendel's
descent from Cain is the fulcrum on which the almost explicitly Christian meaning of the poem's first episode turns. That crucial point seems
to demonstrate the poem's slender grasp but imaginative use of Christian history. Such unfamiliarity with rudimentary biblical history may
seem surprising, but the scribe struggled with the very name of Cain
(107, 1261) first rendering it as "cames" (corrected in the manuscript
to "caines"), then as "camp" (an Anglo-Saxon word for "battle"). E. V.
K. Dobbie's note on line 1261 concludes: "The scribe must have been
unfamiliar with the story of Cain; in 1. 107 he at first wrote *cames,* later
altering it to *caines.*"[8] That scribe was almost surely a monk and a
professed Christian who might be expected to know the Bible better
than most of the poem's secular auditors.

   Antiquity and the greatness of antique kings and princes are the
subjects of the poem's first lines, which memorably place the action's
present in a distant past:

> Hwæt, we Gar-Dena   in geardagum,
> þeodcyninga   þrym gefrunon,
> hu ða æþelingas   ellen fremedon!
>   (1–3)

(Listen, we have heard about the power in former times of the great kings of
the Spear-Danes, how the princes performed deeds of valor!)

That view of the Danes as history hints at a date for the poem's
composition in its surviving form. From about the 830s to the 940s,
the Danes and their spears were news. The argument that during the
first Viking age not all the English were at odds with the Danes and
that an English audience could distinguish the present Vikings and the
generations from Scyld Scefing to Hrothgar seems beside the point.[9]
The poem locates the power and the glory of the Danes in the audience's ancestral past, which implies that *Beowulf* was already on parchment and somewhat resistant to re-creation and updating by the time
the Viking age began in earnest.

The Royalist Bias and Values

The first three lines nicely anticipate the ruling themes of the poem's first section: antiquity, power, dynastic succession, and overlordship. The ancient Danish rulers are "þeodcyningas"—great or national, rather than local, kings. This word has been taken as an indication of the poem's late date since it appears in skaldic poetry we can assign to the ninth and later centuries.[10] However, the prefix "þeod"- can commonly be translated as "great," "national," or "universal," and the compound "þeodcyning" does not require a model in Old Norse skaldic poetry. Greatness is comparative and poetry creates a golden world; we need not suppose that when *Beowulf* was composed, the Danes or the Anglo-Saxons were actually unified under single kings, but that the poem's audience had a strongly royalist bias and found the contemplation of long-continued monarchical power agreeable. The poem throughout focuses on kings and royal dynasties—first the Scyldings, the Danish royal line, then Geatish and Swedish dynasties down to the death of Beowulf and the predicted end of a dynasty. The poem's allusions and digressions also refer to kings of the Angles, the Franks, the Frisians, and others.

The poem presupposes that a people's well-being and their king's power are one and makes the relationship reciprocal. Scyld Scefing arrives, destitute, "feasceaft" (7), and indeed a helpless infant among the Danes who are suffering cruel distress for want of a king. He grows, prospers, and leads them in victorious war until his neighbors pay tribute and obedience to Danish power; at his death, the Danes place Scyld's body in a funeral ship with rich treasures, arms, armor, ornaments, and a royal standard, and return their king of mysterious origin to the deep, the unknowable. The poem's prologue imposes upon the succession of royal lives, the cycle of generation and mortality, a linear movement of Danish imperialism. Despite Scyld's death and funeral, the prologue and first section of the poem seem dominated by images of birth and growth: Scyld "weox under wolcnum" (8; grew up beneath the heavens) and Hrothgar's young retainers "geweox" (66) into a great band of warriors. The poem's close, narrating Beowulf's death, funeral, memorial, and eulogy, like its beginning, describing Scyld's arrival, prosperity, death, and succession, states those themes of antiquity, dynasty, royal power, and a people's prosperity. The dying hero leaves orders for his tomb, a great gravemound that will forever be a landmark for sailors and as "Biowulfes biorh" (2807) his memorial. The poem's

audience finds itself in that "forever after," and the towering earthen
mound raised by the poet's words re-creates the gulf of time and space
and epochal events separating the poem's audience from its subjects.
The poem's royalist bias is subsumed in its vision of human reality; the
glorious line of the Scyldings with which the poem begins has reached
and passed its zenith when Beowulf appears in Denmark and at the
poem's close the line of Hrethel and the Geatish nation itself have
reached their end. The poem's much disputed last word, "lofgeornost"
("most eager for praise"), reasserts the story's antiquity and immediacy.
An Anglo-Saxon audience in responding to the poem fulfills Beowulf's
desire for "lof," the praise of future generations, the poem's audiences'
world to come.

The close of the poem's prologue offers the audience a practical
aphorism seemingly authorized by the story of Scyld Scefing's success
and succession: "lofdædum sceal / in mægþa gehwære, man geþeon"
(24–25) or "in every nation a man can only prosper by doing praiseworthy deeds," but in the poem's close, the praise remains unadulterated
by the prosperity glorious deeds might have deserved and won and held
for a lifetime or a dynasty. The linear thrust of Danish imperialism or
Geatish survival has been overtaken and returned to the eternal cycle.
At the end of *Beowulf* only the praise remains; the hero, the line of
Hrethel, the Geats themselves disappear into that antiquity the poem's
audience contemplates. Scyld was the first of a mighty line, Beowulf
the last of another, but the poem's view embraces the end of both
dynasties; royal families, like royals themselves, are mortal. The poem's
opening and closing link the two heroes with contrasts: a founder and a
last survivor, a mythical hero of mysterious origins returned to the
mystery of the sea, a seemingly historical hero whose princely birth and
kingly burial can be assigned to a definite place. Their very names
differ significantly: Scyld is the eponymous hero of the Scyldings (the
Danes), a mythical figure derived from a name of his supposed people,
but Beowulf's name does not alliterate with the names of the Geatish
royal line (Hrethel, Herebeald, Hæthcyn, Hygelac, Heardred) nor of
his clan (the Wægmundings including Weohstan and Wiglaf). Beowulf's name almost seems a riddle—"who is the bee's enemy?" (or "who
is to the bee as the wolf is to mankind?") to which the answer almost
surely is the bear.[11]

Beowulf has been characterized, by implication at least, as a pastiche,
as something akin to our historical novel, but for all its absorption with
antiquity, the poem almost certainly reflects the social realities of the

Anglo-Saxon audience's world rather than a historian's reconstruction of an earlier society. As far as one can tell from the evidence of archaeology and the poem's sometimes ambiguous details, the material culture of the poem's actors and audience can hardly be distinguished. Swords, shields, coats of ring-mail, helmets with surmounted boar figures, drinking vessels, royal halls capable of accommodating large companies of drinkers, all furnish the poem and are attested to in Anglo-Saxon society; the Sutton Hoo ship burial contains most of these items, and its supply of household artifacts implies a hall and hospitality on a scale like Hrothgar's. The poem's social realities, excepting religious affiliation, seem to be taken from the life of Anglo-Saxon England. Dorothy Whitelock argued powerfully that the poem's values are completely compatible with those of Anglo-Saxon Christianity which, for an important example, recognized the obligation and duty of revenge. That argument baptizes a social institution characteristic of the pre-Christian Germanic world, or attests to the paganization (or secularization) of Anglo-Saxon Christianity. Citing some instances of Anglo-Saxon kings who abdicated and entered monasteries, E. G. Stanley claims that these rulers "thought the pagan glory of pledging in the hall, of victory in the field, of treasure-giving and of loyalty to an earthly throne, a vain ideal."[12] If these ancient pre-Christian and secular ideals and practices are "pagan," we must conclude that Anglo-Saxon England's conversion to Christianity was still incomplete at the time of the Norman Conquest in 1066. *The Battle of Brunanburh* and the *Battle of Maldon* attest powerfully to the survival into the tenth and eleventh centuries of a heroic ideal discernible in *Beowulf;* a sophisticated literary criticism may, as Stanley seems to believe, reveal that the poem rejects that heroic ideal, but many possible Anglo-Saxon audiences would have taken the poem as confirming a traditional and heroic system of values.

The poem's prologue taken literally suggests a royal and noble audience, a value system derived from the heroic age of pre-Christian Germania, and, most appropriately for a poet addressing a noble and royal audience, an epic, public voice repeating those truths universally acknowledged that require authoritative repetition: men need more often to be reminded than to be informed.

The text of *Beowulf* contains only one clear instance of a passage delivered out of this epic voice, the famous "first Christian excursus" of lines 175–88 whose authenticity many older scholars, even including Tolkien, have questioned. Most modern critics of *Beowulf* have insisted on the integrity of the text as preserved in our late copy, rejecting all theories of interpolation, but Stanley, who argues that *Beowulf* rejects the heroic or pagan ideal, makes this passage the cornerstone of his argument: "The poet . . . nowhere states unambiguously (except at lines 175–88) that the pagan ideal he presents is insufficient, and some readers will be reluctant to read the poem in that way (especially if they first delete lines 175–88 as an interpolation)."[13] But the reader need not delete the disputed lines to doubt Stanley's conclusion. The controverted lines first report that many of the "powerful ones" among the Danes frequently considered what to do about Grendel's attacks and that they promised sacrifices (or honors) at pagan shrines if the "gastbona" helped them in this great calamity. Now "gastbona" is usually taken as "soul-destroyer" or devil, but may be "monster-destroyer," an appropriate expression for Thor whom Norse tradition describes as continually engaged in battle with monsters and giants. The narrator's uncharacteristic outburst at this point rejects the worship of pagan gods and defines that worship specifically as performing sacrifices or honoring a pagan god at a temple, but nothing in lines 175–88 rejects the heroic ethos.

Uncharacteristic of the poem's speaker as lines 175–88 are, they may represent a singer's (or poet's or scribe's) attempt to assure his audience that the persons of his poem need not be regarded as eternally lost. The literary treatment of Icelandic or Scandinavian heroes who lived before the conversion seems an instructive parallel. Various sagas specify that their heroes never worshiped pagan gods, that they expressed skepticism about idols, or even that they recognized only the God who created the sun.[14] An example of this theme appears in the *Book of the Settlements* (*Landnámabók*) which reports that when Thorgeir Moon ("one of the noblest heathen that ever lived") lay dying, he "had himself carried out to a shaft of sunlight, and gave himself to the god who created the sun."[15] In a harder case, *The Saga of Hrafnkel Priest of Frey* represents its unidealized hero, a "goði" or pagan priest, as renouncing his faith and rejecting its symbols.[16] These denials or rejections of paganism seemingly assure an Icelandic audience that their heroes and ancestors need not be seen as forever lost. The scrupulous monotheism of Hrothgar's ordinary discourse and the complete lack of any other references to pagan observances among the Danes (or Geats or Swedes) hardly demonstrates that the poem's doctrine of damnation applies to anyone in the poem save those powerful ones among the Danes who promised pagan observances if the "gastbona" succored them against Grendel. Since the "gastbona" did not accept the challenge, we cannot even be sure that those who called on him for help fall under the sentence of damnation. The poem's theology may be faulty, but most popular theology is.

Discovering the Poem's World

The poem imposes many delays on its central story and includes many explorations not directly related to its main business, but despite an indirect movement and moments of leisure, *Beowulf* creates a powerful impression of a great action moving irresistibly forward, advancing not steadily but abruptly in sudden lurches and turns toward a fearful event. Brief summaries of the "basic story" of *Beowulf* conceal its rich variety of forms and matter; the poem captures a vast historical scope, includes a variety of genres or modes of composition, and reveals a constant interplay of tones. The prologue separates the poem's audience from the story—long ago in another country—then presents the audience with a gratifying account of heroic success, of heroism leading to national success, of the hero as founder of a great dynasty. At the height of Scyld's brilliant career, a kingdom won, an overlordship established, and an heir engendered, the narrator proposes as a universal truth the rule that in every nation the successful aspirant to honor must do praiseworthy deeds. On these words, the narrator announces Scyld's death at the fated time; the prologue closes with his people's grief for the great king's passing.

Scyld earned the narrator's accolade—"þæt wæs god cyning!" (11; that was a good king!)—early in the prologue which ends with the universal truth of mortality and an unanswerable question. Scyld returns to the mystery from which he came after his richly laden funeral ship is launched on the unknowable deep. Still, the succession of fortunate generations of Scyld's line contrasts the mystery and the blunt fact of death with an unfolding story of dynastic prosperity extending for generations until the crowning of the Scyldings' success with the building of Heorot. Mortality presses in on the line of Scyld Scefing and the first celebration at Heorot awakens a monster who seems to embody or to represent the force of chaos and old night. That scene, dramatically reversing the stately tone of the poem's prologue, begins with the monster's anger at the sound of joy in Heorot, then traces that joy to the poet's song celebrating the creation of the world, then leaves the Danish ruling elite living in those joys until the monster, Grendel, begins his raids.

Grendel's first raid turns all the successes of the triumphant line of the Scyldings into horror, pain, and humiliation. After Grendel's second raid, the night after his first, the narrator notices that

> Þa wæs eaðfynde   þe him elles hwær
> gerumlicor   ræste sohte
> bed æfter burum,   ða him gebeacnod wæs,
> gesægd soðlice   sweotolan tacne
> healðegnes hete;   heold hyne syðþan
> fyr ond fæstor   se þæm feonde ætwand.
>   (138–43)

(Then it was easy to find the man who got himself a more distant resting place, a bed in a private dwelling, when the hall-thegn's hatred was manifested to him, plainly declared by a sure sign; whoever escaped that enemy kept himself farther away and safer.)

Six full lines remorselessly detail the humiliation of noble warriors among the Danes who, in the face of certain death there, give up sleeping in the royal hall, a kind of mens' lodge, and seek out a more domestic safety. The Danes become double victims, of Grendel's wrath and of the poem's irony; the monster diminishes their manly status; the poem makes that diminishment public and thus real. The audience is drawn toward Grendel, it accepts a certain complicity in calamity to savor the poem's detached irony at the cost of Danish manliness. Warrior societies in many cultures segregate men and women; apparently the all-male fellowship of such lodges contributes to the aggressive spirit a warring society requires.[17] Grendel's interruption of the regular practice unmans the Danish warrior class, calls their heroic status into question, and damages the means of sustaining their traditional calling and their honor.

As the poem moves from the Danes to the Geats, a series of contrasts in the character and tone of the narrative become apparent. The Danish scene represents a whole society in paralysis, the Geatish a man in action. The Danes meet frequently, consider deeply, risk their immortal souls searching for supernatural help, and lament their losses in an agony of helplessness. Immediately following the report of Grendel's first and second raids, the narrator adds that this calamity persisted for twelve years; that the lord of the Scyldings suffered great sorrows; that songs sadly revealed to the world that Grendel waged cruel war against Hrothgar for many years. The narrator (or those songs) reports that

Grendel intended never to make a truce with the Danes. The narrator sums up: Grendel performed "fela fyrena . . . heardra hynða" (164, 166; "many crimes . . . cruel humiliations"), many powerful men among the Danes often considered what should be done (171–74), and Hrothgar's sorrows burned continually in his heart (189–90).

In the Danish setting some forty lines report the unending succession of humiliations and sorrow heaped upon the hapless people and above all their king, but restated among the Geats, the long story of passive suffering and helplessness amounts only to a clause. The Danish complaint ends with Hrothgar's sorrow and inaction:

> ne mihte snotor hæleð
> wean onwendan;   wæs þæt gewin to swyð,
> laþ ond longsum,   þe on ða leode becom,
> nydwracu niþgrim,   nihtbealwa mæst.
> (190–93)

(the wise man was unable to ward off that misery; that distress, that cruel and violent, hateful and long-drawn-out onslaught, that cruel distress, which had fallen upon the people, was too severe)

The scene abruptly moves to the Geats, where the strongest man living on earth, Hygelac's retainer, hears of "Grendles dæda" (195), Grendel's deeds. The strong man at once commands that a ship be readied and announces his intention to visit the famous king of the Danes who has need of men. Between the hero's command, his announcement, and his selection of his companions for the exploit, the Geatish councillors consult the omens and approve his plans even as he leads his picked company to the sea and the ready ship.

The pagan and superstitious practice of consulting omens evokes no negative comment in the poem, though Anglo-Saxon sermons strongly condemned such time-honored observances.[18] From Beowulf's first introduction into the poem to the moment Grendel realizes his impending doom, all signs agree that the hero's victory is certain. The alacrity of the hero's decision, preparations, and setting out bespeaks a self-confidence that seems itself a token of victory. The voyage is swift and easy, which requires strong winds from the right quarter and confirms the favorable omens. The supernatural sign vouchsafed the Geatish councillors and the disposition of nature agree in pointing toward Beowulf's success. The wisdom of the Danes concurs: the coast guard who challenges Beowulf and the Geats at the Danish shore seems to respond to an aura of good luck and good intentions manifested in Beowulf's appearance when he breaks off his formal challenge to observe that one of the seafarers seems a man of unique qualities and exceptional status and to wish: "næfre him his wlite leoge, / ænlic ansyn" (250–51; "may his look, his matchless appearance, never belie him").[19] Given the Danes' dearest wish of the past twelve years, the coast guard must see a resolve to destroy Grendel and the tokens of success in the foreigner at the Danish coast.

Defining Beowulf

The hero's uninvited, unannounced, and indeed anonymous arrival on the Danish coast turns the story's action into a drama of human relationships between characters whose inner lives and motives are not explicitly disclosed. Understanding Beowulf becomes the official business of Hrothgar's royal servants; explaining Beowulf becomes the king's urgent concern, denying him, Unferth's. As he reaches the Danish shore, Beowulf enters a world of anxieties and tensions that vividly contrast his nearly impenetrable calm. The coast guard's tensions are the simplest: his unspoken hope is clearly deliverance from Grendel, his anxiety the possibility that unknown warriors may mean war. Nothing in this good soldier's challenge betrays a fear that these strangers signify his own swift departure for oblivion. The coast guard's words with Beowulf's company recognize the ambiguous significance of their warlike gear, which bespeaks their noble status and their deadly power; the coast guard acknowledges that the hero's appearance is both noble and auspicious, but the good soldier also demands a prompt answer to his challenge (256–57), which could be paraphrased as "Where are you coming from?"

Beowulf's answer responds both to the coast guard's challenge and to his hopes; the good soldier accepts the stranger's words as authentic proof of good intentions, asserting that a well-thinking warrior must distinguish words and deeds, know the difference. The remark has occasioned much commentary; after all, the splendid stranger has offered only words, though welcome ones.[20] The coast guard says both that he understands or knows and that he hears that this troop is loyal to the Danish king: "Ic þæt gehyre, þæt þis is hold werod / frean Scyldinga" (290–91), "gehyre" meaning both "hear" and "understand." The coast guard's actions gloss his words: he agrees to lead the visitors to Heorot, and to assign some of his young warriors to guard their ship. Escorting the newcomers to the point where they can see Heorot (and be seen from Heorot) has an obvious security value; securing their ships almost ensures the visitors' good conduct. These are the courtesies of an age of violence and nobility. The coast guard, the good soldier, betrays no fear and no self-regarding concern for the implications of Beowulf's mission to the Danes.

At Heorot, Wulfgar, a royal officer and member of the Danish court who is apparently a princely foreigner, challenges the visitors, noting their weapons and their evident nobility of spirit. Anxieties and tensions quite unlike those that moved the coast guard come into play. Wulfgar, himself a daring, courageous man ("wlonc hæleð"; 331) surmises at once that these distinguished and noble warriors must, by their air, have come in pursuit of honor and have some daring purpose in mind: "Wen' ic þæt ge for wlenco, nalles for wræcsiðum, / ac for higeþrymmum Hroðgar sohton" (338–39; "I believe that you have sought Hrothgar on account of your daring courage, not on account of exile but because of your great spirits"). Wulfgar takes the word "wlenco," which represents the daring impulse to seek for honor in danger, as an honorific; he intends to praise the hero for a still unstated intention—that praise may be taken as an encouragement for an exploit of extraordinary daring. Wulfgar is clearly anxious lest Hrothgar dismiss these visitors. Having carefully not promised the Geats a royal audience, he urges Hrothgar to receive Beowulf and his company.

Hrothgar's reply, his first direct discourse in the poem, humanizes the king who earlier appeared as a public figure and as a mourner, a sufferer, not quite particularized as a person. Hrothgar recognizes Beowulf unseen: "Ic hine cuðe cnihtwesende" (372; "I knew him when he was a boy") and identifies the hero as the son of Ecgtheow and a daughter of the late King Hrethel of the Geats. Hrothgar knows Beowulf's strength (that of thirty men), guesses his purpose (to defend the Danes against Grendel), and acknowledges both his obligation of generosity to the hero and by implication confidence in Beowulf's success: "Ic þæm godan sceal / for his modþræce madmas beodan" (384–85; "I shall be obliged to give the good man treasures on account of his courageous daring"). Before Beowulf's entrance into the hall, Hrothgar assures his followers that their deliverance is at hand. The delayed disclosure of the hero's name leaves the poem's actors and audience to ponder the hero's identity and significance; Hrothgar proves wisest of the Danes when he recognizes the hero's name and traces his genealogy farther than the narrator has done. Hrothgar's response makes Beowulf part of a social and human context. The hero, a remote and idealized figure among the Geats, becomes a social reality as he enters Denmark and Heorot.

Unlike the Danes and his royal servants, Hrothgar knows Beowulf. Hrothgar's anxiety is not to identify Beowulf but to create a context in which the hero can act to save the Danes' honor from the scourge of Grendel without shaming the Danish aristocracy for its incapacity.[21] Hrothgar creates an explanation for Beowulf's coming consistent with the honor of the aristocratic Danes, among whom he is first. Hrothgar's welcome aims at making Beowulf essentially one of his followers, a man obligated to Hrothgar's service in the manner of Wulfgar, himself a foreigner in the royal Danish service. This agreeable solution might seem less so in the Geatish court.

When Beowulf enters Hrothgar's presence and asks permission to attempt the cleansing of the great hall, the Danish king answers the request obliquely rather than directly. He responds by telling the story, not even hinted at before, of Beowulf's father and his killing of Heatholaf and consequent feud with the Wilfings; of Hrothgar's part in resolving that conflict; and of Beowulf's father's unspecified oaths to Hrothgar. This new accounting for Beowulf makes the deliverance of the Danes from Grendel's ravages the repayment of an old debt, rather than a purely altruistic act of heroism. Hrothgar's revised Beowulf seems quite a different hero from Wulfgar's: the king's hero comes to honor an obligation created by his father's exile and Hrothgar's relief of that condition; Wulfgar's hero comes in the daring pursuit of honor. Preserving the honor of the Danish ruling class despite the inevitable comparison between its helplessness and the hero's power urgently requires Hrothgar's skill. At home Beowulf said that he wanted to visit Hrothgar "þa him wæs manna þearf" (201; "since he was in need of men"), an innocuous remark among the Geats but, if spoken or implied, an insult among the Danes. Hrothgar's concern for his own and his followers' honor attests to his confidence in the hero's victory. If Hrothgar felt the issue of battle doubtful or the hero's prospects grim, the need to identify the heroic deed as part of an exchange of benefits would be less urgent or would not arise. The ruling Danes face a dilemma: Grendel's raids erode their honor and challenge their manliness, while Beowulf's request to be allowed to contest their quarrel with the monster promises to remove the daily horror at the cost of confirming for good their diminished status.

"The wordes Moote Be Cosyn to the Dede"

Hrothgar's speech builds the social web of relationships and of benefits exchanged and to be exchanged, making as clear and as real as
words can a context in which Beowulf's heroism can coexist with
Danish honor. The close of the royal speech calls on the power of words
to create another reality: "Site nu to symle ond onsæl meoto, / sigehreð
secgum, swa þin sefa hwette" (490–91). The passage presents many
difficulties, but if we read the hardest words as "onsæl meoto / sigehreð
secgum," the translation C. L. Wrenn proposed and himself rejected—
"Sit now to the feast and unloose your thoughts, your glorious victories
('sigehreð') to the warriors"—is probably correct. Wrenn objected that
following Hrothgar's invitation the court-poet sings and Beowulf lis-
tens. The last half-line, which Wrenn omitted from discussion, can be
rendered "as your spirit inspires you" or "will inspire you."[22] Hrothgar
suggests that Beowulf make known his mind, thoughts, purpose
("meoto") after first partaking of the "symbel" or feast, which throughout the poem seems to consist of strong drink alone, food never being
mentioned. The glorious victory that Hrothgar particularly wants to
hear Beowulf speak of lies in the future, not the past.

Hrothgar longs to hear Beowulf's formal vow to fight Grendel to the
death since the words of the vow will both bind Beowulf to the attempt
and strengthen him in the act. Formal vows, words spoken in public
and marked as deeply significant, create and sustain the code of honor
and prowess that calls on its members to transcend the "world of
commonsense and nonheroic norms."[23] A minor masterpiece of Anglo-
Saxon poetry, *The Battle of Maldon,* illustrates the importance of formal,
public promises to perform heroic actions, to fulfill the obligations of
membership in a heroic society. In the poem's long concluding section,
one Anglo-Saxon warrior after another vows to avenge his fallen lord,
Byrhtnoth of Essex, or to die beside him, and goes forward to certain
death in the fulfillment of that obligation. The vows spoken in the
course of the battle reaffirm the pledges Byrhtnoth's men had made
earlier that same day and which, at the crucial point in the battle, some
of Byrhtnoth's followers had betrayed.[24] Their own words spoken first
at a public assembly and restated on the field of battle steel Byrhtnoth's
loyal followers to their final acts of heroism. Thus Hrothgar anticipates
the words that will commit Beowulf to overcome the monster who has
blighted Heorot for twelve years. The poem explicitly confirms
Hrothgar's wisdom in inviting the hero to speak: when the hero (still

lying in bed) has gripped Grendel's groping hand, the monster's spirit fails in the instant. Grendel thinks only of escape, Beowulf of his vow: "Gemunde þa se goda, mæg Higelaces, / æfenspræce, uplang astod / ond him fæste wiðfeng" (758–60;" Then the brave man, Hygelac's kinsman, thought of his speeches that evening, stood up, and laid firm hold on him"). The words he spoke in the hearing of all Heorot inspire Beowulf to a still more deadly grip on the enemy whose spirit has already failed.

Just before welcoming Beowulf to the hall's hospitality and alcohol, and before hinting that the hero should state his heroic intentions formally, Hrothgar cites precedents for just that progression, from the drinking cup to a formal and binding promise to defend Heorot from the monster. The king relates that his own followers frequently proceeded from their drinking to vows of cutting off Grendel with the sword:

> Ful oft gebeotedon   beore druncne
> ofer ealowæge   oretmecgas,
> þæt hie in beorsele   bidan woldon
> Grendles guþe   mid gryrum ecga.
> (480–83)

(Very often warriors drunk with strong liquor vowed over the ale-cup that they would await with the terrors of swords Grendel's onslaught in the drinking-hall.)

With grim candor, Hrothgar reports the outcome of those pledges:

> Ðonne wæs þeos medoheal   on morgentid,
> drihtsele dreorfah,   þonne dæg lixte,
> eal bencþelu   blode bestymed,
> heall heorudreore;   ahte ic holdra þy læs,
> deorre duguðe,   þe þa deað fornam.
> (484–88)

(Then in the morning when day dawned this mead-hall, the noble building, was stained with gore, all the bench-planks wet with blood, the hall with men's life-blood; I had the fewer loyal followers in my beloved band since death had taken them away.)

The last two lines include a construction like "the more the merrier"—the more death took away, the fewer Hrothgar had left—which seems a mathematical tautology but powerfully expresses the emotion building up in the old king as he speaks. Just at this point, Hrothgar invites Beowulf to sit down to the feast.

Hrothgar's candid acknowledgment that previous attempts to rid the hall of Grendel ended in bloodstained disappearances counterpoints the horror of the past against the recurring suggestion that Beowulf's victory is inevitable. Hrothgar's openness powerfully reminds his followers of their collective failure and dreadful predicament. The reminder seems all the more necessary for being ignored in the next scene—Unferth's interruption. Hrothgar recognizes that Beowulf's intention to attempt the action no Dane could perform in the past or dares venture in the present affronts every Danish warrior in the great hall, and he realizes that the hero's vow will shame them all. The fate of Danish warriors past presents the alternative to accepting an outsider's help with its painful implications, hence Hrothgar makes that fate vivid. As he does, he feels the old pain anew. The sound of the scop's song and of human joy fills Heorot once more and for a moment (496–98) the scene recalls the great celebration before the beginning of Grendel's raids. The conclusion of the scop's performance seems to be Beowulf's cue. The poet's song makes a decorous and appropriate prelude to the words Hrothgar keenly anticipates Beowulf's speaking; Heorot's poet is described as "gilphlæden" (868) as the Danes ride back in triumph from the mere after seeing its waters boiling with Grendel's blood. The adjective "gilphlæden" seems to mean both that the poet was loaded ("hladen") with fame or glory ("gilp") and laden with poems expressive of the fame and glory won by vows of great deeds subsequently performed.[25] The word "gilp" can mean a vow or boast and the glory or fame characteristically won by its fulfillment. Indeed, after the prelude and interruption, Beowulf's long-awaited words are called a "gilpcwide," the formal statement of a vow to do a glorious deed (640).

Before the poet's song and strong drink (Hrothgar's program) can inspire Beowulf to speak, Unferth, Hrothgar's "thyle" (perhaps "spokesman"), breaks in with a story of an alleged defeat Beowulf suffered in the past and concludes from that event that the hero will not survive the encounter if he dares to wait in the hall for the monster's nightly visit. This intriguing instance of dramatic interplay in the poem's action has set off much dark interpretation: Unferth's name has been taken to signify "un-peace," that is "strife" or "discord," the apparent truth that he killed his brothers with the sword has been seen as establishing a spiritual affinity between Unferth and Grendel, whose descent the poem traces back to Cain.[26] Some hints in the poem and the legendary-historical fact that the poem's Hrothulf must be Rolf Kraki, the greatest of the legendary Danish kings, have persuaded various scholars that Hrothulf, Hrothgar's nephew, deposed the old king's sons after their father's death, and Unferth is often suspected of being a party to treason in the Danish court.[27] But Unferth's apparently indecorous outburst has its own unruly propriety. His profession or perhaps his office, like the scop's, requires an extraordinary gift for words, hence an appropriately ornate circumlocution introduces his speech: "Unferð maþelode, Ecglafes bearn, / þe æt fotum sæt frean Scyldinga, / onband beadurune" (499–501; "Unferth, the son of Ecglaf, who sat at the feet of the lord of the Shieldings, spoke, unbound his battle-runes"). The "beadurune" or "battle-runes" are Unferth's hostile speech, but "runes" suggest the Germanic alphabet invented, according to tradition, by Othin (Anglo-Saxon Woden), god of wisdom and poetry, war and strife.[28]

Unferth interrupts and attempts to forestall Beowulf's "beot" when he transforms the perfect moment for the vow or binding promise solemnly taken—especially taken with strong drink—into a "flyting." Both the "flyting" and the "beot" are traditional verbal forms, though of antithetical character. The first completes itself in words, the second looks forward to deeds and finds its meaning in action: performed, the "beot" means fame; unperformed, disgrace. Carol Clover argues that the recurring structure of flytings can be summarized as "Claim, Defense, and Counterclaim" in which the opponents interpret past incidents in each other's lives. Each speaker interprets his past as favorably as the background of fact permits, the opponent's past as unfavorably as possible. The "flyting" ends with an unchallenged claim of victory and generally without violence.[29]

Unferth quarrelsomely claims that Beowulf entered into a competitive swimming match with Breca (Breoca who in the Anglo-Saxon poem *Widsith* ruled the Brondings) and lost. From that defeat Unferth infers that Beowulf will suffer one still harsher if he dares await Grendel's nightlong visit to the hall. In a sense, Unferth's intention seems thwarted from the outset because Beowulf has already, in the course of asking Hrothgar's permission to cleanse the hall, announced his intention to fight Grendel hand-to-hand in the monster's own style, digressed with macabre humor on his fate should Grendel be the victor ("you needn't worry about my dinner since I'll be his" and "he's a messy feeder"), given instructions for the disposal of his heirloom mailshirt, and asked Hrothgar's care for his followers. But Beowulf later makes three formal statements vowing or promising to fight Grendel, the last two pledging to defeat the monster or die in the attempt (601–3, 632–38, 677–87). Unferth's interruption assumes that Beowulf could indeed be discouraged from repeating the vow and thus from performing the heroic act that will reduce Unferth's—and every Danish warrior's—status. Hrothgar and Unferth embody two contending impulses in the Danish court: a fervent hope that the newcomer will cleanse the hall and end the blight, and a recognition that Beowulf's "beot" will inevitably shame the Danish ruling class, and his victory will make that shame indelible. Unferth, the Danes' eloquent spokesman, speaks what many Danish nobles must feel. He picks up the dominant themes of the preceeding narration, the identification of Beowulf and the relationship of words and actions:

> Eart þu se Beowulf,   se þe wið Brecan wunne,
> on sidne sæ   ymb sund flite,
> ðær git for wlence   wada cunnedon
> and for dolgilpe   on deop wæter
> aldrum neþdon?
>
> (506–10)

(Are you the Beowulf who competed against Breca in a swimming match on the wide sea when the two of you tested the seas because of your high spirits and for a daring vow risked your lives in deep water?

The challenge concludes with (1) an assertion that Breca succeeded in his vow against or in rivalry with Beowulf—by implication a vow to excel Beowulf in swimming (523–24), and 2) with the inference that defeat in that contest indicates Beowulf has no chance against Grendel.

Postwar criticism typically sought Unferth's motive for his challenge ("Are *you* the Beowulf who . . .") in his supposed status as a symbol of strife or discord, and located the significance of the episode in Beowulf's riposte that Unferth had killed his brothers and would suffer punishment in hell.[30] Christian interpretations made Unferth a type or reflection of Cain, the first fratricide; that argument links Unferth and Grendel, whom the poet identifies as a descendant of Cain and consigns to hell (105–8, 852). Thus Unferth becomes an embodiment of the moral guilt of the heroic world.[31] At a more literal level, Unferth has been described as a buffoon, a court jester, a coward, and a murderer.[32] But he is none of

the above. The argument that Unferth is an allegorical figure has become
untenable; his name poses deep philological problems, but the first
element (*Un-*) is probably related to the Icelandic *hunn* meaning "bear-
cub," and almost surely *not* to the prefix *un-* meaning "not." The meaning of the second element of Unferth's name, sometimes explained as
"-frið" or "peace," sometimes as "-ferhð" or "spirit," remains obscure,
but Unferth bears an authentic Germanic name that would not have been
coined in Anglo-Saxon times.[33] In short, the name "Unferth" illustrates
the poem's traditional roots, not the poet's allegorical intentions. Beowulf's supposed claim that Unferth will suffer punishment in hell for
killing his brothers rests on a conjecture. The word "hell" has disappeared from the manuscript (the result of damage sustained in the fire of
1731) and Fred C. Robinson has suggested that it may have been
"healle," hence Beowulf's retort predicts that Unferth will suffer reproach in the hall, not punishment in hell, for kin-killing.[34] That argument makes Beowulf's words a "speech act" since the hero's statement
itself reproaches Unferth and in the hall. Beowulf's charge against
Unferth fits the rhetorical form of their exchange: accusations of kinship
crimes (fratricide, patricide, incest) are typical elements in a form that
opposes the worst and best possible interpretations of external realities.

Unferth needs first of all to be taken literally and seriously. He is part
of the heroic world's gritty reality, and probably Hrothgar's official
spokesman; in the exchange with Beowulf, he may be taken as speaking
for many of the Danes. The poem makes Unferth's motive for this
hostile speech explicit:

> wæs him Beowulfes sið,
> modges merefaran,   micel æfþunca,
> forþon he ne uþe,   þæt ænig oðer man
> æfre mærða þon ma   middangeardes
> gehedde under heofenum   þonne he sylfa.
> (501–5)

Beowulf's, the brave seafarer's, journey / undertaking / conduct was a vexation
for him because he would not grant that any other man on earth should aim at
accomplishing more in the way of glorious deeds beneath the sky than he
himself [aimed at].)[35]

Unferth resents and intends to forestall the "beot" or "gilp" in which
Beowulf would make his intention formal and binding. Unferth claims
that daring and the pursuit of honor led Beowulf to an earlier defeat:

Beowulf and Breca entered a swimming competition "for wlence" and "for dolgilpe" (508–9). Critics and translators have sometimes given Unferth's words "wlencu" and "dolgilp" pejorative meanings derived from homiletic contexts, but the honorific and heroic senses of the words seem at home in Heorot and the poem. Wulfgar greeted Beowulf at the door of Heorot guessing that the Geats must have come "for wlenco" (338; "because of daring") and clearly intended a compliment. That "dolgilp" articulated by Beowulf and Breca was a promise to do a "dollic" or daring deed; much later in the poem (2645–46), Beowulf's young kinsman and follower, Wiglaf, observes that the hero had performed more glorious actions ("mærða"), more daring deeds ("dæda dollicra") than any other man.[36] Unferth gives these words their heroic meanings since he argues from Beowulf's alleged defeat that the hero has no chance of successfully fulfilling a vow to defend the great hall against Grendel. Unferth seems to be saying "send Breca not Beowulf." As he closes his claim against Beowulf, the word that sums up Unferth's chagrin rises to his lips: "Beot eal wið þe / sunu Beanstanes soðe gelæste" (523–24; Beanstan's son truly performed his whole vow to rival you").

Beowulf's reply accepts and responds to Unferth's challenge as a traditional form of discourse and also recognizes Unferth's motif for the challenge, chagrin. Beowulf conventionally redefines the swimming match, corrects Unferth's misstatements and omissions, charges the Danish spokesman with a kinship crime, buffets the rawest nerve of all, Unferth's, and the Danes', inadequacy in the face of Grendel's raids, and abruptly closes coupling a claim of victory in the flyting with a vow to offer Grendel battle. Beowulf begins cordially, "my friend Unferth" (530), and observes that Unferth has spoken "beore druncen" (531), under the influence of strong drink. The sting of the remark does not lie in an accusation that Unferth has drunk too much but that he has not proceeded from the "beor" to the "beot," a vow to defend the hall against Grendel.[37] Beowulf's retelling of the Breca story nicely echoes details, words, and phrases of Unferth's but with an utterly different cast and with a conclusion—battle with a sea-monster—Unferth omitted altogether. Beowulf denies Unferth's characterization of the enterprise as a competition. In their boyhoods (535, 537; "cnihtwesende . . . on geogoðfeore," that is, "being boys . . . in youth") Beowulf and Breca agreed (535; "gecwædon") and vowed (536; "gebeotedon") to risk their lives in a venture on the sea. That "gebeotodon" followed by "ond þæt geæfndon swa" (538; "the two of us vowed and performed it exactly") returns the painful word to Unferth. The deed Beowulf reports more resembles a "dare" than a race or competition, hence the first ashore might be called the loser. Breca could not swim more strongly than Beowulf nor would Beowulf outswim Breca.[38] Thus the two proceeded companionably until separated by storms; Unferth's uncorrected report that Breca was washed ashore and returned to his people, having performed his vow, apparently stands. The pointed difference between Unferth's report that the enterprise took seven days and Beowulf's that he and Breca were on the sea together for five days hints that Breca was the first out of the water, though involuntarily.

Beowulf claims a kind of victory in this feat of endurance and daring when he asserts he had greater strength and severer hardships (533–34; "merestrengo maran . . . earfeþo") on the sea than any other man. That victory was given, not sought. Once storms separated the companions, sea-monsters attacked Beowulf and the boyish exploit turns into a mythical struggle against what may seem the forces of the deep, the realm of chaos itself. Beowulf's victory at the bottom of the sea was also given:

> . . . me gyfeþe wearð,
> þæt ic aglæcan   orde geræhte,
> hildebille;   heaþoræs fornam
> mihtig meredeor   þurh mine hand
>   (555–58)

(it was granted to me that I struck terrible enemies with my sword, battle destroyed powerful sea-beasts through my hand)

In five lines (569–73) Beowulf seems to credit his victory to God and to fate ("wyrd"). In his defense, Beowulf reinterprets his adventure with Breca as a portent of victory over Grendel.

Beowulf's brisk counterclaim denies Breca and Unferth any exploits like a victory over the monstrous and accuses Unferth of a monstrous victory, the killing of his brothers. In an early Germanic or Anglo-Saxon understanding of law, Unferth was probably not guilty of Cain's crime, a brother's murder. Cain, after all, killed Abel and attempted to conceal the fact. In the old Germanic world generally murder is a concealed, secret killing. We cannot doubt that Unferth killed his brothers, but until Beowulf's speech he apparently suffered no reproach in the hall where his heroic qualities were highly esteemed despite his fratricide. At the celebration following Beowulf's victory over Grendel, the poet reports that both Hrothulf and Hrothgar (nephew and uncle) trusted Unferth: "gehwylc hiora his ferhþe treowde, / þæt he hæfde mod micel, þeah þe he his magum nære / arfæst æt ecga gelacum" (1166–68; "both of them trusted his spirit, trusted that he had great courage even though he was not gracious to his kinsmen in the play of swords"). The claim made now and then that Unferth was a coward cannot be seriously maintained: both Hrothulf and Hrothgar believed in his courage and the "play of swords" makes an adequate test of courage. The seeming anomaly between Unferth's crime and his social status would have been familiar to an Anglo-Saxon audience. The literature of the heroic age took conflicts between the inherited obligations of kinship and obligations of loyalty voluntarily entered into as a great tragic theme. The *Anglo-Saxon Chronicle* entry for the year 757 reports the accession of the West-Saxon king, Cynewulf, but also includes the dramatic events of 786 that ended his reign and life. In this brief epic three groups of Anglo-Saxon warriors, followers of King Cynewulf and Prince Cyneheard, fight two mortal battles in succession. Prince Cyneheard and his company win the first round, killing King Cynewulf and a small troop of the king's bodyguard, but lose the second to a large company of royalists. The eventual winners offered to spare those of their kinsmen who were among the winners of the first round. The kinsmen insisted on remaining with their lord, Prince Cyneheard; the royalists placed their duty to revenge King Cynewulf above their kinsmen's lives. The same harsh choice and the same decision had marked the first encounter. Cynewulf's and Cyneheard's followers killed their kinsmen in their lords' causes, but did no murder. Unferth's fault was common on that bloody day in 786, by which date *Beowulf,* perhaps in something like its present form, may have been in circulation.[39]

Beowulf's claim of victory in the flyting moves quickly from the reproach aimed at Unferth to an unanswerable accusation that were the Dane's courage up to his pretensions, Grendel would not have humiliated Unferth's lord in Heorot and to a general charge that Grendel has not needed to fear the prowess of the Danes. Before his auditors can respond, Beowulf makes his "beot," a formal and binding promise to fight Grendel, in just four half-lines (601–3). The hero's vow and his claim of victory in the flyting with Unferth become one. As he brusquely makes explicit the implicit affront to Danish honor his presence means, Beowulf asserts the necessity of his prospective victory over

Grendel. The success of Beowulf's rhetoric becomes plain the instant
Hrothgar responds with joy to the hero's seemingly undiplomatic
speech:

> Þa wæs on sælum   sinces brytta
> gamolfeax ond guðrof;   geoce gelyfde
> brego Beorht-Dena;   gehyrde on Beowulfe
> folces hyrde   fæstrædne geþoht.
>
> (607–10)

(Then the grey-haired and battle-brave distributor of treasures was joyful; the
prince of the Bright-Danes counted on help; he, the guardian of the people,
had heard Beowulf's firmly resolved intention.)

Hrothgar's delighted reaction to Beowulf's speech sweeps the hall:
"Ðær wæs hæleþa hleahtor, hlyn swynsode, / word wæron wynsume"
(611–12; "There was men's laughter, the sound was pleasing, and
words joyful"). The Danes rejoice at their impending deliverance; the
immediate juxtaposition of Beowulf's insult to their martial prowess
and his promise to destroy their enemy, coming as the climax to a
traditional form of verbal play, resolves the contradiction between
manly honor and need.

Precisely the same pattern, a well-pleased royal and the sound of
general approval, follows Beowulf's second statement of his vow, but
with the repetition of his heroic statement, Beowulf's mood seems
fiercer, his readiness for battle greater. In what seems a formal ceremony, Wealtheow passes a drinking cup round the company, beginning
with Hrothgar. She offers the cup last to Beowulf, and sets off the
strongest emotions of the drama in Heorot: as he accepts the cup,
Beowulf restates his vow, but he is now "wælreow" and "guþe gefysed"
(629, 630; "slaughter-fierce," and "impelled toward battle").[40] He announces that in setting out for Denmark he intended to fulfill the desire
of the Danish people or die in the enemy's grip, and promises to
perform a deed of noble courage or end his life in the hall. The commitment is absolute, yet allows for failure. The narrator notes Wealtheow's
pleasure in Beowulf's vow: "Ðam wife þa word wel licodon, / gilpcwide
Geates; eode goldhroden / freolicu folccwen to hire frean sittan (639–
41; Those words, the Geat's spoken vow, pleased that woman very
much; gold-adorned, the people's noble queen went to sit beside her
lord). The sound of heroic assembly resumes, again great words are

spoken, the company rejoices—but only for two and one-half lines when a significant change of mood is announced with "oþ þæt" or "until," which repeatedly sounds in the poem (Hrothgar ruled happily "oþ þæt" Grendel began his raids).[41]

The phrase "oþ þæt semninga" (644; "until suddenly") leads at first to an intrusion of the commonplaces of domesticity on the heroic ceremony joyfully concluded in the great hall. Hrothgar wishes to seek his bed; the almost mock-heroic juxtaposition of the fateful phrasing and the quotidian result turns grim as Hrothgar's wish to retire seems to spring from his awareness that night, and Grendel's nightly visit to the hall, is almost at hand. This juxtaposition of domesticity and horror reappears as Beowulf readies himself for the struggle. With Hrothgar's going to bed, the tone and even the setting of the story change abruptly. In just seven lines the king entrusts Beowulf with the royal hall, charges him to hold it well by keeping watch against the savage enemy, and assures the hero that the rewards of victory will be generous. Hrothgar seems not to wait for an answer:

> Ða him Hroþgar gewat   mid his hæleþa gedryht,
> eodur Scyldinga   ut of healle;
> wolde wigfruma   Wealhþeo secan,
> cwen to gebeddan.
>
>   (662–65)

(Then Hrothgar, the protector of the Scyldings, departed out of the hall with his company of warriors; the battle-commander wished to visit Wealhtheow, his queen as bedfellow.)

The alacrity of the king's departure, his connubial plans for the night, add a touch of near-comedy to a reminder of fear. In what seems moments, the hall has changed utterly.

Heorot resounds with voices from the time Wulfgar, having spoken to Beowulf outside the building, speaks of the hero to the king within it; Hrothgar, Unferth, Wealththeow, the poet, and a multitude of Danes contribute to a sense of Heorot as a place of many voices, many sounds. But with Hrothgar's brisk departure, the hall seems almost silent, the place of joy and noisy merriment ("dream" in an Anglo-Saxon word) that first aroused Grendel's anger now seems hushed in fear. The hero alone speaks and Heorot seems again a place besieged and endangered as it was before his arrival. Beowulf makes his longest statement of his vow; having handed his arms and armor to a servant, he specifies his intention to fight Grendel without arms or armor since the monster cannot wield weapons like a warrior. Beowulf concludes this third and final statement of his vow saying (to paraphrase lines 685–87) "let God adjudge the glory to whomsoever it pleases him." Though neutral in form, the statement suggests the inevitability of the hero's victory. The narrator has previously noted that Grendel was cursed by his descent from Cain (104–10). This time the vow finds no audible response; the silent Geats, like Heorot itself, make no reply.

Chapter Four

The War against the Monsters

Entrances and Exits

The Road to Hel   From Hrothgar's brisk departure out of the
hall to Grendel's fearful, fatal entrance, the narrative balances the
audience's apprehension at the monster's inexorable and malevolent
approach with dramatic irony based on the audience's foreknowledge
that this terrifying approach brings the enemy step by step to his well-
deserved destruction. Some touches of humor or black comedy set off
both the irony and the terror[1] of Grendel's last visit to Heorot. Beowulf
begins his final vow "ær he on bed stige" (676; "before lying down in
bed") and on completing it, "Hylde hine þa heaþodeor, hleorbolster
onfeng / eorles andwlitan" (688–89; "The man brave in battle reclined,
the pillow received the nobleman's face"). The nearly mock-heroic
juxtaposition of the heroic vow and the domestic situation highlighted
by placing the bed at the beginning and the pillow at the end of the
hero's speech gains a special resonance juxtaposed with Grendel's expected arrival. And the poem moves directly from Beowulf's pillow to
his followers' going to bed in silent anticipation of the worst: none of
them expects to see home again after having heard the fate of so many
Danes in this hall (691–95). Unferth's envy, Hrothgar's joy, and
Wealhtheow's confidence in the hero's vow set in motion an audible
wave of hope and optimism, but the Geats' silent anticipation of a
violent death in Heorot reawakens the audience's apprehensions.

The essential design for irony in the representation of Grendel's last
visit to Heorot counterpoints, as Richard Ringler points out, the monster's expectations of feasting unopposed as usual in Heorot and the
audience's knowledge that he will not live out the night. Grendel
violates an essential precept of Anglo-Saxon prudential wisdom that
Beowulf scrupulously observes: bear in mind the possibility that the
future may not fulfill your hopes. Beowulf's daring vows commit him
to attempt deeds requiring the utmost courage, but acknowledge the
possibility and consequences of failure. Grendel's panic and terror at

the moment he perceives that his hand is in a stronger grip than his own realizes in an instant the ironies to which a reckless expectation uncorrected by understanding and forethought is liable.[2] At each significant step of Grendel's journey to Heorot (those approaching steps being central to the poem's design for terror), the narrator makes clear that God, the hero, or fate are prepared to thwart Grendel's purpose. When Grendel sets out for Heorot, the narrator notes that one of the warriors is not sleeping but awaits the battle in anger, and that it is well known that the monster cannot destroy the men in the hall if God does not wish it. At the next stage of the advance, the narrator notes that Grendel "bore God's anger" (711), an awkward burden to carry into mortal battle. When Grendel reaches Heorot, the narrator, with a mocking rhetorical flourish, observes that the monster had never in his life met "heardran hæle, healðegnas" (719; "tougher luck, [tougher] warriors"); the comparative adjective ("harder" or "tougher") describes both Grendel's luck and the warriors. As Grendel steps on the floor of Heorot, rejoicing in the expectation of a great feast, the narrator reassures the audience that it is not fated that Grendel should devour more men in the hall and that the hero is watching the monster's attack.

Grendel's approach to Heorot creates a sense of terror or apprehension as the monster becomes a juggernaut bearing inexorably down on the silent hall, moving inevitably toward Heorot and, as it were, the poem's audience. The approach falls into sections marked by verbs of motion and particularly by the triple repetition of a verbal sequence "com" ("he came") plus another verb of motion: "Com on wanre niht scriðan sceadugenga . . . Đa com of more . . . Grendel gongan . . . Wod under wolcnum . . . Com þa to recede . . . rinc siðian . . . on fagne flor feond treddode" (702–3, 710–11, 714, 720, 725; "The walker in shadows came advancing in the dark night . . . then Grendel came walking from the moor . . . he moved beneath the sky . . . then the warrior came advancing to the hall . . . the enemy trod the adorned floor"). Grendel's palpable advance follows a definite path that leads closer and closer to Heorot, to us. First he moves in the dark night ("on wanre niht") of the moor, then issues from it ("of more"), and moves beneath the open sky ("under wolcnum"); he is moving from the waste, an image of chaos, and crossing cleared land, the realm of mankind, "to þæs þe he winreced, / goldsele gumena gearwost wisse / fættum fahne" (714–16; "to the place where he knew very well the wine-building was, the goldhall of men adorned with ornaments").[3] Like a creature of permanent darkness, Grendel senses the location of the hall unlike

Beowulf and his company who perceived its gold-adorned splendor. At last Grendel steps on the beautifully adorned floor of Heorot (probably suggested by mosaic floors found in Romano-British villas built before the Anglo-Saxon conquest). Grendel's dreadful footfall on such a work of human art seems grotesque, and tellingly opposes images of destruction and creation.

As Grendel approaches and enters Heorot, the narrator successively describes the monster's intentions in more horrific detail until at last, and for the first time, the story directly represents the fate of many victims of the monster's raids. The graphically detailed account of Grendel eating one of Beowulf's unresisting, apparently unconscious followers becomes the final statement of the monster's intentions and makes good that nice reticence by which the poem has reported and not depicted the fate of Hrothgar's retainers. By keeping Grendel's deeds, like the monster himself, in the darkness—felt, but not pictured—the poem makes Grendel all the more terrible. The dramatic power of the single graphic, gross, and horrific instance of Grendel biting through a victim's muscles, drinking the blood, consuming the body to its extremities—"feet and hands"—gains all the more force from the episode's placement at the moment when retribution for those murderous acts committed in Heorot is about to overtake the monster. This horrific finale to the poem's ironic contrasts between Grendel's careless confidence and the actual outcome of his visit to Heorot confirms the audience's horror even as its anticipation is about to be gratified.

\Readers shocked at the gruesome realization of Grendel's crimes have frequently wondered why Beowulf passively allows one of his followers to be killed and devoured before his eyes or why the poet leaves the question open.\ If one supposes that the action takes place too rapidly for Beowulf to intervene and save the hapless man's life, the hero might at least have interrupted Grendel's dreadful feast.[4] An answer once in explicit favor and perhaps still implicitly accepted claims that the poet could not alter the traditional tale that represented the failure of earlier champions to cleanse the hall. But if we agree with Richard N. Ringler that the poem represents Grendel's fate as sealed even as he anticipates a feast in Heorot,[5] and with Hrothgar that God could easily put an end to the monster's outrages (478–79), we are invited to ask, Why does God permit still another crime and outrage in the high hall? Just as Hrothgar abruptly quits the hall, the narrator assures the audience all will be well: "Hæfde Kyningwuldor / Grendle togeanes, swa guman gefrungon, / seleweard aseted" (665–67; "The most glorious of Kings, as men learned, had set a hall-guard against Grendel"). Hondscioh's grisly death interrupts the "design for irony" and momentarily suspends the audience's anticipation of grim satisfaction in a shattering reversal of Grendel's fortunes. Though the question "Why does Beowulf (the poet, God) let Hondscioh be killed and eaten?" seems muted by the great struggle in Heorot, that disturbing, dissonant note seems a highly appropriate hint of the challenges to an optimistic reading of Grendel's story.

Hondscioh's Death and Other Mysteries   If Grendel is a symbol of evil, and the poem's language suggests that we can take him so, the pattern of irony that hangs heavily upon him as he proceeds to Heorot and his unexpected execution powerfully communicates an optimistic reading of this event and of the world. The Danes hope, but the audience knows, that Grendel is doomed; the audience's superior knowledge rests on the narrator's commentary but is also founded on a better understanding of the monster made possible by Christian insight. For the Danes, Grendel is an affliction of unknown origin; for the audience, he is one of the race of Cain. The audience of the poem can feel itself in possession of the essential truth of Grendel denied the Danes, the Geats, and Beowulf himself. The poem's audience can indeed see the irony enveloping Grendel as part of a larger pattern, a benevolent providence that embraces all mankind. The battle itself and Beowulf's victory, though seeming to represent the defeat of evil and to confirm an optimistic reading of the world, unravels the texture of the audience's seeming knowledge of Grendel. His mother's revenge challenges the apparent meaning of the monster; the terms of the battle in Heorot redefine or undefine Grendel, but the inevitable question "Why Hondscioh's death?" almost refutes the optimism implicit in the story of Beowulf's first great victory.

In our experience of the poem, however, the significance of Hondscioh's death seems suspended by the rapid movement of the action following Grendel's last meal. After finishing Hondscioh, Grendel reaches out toward the reclining Beowulf who takes that grasping hand and "wið earm gesæt" (749; "sat up on his arm"), that is, probably, propped himself up in bed on one arm. The effect of this casual, domestic pose is electric:

> Sona þæt onfunde   fyrena hyrde,
> þæt he ne mette   middangeardes,

```
          eorðan sceata      on elran men
          mundgripe maran;   he on mode wearð
          forht on ferhðe;   no þy ær fram meahte.
                                                (750–54)
```

(Immediately the guardian of crimes realized that he had not met anywhere on earth a more powerful grip in another man; in his heart, his spirit, he was afraid; none the sooner for all that could he get away.)

The poem creates two quite different impressions of the battle, neither of which completely or clearly becomes incompatible with the other. One can understand the entire account of the struggle as essentially one of spirit, as the citation above suggests. At the instant Grendel apprehends the strength of Beowulf's grip, the monster's whole intention is to escape. In the course of his frantic attempts to break free, Grendel upsets the hall, even damages its structure, and eventually frees himself from Beowulf's iron grip when his arm comes off at, or with, the shoulder.

But the poem also creates an impression of a battle between Beowulf and Grendel in which two mighty opposites who resemble one another in savage spirit and force grapple in a elemental struggle:

```
                     Yrre wære begen,
          reþe renweardas.     Reced hlynsode.
          Pa wæs wundor micel,    þæt se winsele
          wiðhæfde heaþodeorum,      . . .
          . . . . . . . . . . . . . . . . . . . . . . . . . . . . . . .
                     Pær fram sylle abeag
          medubenc monig      mine gefræge
          golde geregnad,     þær þa graman wunnon.
                                                (769–77)
```

(Both of the fierce house-guards were angry. The building resounded. It was a marvel that the drinking-hall withstood the battle-brave ones . . . There, as I heard, many a gold-adorned drinking bench flew from the floor where the hostile ones struggled.)

The word "both" ("begen") links the hero and the monster in a kind of parity reinforced by the adjectives they share, "angry," "fierce," "battle-brave" and "furious" ("yrre," "reþe," "heaþodeor," and "gram"); the significant noun designating them both, "renweardas," "house-guards" or "guardians of the building" gives the hero and monster the same spirit and function.

The audience of the poem seems at first to understand Grendel more deeply than do the Danes, his victims. Yet the story of the battle in Heorot presents the poem's audience with a Grendel it cannot understand in action. The monster's descent from Cain, a truth known to the audience but not to Hrothgar, proves an illusory guide to Grendel's reality. The two versions of the "first great fight" alternatively cast him as utterly unheroic, or as the hero's monstrous peer. One version of Grendel, the victim of the poem's dramatic irony, feels himself in a grip stronger than his own and abandoning his hopes of a great feast in Heorot thinks only of flight; the other, a terrible warrior, fights in a heroic rage of battle exactly matching Beowulf's. This indefiniteness surrounding Grendel's reality appears in the terms characterizing him as he approaches Heorot: he is a "sceadugenga" (703; "walker-in-shadows"), a "manscaða" (712; "evil destroyer"), and a "rinc" (720; "warrior")—this last seems more appropriate to Beowulf than to Grendel. Yet when the Geats and Danes examine Grendel's arm the morning after the great victory, the monster's claws are identified as the "hilderinces" (986; "battle-warrior's") sword;[6] at this examination, everyone agrees that no iron weapon could injure the monster's "battle-hand" (987–90). The context seems to make clear Grendel's nonhuman nature and almost supernatural force, but terms like "battle-warrior" also link him with men of the heroic world. Like the Danes themselves, the poem's audience cannot know whether Beowulf and Grendel fought a great battle in Heorot, or whether the monster tore off his own arm in his frantic attempt to escape.

The details of Hondscioh's death and Beowulf's battle cast a retrospective doubt on Grendel's earlier raids on Heorot, which are avenged but not explicated with Beowulf's victory. Neither the Danes nor the poem's audience knows whether Grendel overcame the watchers in the hall with strength, or devoured them sleeping like Hondscioh. As Grendel approaches Heorot for the last time, all the Geats save Beowulf fall asleep, a reaction some readers have understandably found surprising. The monster's approach may have had the power to charm his intended victims to sleep and Beowulf's wakefulness (noted at line 708, recalled at line 1268) may represent a victory of his will over Grendel's power. In line 1268, Beowulf's wakefulness appears as the cause of Grendel's death: the monster met "a waking man awaiting battle" in Heorot, a hint that Grendel's victims slept helplessly, passively into death. In his stinging reply to Unferth and the Danes in the flyting, Beowulf describes Grendel's habitual crime in Heorot: "he lust wigeð, / swefeð and sendeþ, secce me weneþ / to Gar-Denum (599–601; "he carries out his desires, puts to sleep and slaughters [or 'sacrifices'], expects no fight from the Spear-Danes").[7] When Beowulf speaks, "swefeð," meaning literally "puts to sleep," may be a familiar metaphor signifying "kills," but after the death of Hondscioh, "puts to sleep and kills" becomes a possible interpretation of "swefeð and sendeþ." The story of Grendel's outrages against the Danes is not explicitly defined as a tale of demonic or supernatural haunting or a story of almost realistically conceived, almost human force superior to the strength of the once-victorious Danes. The nature of Grendel's power never becomes a question, although the question only needs an invitation to arise. The half-line "swefeð and sendeþ," the reference to Beowulf's wakefulness as the cause of Grendel's death, and Hondscioh's passive entrance into the jaws of death taken together indicate the possibility that Grendel's strength was supernatural, magical as well as physical.

In the course of the encounter between Beowulf and Grendel the sleeping hall reawakens; the suggestion of a deep or even supernatural silence gives way to tumult; the progressive isolation of Beowulf in a narrowing field of vision yields to a re-creation of a large view and spacious context like that of the public gathering in Heorot before the approach of darkness and the monster. Indeed Grendel's approach, entrance, and last meal seem utterly silent—no reference to noise marks any action in that progression. The door of Heorot opens at his touch, but his powerful touch seems silent. The palpable sense of silence and darkness isolates Beowulf from the world, the Danes, and even his sleeping companions. That isolation, greatest when the hero alone is awake in the featureless hall, hardly lessens when Grendel steps on the adorned floor or tears and devours the passive Hondscioh. When Beowulf grasps the enemy's reaching hand, the struggle begins, the hall resounds, its furniture flies from the floor, the human context of Heorot becomes tangible if not visible; the social context recreates itself as the Danes respond immediately to the hubbub (767–69) and then hear with terror Grendel's defeated "song," the monster's cry. The Geats, as their loyalty requires, press round their leader, attempting to kill Grendel with swords the monster may have charmed into impotence.[8] The heroic world begins to reconstitute itself as Beowulf's powerful grip dismembers Grendel.

The poem represents the violence and power of the struggle between

Beowulf and Grendel obliquely rather than with an abundance of
graphic images, just as the horror of Grendel's long reign of terror
appeared chiefly through the distress of the Danes. Their anguish and
its cause were concretely rendered only once, when, almost at the last
possible moment, Hondscioh's death validates the horror of Grendel's
deeds. So, too, one grisly, graphic sequence realizes the power of the
struggle between the hero and the monster generally expressed by its
impact on the hall, its furniture, the astonished Danes, and the loyal,
ineffective Geats. Grendel's mortal wound becomes the final detail in
the story of the encounter and the token of the power of the conflict:

> Licsar gebad
> atol æglæca;   him on eaxle wearð
> syndolh sweotol,   seonowe onsprungon,
> burston banlocan.
>
> (815–18)

(The terrible monster endured a wound; a great injury appeared on his shoulder, his sinews snapped, his muscles tore apart.)

Grendel flees mortally wounded, knowing that his life has reached its
end. In ten lines the narrator sums up the several meanings of the
event: the fulfillment of the Danes' wish, the cleansing of Heorot, the
hero's joy in the night's work, the fulfillment of his vow to the Danes,
the satisfaction taken for Danish suffering. From the meanings of Grendel's defeat, the story returns to the graphic proof of victory that
Beowulf publishes when he hangs Grendel's arm up under the roof of
the great hall.

Restoring a Heroic World

The Proof of Victory   The narrator's black humor repeatedly
identifies the restoration of the heroic world and the mutilation of Grendel. The hero exhibits the monster's "hond . . . earm ond eaxle . . .
Grendles grape" (834–36; "hand . . . arm and shoulder . . . Grendel's
grasping member"); the leisurely sequence enumerating those losses
makes clear for the first time that he escaped, as trapped animals sometimes do, by leaving a limb behind. The narrator's ascending order—
hand, arm, and shoulder—moves steadily toward the heart. Many fighters have survived the loss of a hand, some of an arm, but an arm taken off

with the shoulder means death. The hero himself restates the sequence when he assures Hrothgar that though he had intended to hold Grendel fast, the monster moved too powerfully to be held: "Hwæþere he his folme forlet / to lifwraþe last weardian, / earm ond eaxle" (970–72; "Nevertheless, he left his hand behind to save his life, his arm and his shoulder"). Beowulf assures Hrothgar that Grendel's escape was in vain, that the wound, the loss of his gripping member, holds the monster in a mortal grip (975–77).

With Grendel's defeat, a moment marked by his wounding, his body's failure, and the shattering of his tissues, the pace and character of the narration abruptly changes, becomes circumstantial and leisured—until Grendel's mother brusquely gives the story a new pace and tone. The story moves from Grendel's wound to the dawn in which his hand, arm, and shoulder mutely proclaim the hero's victory and that dawn becomes a central moment to which the narrative returns. Leaders of the Danish people gather from far and near to view Beowulf's trophy and inspect the beaten enemy's bloody tracks; returning from this expedition to Grendel's pool, a poet identified as the king's retainer composes a poem about Beowulf's exploit, Sigemund's dragon killing, and Heremod's promising beginning and bad end. At the close of that song, the narrator returns to the morning—"Đa wæs morgenleoht / scofen ond scynded" (917–18; "Then the light of dawn was hastening onward")—and the royal inspection of Grendel's hand that leads to Hrothgar's speech of thanksgiving praising both God and Beowulf:[9]

> Nu scealc hafað
> þurh Drihtnes miht   dæd gefremede,
> ðe we ealle   ær ne meahton
> snyttrum besyrwan.
> > (939–42)

(Now a warrior has, through God's power, performed the deed which all of us could not encompass by our wisdoms before.)

After Beowulf's gracious acceptance of Hrothgar's eloquent praise, Unferth's dramatic silence accepts the tangible evidence of Grendel's murderous power:

> Đa wæs swigra secg,   sunu Ecglafes,
> on gylpspræce   guðgeweorca,

siþðan æþelingas   eorles cræfte
ofer heanne hrof   hand sceawedon,
feondas fingras.

(980–84)

(Ecglaf's son was more silent on the subject of heroic vows about deeds of
battle after the noblemen had, thanks to the warrior's strength, viewed the
hand over the high roof, the enemy's fingers.)

The succeeding description of that armed hand and sword-proof arm
assuages the chagrin Beowulf's offer of help posed and Unferth's earlier
eloquence attested.

The doubled representation of the morning in which Danish nobles
from far and wide, then Hrothgar, Wealhtheow, and Unferth view the
evidence of Grendel's defeat gives the narrative an unfamiliar sense of
leisure. This change in the pace of narration after Beowulf's victory
appears clearly in our account of Danish poetry. When Beowulf first
joined in the drinking ceremony at Heorot, a court poet performed
more than one poem—"Scop hwilum sang / hador on Heorote" (496–
97; From time to time the poet sang clearly in Heorot)—but no further
account of those songs appears. At the celebration of Beowulf's triumph, a court poet sings of the Danes' great victory at Finnsburg and
an impressionistic but detailed account of that song becomes part of the
Beowulf story. From Grendel's defeat to his mother's first appearance,
the victory celebration claims more space than the original encounter of
the hero and the monster. In this recursive, leisurely, and expansive
section of the poem, the narrative reconstructs a heroic world. Recurring black humor based on Grendel's mutilation becomes part of the
regenerative process. Following Hrothgar's satisfied examination of Beowulf's trophy, the narrator reports the command to prepare Heorot for
the great celebration: "Ða wæs haten hreþe Heort innanweard / folmum
gefrætwod" (991–92; "Then the order was quickly given that the
interior of Heorot should be adorned by hands"). Those who heard and
obeyed that order could, like the audience of the poem, reflect comfort-
ably that Grendel's single hand (arm and shoulder) had already adorned
the exterior of the great hall.

The Healing Art of Poetry   The celebration itself, the first
drinking ceremony in Heorot in twelve years not subject to a disorderly
curfew, becomes part of the reintegration of the heroic world of Den-

mark. The opulence of Hrothgar's gifts to Beowulf, tokens of the old king's former prowess and present power, of his acknowledged correctness in kingly conduct, also asserts the restoration of the Danish court's heroic status. Most of all, the Finnsburg episode re-creates the Danish heroic world. The scop's song of the events at Finnsburg restores their heroic past to the Danish warrior class after twelve years of absorption in a humiliating, inescapable present. Modern criticism has often read the episode as a tragedy and as an indictment of the heroic code of revenge and of the ethos of the heroic world.[10] Within the poem, however, the Danes clearly hear their scop's song as a celebration of their heroic past and account the event at Finnsburg as a great victory. As the performance ends, poetry and strong drink jointly renew Heorot's morale:

> Leoð wæs asungen,
> gleomannes gyd.   Gamen eft astah,
> beorhtode bencsweg,   byrelas sealdon
> win of wunderfatum.
>
> (1159–62)

(The song, the gleeman's poem, was sung to its end. Once more joy was raised aloft, the noise from the benches brightened, servants poured out wine from splendid vessels.)

The identification of music, poetry, and joy seems implicit in the word "gleomann" ("joy-man, music-man") for "poet," and explicit in the second sentence that celebrates the restored happiness of the Danish nobility in a well-ordered society. The performance of the poem about Finnsburg sets off a harmonious and well-ordered outburst of high spirits, of euphoria in Heorot. The response of an Anglo-Saxon audience to the Finnsburg digression might not have agreed entirely, of course, with the hearing Hrothgar's Danes gave the song.

An Anglo-Saxon audience ought to have found as much immediate interest in the Finnsburg song as did Hrothgar's court: Hengest, the Danish hero of the episode, bears the name of one of the archetypal founders of Anglo-Saxon England, the first great leader in the Anglo-Saxon conquest of Celtic Britain. The Finnsburg story creates a familiar world of gritty realities and conflicting obligations, of a battle both lost and won. The Danish poet's Finnsburg song, as reported in *Beowulf,* implies rather than tells its story. In Denmark's ancient and heroic past, a Danish prince, Hnæf, visited his married sister Hildeburh and his brother-in-law, Finn, the Frisian king. At Finn's stronghold, Finnsburg, a battle somehow broke out between Hnæf's followers and Finn's. In the battle, Hnæf, his nephew (or nephews), the son(s) of Finn and Hildeburh, and many others fell. The cause of the battle is suppressed, leaving the adjudication of guilt, praise, or blame to silence. The military outcome is no clearer than the moral responsibility for its beginning; the opposed parties were unable to fight the battle to a finish and accepted a truce, although the text is not completely clear as to who first proposed it. The agreement made Hengest the Dane a follower of Finn the Frisian king and specified that under penalty of death no Frisian was to taunt any of the Danes for taking service with one who was responsible for the death of their own lord. The position the Danes accepted at Finnsburg is precisely the one that followers of King Cynewulf and Prince Cyneheard rejected, at the cost of their lives, in 786.

Modern students of Beowulf have frequently claimed that the tragic force of the Finnsburg song arises from its concentration on Hildeburh, with whom the song begins and ends.[11] The morning after the battle Hildeburh discovers that the place where she had experienced her greatest joys had become a battlefield on which she suffered the heaviest losses: "unsynnum wearð / beloren leofum æt þam lindplegan / bearnum and broðrum" (1072–74; "though innocent she was bereaved of her beloved sons and brothers in that battle"). At Hnæf's funeral, which seems to follow immediately on the terms of the truce, Finn and then Hildeburh make what must seem strong attempts to restore peace. The funeral pyre is kindled and gold brought from the hoard, evidently Finn's treasury. The gold is apparently meant to honor Hnæf and to pay compensation ("wergeld" or "man-money") for his death and thus settle the feud even though the Danes seem not to have compensated Finn for the death of his son.

The poem assuredly accepts the general conviction that the death of kinsmen ought to be avenged; "The Father's Lament" (2444–62) of part II represents the heartbreaking grief of a father who cannot take vengeance for the violent death of his only son, yet Finn apparently prefers peace to vengeance and apparently is prepared to pay and not receive wergeld. Hildeburh follows Finn's move to reestablish peace with her own: she orders that the body of their son be placed on Hnæf's pyre, perhaps at his uncle's shoulder (1117; "eame on eaxle"). The common pyre and perhaps their positions on it seem to make the two kinsmen comrades once more, though now in death. Hildeburh's gesture apparently is intended to reconcile the living as well as to honor the dead. Hildeburh clearly exercises some authority among the Danes and the Frisians and devotes her diplomatic skill to securing peace and Finn's survival. Hildeburh makes a strong contrast with Signy of the *Volsunga Saga* who, having lost her brothers (and father) to her husband's treachery, slaughtered their sons and bore a hardier one to her surviving brother, Sigmundr, named in *Beowulf* as the dragon-killing Sigemund. With his nephew-son at his side, Sigmundr avenged his father and brothers—as the audience of *Beowulf* probably knew.

After the truce and funeral at Finnsburg, Hengest spends the winter brooding on the revenge a prudent seafarer lodged in a foreign country would defer until the end of the stormy season; in the spring, opportunity and incitement press Hengest forward to the enactment of his duty to avenge his late lord, Hnæf, which requires the killing of his new lord, Finn. With the truce, Hengest had sworn himself into a moral dilemma: his oaths of loyalty to his lord, Hnæf, and his promises to Finn were irreconcilable. But the Danish poet's reported song represents Hengest's dilemma in different terms:

> Ða wæs winter scacen,
> fæger foldan bearm;   fundode wrecca,
> gist of geardum;   he to gyrnwræce
> swiðor þohte   þonne to sælade,
> gif he torngemot   þurhteon mihte,
> þæt he Eotena bearn   irne gemunde.
> (1136–41)

(Then winter had departed, the lap of the earth grew fair; the exile longed to leave that dwelling-place; he thought more on revenge than the sea-journey— if he could bring about a hostile encounter so that he could remember the Jutes with iron.)

As the Danish poet saw it, Hengest struggled with conflicting impulses to take revenge or to sail away. For the Danish poet, the essential conflict lay between the instinct for self-preservation and the social duty of revenge. Personal courage, the willingness to risk all in battle, seems at the heart of Hengest's story as the Danes of Heorot heard it. The moves toward peace made at the funeral of Hnæf and Finn's son are set against a demand for war and vengeance. In an obscure but almost surely symbolic act, Hunlafing presents Hengest with a sword (or someone presents Hengest with a sword named Hunlafing) whose mute logic convinces Hengest to accept the universally recognized duty of revenge.

The gathering at Heorot and the Danish poet himself celebrate that story we have often seen as tragic and recall those events in reclaiming their own heroic status. In the spring, just when, as the Danish poet notes, the Father releases the murderous bonds of ice that have bound up the waves and returns the world to glorious summer—just as He still does—Hengest's deadly onslaught falls upon Finn and his followers. Hengest was a hero to the Danes of Heorot; Hengest was a hero in the *Anglo-Saxon Chronicle* and in Bede's history of the English. The possibility that the audience of *Beowulf* admired Hengest as much as it pitied Hildeburh seems real. The Danish poet juxtaposes the eternal proof that a benevolent God presides over the world with Hengest's heroic revenge. The world is neutral. Spring returns, and spring is the season of war and violence, the appropriate moment to begin a campaign or launch an attack.

The Danish Future

At home among the Geats, Beowulf's report to Hygelac adds to Hildeburh's another story of a Danish princess caught up in a conflict of kinship loyalties and the duty of revenge. For the audience of *Beowulf* this was evidently an old story, but to Hygelac it is new.[12] Beowulf reports that Hrothgar has engaged his only daughter, Freawaru, to Ingeld of the Heathobards in order to settle their long-standing feud, and in a chilling aphorism states the principle of failure applicable to diplomatic marriages: "Oft seldan hwær / æfter leodhryre lytle hwile / bongar bugeð, þeah seo bryd duge!" (2029–31; "Seldom does the murderous spear rest after the fall of a prince even though the bride is good").

Beowulf's prediction that the attempt to settle Ingeld's feud with the Danes by giving him a Danish princess will fail takes the form of a condensed, almost lyric, narrative of extraordinary power. Beowulf creates a scene in which a nameless Danish nobleman bears, to the displeasure of the ruler of the Heathobards and his noble followers, a well-known and valuable heirloom sword that the Heathobards had lost to the Danes in an earlier battle. For the Danish possessor, the sword is an heirloom inherited from his father, a token of love and of success in war. For the Heathobards, the sword betokens defeat and violent death, and the feud Freawaru's marriage was designed to settle. An old spear-warrior (2042) whom Beowulf appropriately leaves unnamed addresses the son of the sword's late owner, eloquently urging the duty of revenge:

> Meaht ðu, min wine,   mece gecnawan,
> þone þin fæder   to gefeohte bær
> unde heregriman   hindeman siðe,
> dyre iren,   þær hyne Dene slogon,
> weoldon wælstowe,   syððan Wiðergyld læg,
> æfter hæleþa hryre,   hwate Scyldungas?
>
>   (2047–52)

(Can you, my friend, recognize the sword, the precious iron, which your father carried going for the last time into battle beneath his helmet where the Danes killed him?)

The grim and gloomy speaker remembers all, and at the beer-drinking he makes his young auditor aware of the sword's great value, its present status as a trophy of victory—and a reminder of defeat—and its rightful ownership.

Beowulf creates the scene just once but suggests its repetition until at least the old warrior's wounding words impel his young companion to strike: Withergyld is avenged, the slayer flees, the truce will be broken, the feud will break out afresh. Beowulf's prophetic story must fall on the ears of an Anglo-Saxon audience as a version of historical truth: a similar scene appears in Saxon Grammaticus's *History of the Danes* with the intriguing difference that the young auditor is Ingeld, the ruler of the Heathobards and the bridegroom. The old spear-warrior is Starkaðr (Starcatherus), a legendary hero whose single long speech persuades Ingeld (Ingellus) to avenge his father on his brothers-in-law whom he has been entertaining at a feast.[13] The anonymity of Beowulf's speaker and auditor makes his prophetic statement seem the result of a human wisdom rather than a supernatural gift, but that realistic generality also makes the hero's vision of the Danish future a plausible account of its past: the scene Beowulf sketches for the collapse of Freawaru's diplomatic marriage and the reopening of an old war could, with few changes, become the omitted first act of the drama at Finnsburg where the possibility that neither Finn nor Hnæf intended a battle is quite real.

An Anglo-Saxon audience could hear Beowulf's future story as a

powerful illustration of his human foresight and wisdom, his understanding of the world, but an Anglo-Saxon audience would presumably
also know that though Hrothgar's diplomacy failed, the king and his
nephew Hrothulf defeated Ingeld's army in battle. That legendary fact
appears in the Anglo-Saxon poem *Widsith*. [14] As ever, Beowulf's wisdom is human and subject to error, but the gloomy perspective he casts
on the Ingeld story harmonizes with other suggestions that the poem
envisions an endangered dynasty in Heorot, a hall doomed to perish in
flames probably kindled during Ingeld's attack (82–85). From the first
the brilliance of Heorot and the greatness of Hrothgar seem precarious,
beset by dangers. The dark telling of Freawaru's story seems to confirm
the darker readings of earlier events in Heorot.

The Diplomacy of Anxiety   Kenneth Sisam rejected a once-
popular view that the shadow of future treason hangs over the joyful
celebration of Grendel's defeat in Heorot. Sisam correctly notices that
only conjecture confirms the belief that Hrothulf, Hrothgar's nephew,
seized the Danish throne after killing Hrethric and Hrothmund,
Hrothgar's sons, and possibly the old king as well. Hrothulf, the son
of Halga the Good, youngest of the three sons born to Healfdene (59–
62), eventually succeeded to the Danish throne and is known in later
Scandinavian tradition as Hrólfr kraki (Rolf Kraki), greatest of the
legendary kings of the Danes. Sisam's learned doubt that the audience
of *Beowulf* should have seen an ironic hint of Hrothulf's future dis-
placement, betrayal, or murder of Hrothgar's son in the celebration at
Heorot assumes that a glorious hero like Rolf Kraki would not have
had a great crime in his background. Sisam indeed expected straightforward moral judgments plainly expressed on the part of the *Beowulf*
poet, like other poets of the age: "The Ganelons and Modreds of other
medieval poems are called traitors in plain words." [15] Still, *Beowulf*
might contain more moral ambiguity than some other medieval poems. If *Beowulf* suggests approaching misfortune for the sons of
Hrothgar even as the Danes celebrate Grendel's death, the Anglo-
Saxon audience might have also anticipated that lying beyond that
particular catastrophe was the glorious age of Rolf Kraki which
ended, to be sure, in his defeat and death.

The narrative manner and moral vision of the first and second of
Beowulf's battles with monsters seem strikingly dissimilar. Ironies of
the kind Sisam attempted to banish from the poem seem part of those
contrasts. In the celebration of Grendel's defeat, the song of Finnsburg,

and the revenge of Grendel's mother, an ironic current runs strongly
against the Danes rather than against the monstrous enemy, and moral
judgment seems clouded rather than straightforward. The scene in
Heorot at the beginning of the great victory celebration includes some
hints of betrayal and future enmity among the Danish celebrants if we
assume an Anglo-Saxon audience would know that Hrothulf succeeded
his uncle Hrothgar, as seems likely, and suppose that the poem creates a
reasonably consistent vision of a social and human context. The drinking ceremony in Heorot begins with Hrothgar and Hrothulf, the reign-
ing king and his nephew; the vocabulary of treason appears early in the
scene:

> Heorot innan wæs
> freondum afylled;   nalles facenstafas
> Þeod-Scyldingas   þenden fremedon.
> (1017–19)

(Inside Heorot was filled with friends; at that time the Danes did not at all
practice treachery.)

A retrospective irony might even lurk in the first clause: though those
within Heorot were friends, an enemy, Grendel's mother, waited in the
darkness outside as the poem's audience and the Danes were soon to
learn. The second clause seemed, at least before Sisam, deeply laden
with ironies. The single word "þenden" ("then, at that time") took on
an enormous weight of ironic implication.

Wealhtheow: Negotiating the Future   At the end of the
Finnsburg song, Wealtheow approaches the royal kinsmen and the
poem's sketch of the scene again includes a verbal touch that suggests
treason among the Danish royalty, and now adds a hint of Unferth's
possible treachery:

> Þa com Wealhþeo forð
> gan under gyldnum beage   þær þa godan twegen
> sæton suhtergefæderan;   þa gyt wæs hiera sib ætgædere,
> æghwylc oðrum trywe.   Swylce þær Unferþ þyle
> æt fotum sæt frean Scyldinga;   gehwylc hiora his ferhþe treowde,
> þæt he hæfde mod micel,   þeah þe he his magum nære
> arfæst æt ecga gelacum.
> (1162–68)

(Then, wearing her golden diadem, Wealhtheow came to the two brave men, the uncle and nephew; then their loyal kinship was still intact, each true to the other. There too was Unferth the spokesman sitting at the feet of the lord of the Scyldings; both trusted in his spirit, believed that he had great courage even though he was not gracious to his kinsmen in battle.)

The adverbial phrase "þa gyt" (still) bears, like "þenden" (at that time) a considerable critical burden; moreover, even granting the maximum of interpretative weight to these words, neither passage indicates which kinsman betrayed the other. The adverbial hints of future treason in themselves are merely disquieting, like the reference to Unferth's unkindness, but their muted affect becomes audible in the great celebration of Beowulf's victory over the race of Grendel.

Wealtheow's speeches, anxious, diplomatic attempts to control the future by telling its story, imply Hrothulf's future treachery, the exclusion of her sons from the succession, and possibly their violent deaths. Wealtheow addresses Hrothgar, Beowulf, and indirectly Hrothulf himself as she implies her fears and voices her petitions. She fears Hrothulf's ambitions and at the same time dreads that in his relief at the end of Grendel's humiliation of the Danish royal house and in his gratitude to Beowulf for that relief her royal husband might have compromised her sons' rights. She wants to enlist Beowulf's help for her sons and also to warn Hrothulf. She brings the drinking cup to Hrothgar, and, as if she had not been present to hear for herself, diplomatically mentions a report that Hrothgar had taken Beowulf as a son, then admonishes her husband to treat the Geats generously with gifts and to leave to his kinsmen (not, we may guess, to a newly adopted "son") the kingdom and its people: "and þinum magum læf / folc and rice" (1178–79). Sisam reasonably claimed that Hrothulf was one of Hrothgar's kinsmen, too, and concludes that Wealhtheow betrays no fears for her sons' future and does not even insist on Hrethric's succession. In her continuation, Wealhtheow's speech to Hrothgar seems intended for a wider audience, one including both Beowulf and Hrothulf, and her clear intention is that *her* son or sons succeed their father.

As if still addressing Hrothgar, Wealhtheow states as a belief, indeed as a certainty, that should Hrothgar not survive his nephew Hrothulf, the latter would act graciously to the young nobles (her sons) and would, in his conduct toward them, repay the benefits he had received from both herself and Hrothgar. But even as she reaches the final clause asserting a valid claim on Hrothulf's loyalty, Wealhtheow slips into the conditional: Hrothulf will be true, "gif he þæt eal gemon, / hwæt wit to willan ond to worðmyndum / umborwesendum ær arna gefremedon (1185–87; "if he remembers all the good things that we did to please and honor him earlier on when he was a boy"). To match the positive rhetoric of her beginning, Wealhtheow might have continued with a declarative clause (something like "remembering all those benefits, he will . . ."), but the uncertainty she would overcome with words has infected her words themselves. The statement meant to shape the future becomes a petition addressed to Hrothulf, a plea, an admission of doubts about the future.

In her address to Beowulf (seated between her sons, surely an indication of his loyalty to them), Wealhtheow's grip on her self-possession and tact seems unsteady, her speech infected with uncertainty and tension. Wealhtheow's syntax and rhetoric seem almost out of control, yet the verbal devices indicating this distraction, repetition and abrupt changes of tone and topic, have an artful and controlled deployment. As she speaks to Beowulf, Wealhtheow wishes him joy of the great rewards he is receiving, wishes for his prosperity, "and þyssum cnyhtum wes / lara liðe!" (1219–20; "and be gracious to these boys in your counsels!"). In what seems a sudden change of tone, Wealhtheow promises to reward Beowulf for those future counsels, then announces that he has achieved a worldwide fame, again wishes him lifelong good fortune, and once more pleads: "Beo þu suna minum / dædum gedefe, dreamhealdende!" (1226–27; "Fortunate man, treat my son kindly!"). The depth and intensity of Wealhtheow's emotional response to the victory celebration seems thoroughly human. Beowulf is everything she would want her sons to be; his future seems assured, theirs imperilled. The contrast seems all the more powerful because only a few years separate the Beowulf whom she calls "hyse" (1217; "young warrior, youth") from her sons whom she calls "cnyhtas" (1219; "boys"). Beowulf's nearly supernatural strength, his victory over a monster who seemed to challenge the heroic world itself, and his aura of good fortune that seemed from the first to augur his success against Grendel make a powerful contrast with Wealhtheow's position and her fears for her young, endangered sons. The contrast between their untested youth and Beowulf's fame, their insecurity and his assurance, affects Wealhtheow powerfully.

The coda to her nearly distraught appeal to the hero asserts the reality of the order Wealhtheow desires and intends to create, and

regains the self-possession that marked her words to Hrothgar. This
striking assertion of order and control in the Danish court, of loyalty
and harmony in Heorot, is itself well-ordered. Wealhtheow's coda includes four honorifics and one problematic term that has exercised
modern readers. The passage depicts a heroic utopia in Denmark:

> Her is æghwylc eorl   oþrum getrywe,
> modes milde,   mandrihtne hold,
> þegnas syndon geþwære,   þeod ealgearo,
> druncne dryhtguman   doð swa ic bidde.
>   (1228–31)

(Here every nobleman is faithful to the other, generous in spirit and loyal to
the liege lord; the retainers are united, the nation alert, the drunken warriors
do as I command.)

The honorific adjectives, "getrywe . . . milde . . . hold . . . geþwære"
("faithful," "gracious/generous," "loyal," "united"), suggest the four superlatives conferring the poem's final accolade on Beowulf. The last line
holds a lexical problem scholars have often addressed—how to understand "druncne," translated as "drunken" just above—and an interpretative problem almost never mentioned: to whom is the coda addressed and
what does it mean?

One of the poem's most astute and witty students, T. A. Shippey,
translates "druncne" in the last line of Wealhtheow's coda as "drunken,"
and notes that "Nervousness breaks out among many translators at this
stage, with *druncne* rendered as 'carousing,' or 'cheered with drink' or
'wine-glad' or even more circuitous paraphrase. But the problem is a
cultural one; we cannot translate *druncne* as 'drunken' only because it
seems not to collate with words like 'true' and 'loyal' and 'united.' "[16]
Shippey rightly reminds us that the standards of the poem are not
always ours, but his interpretation of the passage leaves its general
import within the poem unexplained: how would the Danes in Heorot
or an Anglo-Saxon audience have understood Wealhtheow's coda or its
most puzzling adjective? Another astute and witty critic, Fred C.
Robinson, approached the difficult adjective in the context of the
speech as a whole: "After thanking Beowulf for having achieved what
she and her people requested of him, she repeatedly asks that he support her royal sons." In the conclusion of her speech "as is her wont, she
adds anxious public assurances that the Danish retinue around her

(including, no doubt, Hrothulf) will prove loyal to prince and comrade and eager to obey the royal will." Robinson concludes the last line should be understood as: "having drunk [the royal mead], the retainers will [surely] do as I ask."[17] Drinking the royal mead creates an obligation which obedience will repay. The drinking ceremony, in short, both creates and acknowledges the retainers' obligation, confirms the oaths of loyalty between lords and followers. When she describes the loyalty of the Danish "dryhtguman," or retainers, Wealhtheow does not slip into the conditional mood as she did in predicting Hrothulf's fidelity. Robinson's suggestion adds a new dimension to the passage, but does not address the question: if drinking the king's beer binds the Danish nobility to his cause, and to Wealhtheow's, why does she make this speech?

The nearly distraught urgency of Wealhtheow's appeal to Beowulf for his favor for his sons, her anxiety about Hrothulf's loyalty, and the emphatic assertion of power Wealhtheow's coda becomes converge in an interpretative crux. A conjecture that Wealhtheow's closing words ostensibly addressed to Beowulf warn Hrothulf that she will not hesitate to call on the power of the sword to secure her sons' safety and succession seems a solution to the paradoxes of her intricate speech. Her last line can be heard as a public warning to Hrothulf. Wealhtheow claims and in fact exercises considerable real power in Heorot as the present dramatic action makes clear. Her admonition to Hrothgar urges him to reward the Geats generously and leads immediately to a golden shower, but for all Wealhtheow's apparent authority, we may guess that many Anglo-Saxon audiences would have believed that she failed to secure her sons' succession and perhaps even their lives.

If Hrothulf understood himself to be addressed in Wealhtheow's speech to Hrothgar and warned in her words to Beowulf, he makes no response. Beowulf's silence seems more surprising since the queen addresses him openly, by name, and urgently. Discretion might suggest some delay and some obliqueness in replying to this appeal; before the next day dawns, the crisis of Grendel's mother intervenes. The hero's farewell speech to Hrothgar makes an answer to Wealhtheow's petition which the queen should have approved and which Hrothgar receives with deep gratitude. Beowulf grants Wealhtheow's petitions as fully as his status allows. Though he addresses Hrothgar, Beowulf's words (1818–39) move indirectly and discreetly toward an answer for Wealhtheow. First Beowulf briefly announces his desire to return to Hygelac; his word for himself and his company is "sæliðend" or "seafarers," and naturally they must be off. Then, like a good guest, he thanks his host and adds a promise to perform any further deeds of war as may earn Hrothgar's love. Moreover, Beowulf engages that if he learns that external enemies should threaten Hrothgar, he will bring a force of a thousand warriors, an enormous army for the heroic age,[18] to help; the hero assures Hrothgar that though young, Hygelac will assist Beowulf to bring an army, a "garholt" (1834) or "forest of spears," if Hrothgar has need of men, and closes with an assurance that Hrethric can count on many friends among the Geats should he visit them.

Beowulf: Proposing a Future   Beowulf's engagements in delayed response to Wealhtheow's petitions are clearly important: they take up more lines than the hero's goodbye and thanks (eighteen against four) and their seriousness justifies his delay in speaking; such promises are hardly to be made on short notice since they commit more to Hrothgar's cause than Beowulf's own life or personal retinue. The delay, moreover, separates the promise of military aid and the offer of political asylum from the immediate context of Wealhtheow's speech and clothes that promise of refuge in the language of conventional courtesy. The poem has other instances of political exile: Beowulf's own father Ecgtheow whom Hrothgar received and protected, and the nephews of the Swedish king Onela whom Heardred of the Geats received but could not protect. In that case, still in the future as Beowulf says farewell to Hrothgar, Onela invaded the Geats and killed one of his nephews and young King Heardred. The unqualified commitment to receive Hrethric involves the Geats, on Beowulf's decision, quite as seriously as his promise of military aid to Hrothgar.

Wealtheow's petitions could hardly have found a more complete and satisfying answer and her diplomatic effort to secure Beowulf's support for her sons seems to succeed in full. The intensity of Hrothgar's immediate response to the hero's words abruptly make clear that the old king has shared Wealhtheow's anxieties:

> Þe þa wordcwydas   wigtig Drihten
> on sefan sende;   ne hyrde ic snotorlicor
> on swa geongum feore   guman þingian.
> (1841–43)

(The wise Lord sent those words into your heart; I have never heard so young a warrior discourse more wisely.)

Hrothgar did not respond more strongly to Beowulf's vow to fight Grendel in Heorot, but the poem's audience knows that Beowulf's commitments rest on an assumption the future will confute. In tracing the future history of the great neck-ring Beowulf received in Heorot, the poem has already revealed that Hygelac would fall in Frisia rather than support Beowulf in a Danish expedition. On the evidence of later Scandinavian traditions and allusive hints in the text of the poem, an Anglo-Saxon audience probably placed the poem's images of the Danish heroic age in a context of future disasters and glories—Heorot burned, but Ingeld defeated, Hrethric disappointed (or worse), but a new heroic age under Hrothulf. In this whirligig of time and revenges, an Anglo-Saxon audience might more easily have seen the shape of the world's features, an endless cycle of men, generations, dynasties, and nations, than a conflict of good and evil defined in terms of Christian doctrines.

Grendel and His Mother: Contrasts

From Beowulf's arrival in Heorot to the celebration of his victory over Grendel, the mood of the poem alternates between terror and horror at the monstrous enemy who evokes an audience's fears—of the dark, of death and nonbeing, of engulfing disorder—and who also arouses the audience's sense of irony, a gratified realization that terror, agony, and the abyss itself await that unsuspecting demon. From the celebration of that first great victory to the end of Beowulf's report to Hygelac, surprise, suspense, and anxiety dominate the telling of the story. In the Grendel story, the movement onward to the anticipated encounter of the hero and the monster has a continuing hold on an audience's attention and thus defers the moment when the human context of action will become the central narrative subject. After Grendel's death, the human context of the action seems almost as much the subject as Grendel's mother. Indeed, since an audience has no warning of the existence of Grendel's mother until nearly the end of the celebration in Heorot, the depiction of a Danish present in the hall and the heroic Danish past in the singer's tale of Finnsburg becomes the narrative foreground. The first announcement that an avenger still lives after Grendel's death comes as a surprise, and makes the Danes rather than the race of Grendel the objects of irony, a notable reversal.

Grendel seemed to rise up from the mere as the antithesis to Heorot, that great structure founded on order, born of Hrothgar's thought, and raised in answer to his commands. The monster manifests his descent from Cain and status as a part of an archetypical opposition to creation itself when the poem represents his war against the great hall and its people as the expression of his savage anger at the sound of the Danish poet's song praising the Creation and the Creator. In contrast, Grendel's mother attacks Heorot and kills the noble Æschere to avenge her son's death, a motive the Danish audience, which approved the Finnsburg song, recognized. Indeed, Hrothgar explicitly informs Beowulf that in killing Æschere Grendel's mother had continued the feud the hero initiated when he slew the monster with violence the night before. The contest of Grendel's mother and Beowulf more resembles the morally ambiguous or neutral clashes between the Danes and the Frisians at Finnsburg than it does the struggle of the hero and the monster. As J. R. R. Tolkien observed in the appendix, "Grendel's Titles," to his famous essay, the poem's terms for the monster make him a descendant of Cain, a sinful creature, a pagan, and doomed to damnation but not quite "a mediaeval devil."[19] Tolkien adds parenthetically that Grendel's mother is characterized "in precisely similar terms" without making quite clear the similarity he means.[20] The terms for Grendel's mother identify her as a woman (or perhaps even lady), as terrible, and as nonhuman, but contrast dramatically with the terms for Grendel. Grendel's mother, in fact, is not clearly described as a descendent of Cain (but lines 1258–66 might have this implication) and clearly is never called God's enemy or described as destined for hell.

Grendel's mother's attack, quite unlike Grendel's last visit to Heorot, comes as an unanticipated and shattering surprise to the Danes. The poem's audience has only brief forewarning of the onslaught: a generalizing remark that the celebrants in Heorot did not know the grim fate that had befallen many (1233–35) yields to the mild observation that after Hrothgar's withdrawal many men occupied the hall as they had often done in the past. But they had not, of course, since Grendel made the hall uninhabitable at night; the inconsistency reorders the past to fit the dominant impression of the moment: the renewal of the heroic society of Heorot. The narrator describes the domestic preparations for going to bed and the warriors' disposition of their arms and armor in readiness for any emergency in accordance with their traditional martial custom. The narrator commends this military virtue—"wæs seo þeod tilu" (1250; that was a good nation). But then, just as the heroic society of Denmark has restored itself to a pristine military virtue and its habitual occupation of the once-challenged hall (an inconsistency readers might catch), the monstrous reign in Heorot seems at the point of resuming: "Sigon þa to slæpe. Sum sare angeald / æfenreste, swa him ful oft gelamp, / siþðan goldsele Grendel warode" (1251–53; "They fell asleep. One of them paid dearly for his night's rest as had often befallen them after Grendel occupied the gold-hall"). The abrupt transition from comfortable domesticity—"they fell asleep"—to the mortal cost of that sleep introduces a brief recapitulation of the Grendel story, closing with Grendel's mother's intention to avenge her son's death.

The poem's action turns from celebrating Grendel's defeat and renewing the heroic spirit of the Danes to an unexpected and shattering renewal of the monstrous assault. As an unexpected avenger approaches the hall, the narrator reawakens the audience's sense of the horror of Grendel's long campaign against Heorot. The audience hears first of a grim and unknown fate, then that one of the warriors goes doomed to his bed, then that men are soon to learn that an avenger survived Grendel, and at last the avenger's identity. That revelation retraces Grendel's lineage to Cain and briefly recounts the monster's death before returning to his mother's savage grief and purpose. Her approach to the hall briefly echoes the poem's account of Grendel's last, fatal visit to Heorot:

> Com þa to Heorote, ðær Hring-Dene
> geond þæt sæld swæfun. Þa ðær sona wearð
> edhwyrft eorlum, siþðan inne fealh
> Grendles modor.
>
> (1279–82)

(Then she came to Heorot where the Ring-Danes were sleeping throughout the hall. There was a reversal for the noblemen as soon as Grendel's mother got inside.)

The opening half-line, "Com þa to Heorote," recalls the extended representation of Grendel's last approach to Heorot, but now the residents of the hall rather than the approaching monster become the objects of the story's ironies, the victims of a reversal. The renewed march on Heorot realizes the aura of foreboding and of future sorrows hanging over the celebration of Beowulf's first victory.

The battle between Beowulf and Grendel seemed ambiguous or undefined but assuredly not at all like ordinary warfare fought out with spears and swords clashing against coats of mail and helmets. In the event, the battle with Grendel's mother seems less tinged with the supernatural and more like ordinary armed conflict despite its setting in a hall or antihall at the bottom of the mere. The opening of the earlier battle—if indeed battle is the right word—with Beowulf grasping Grendel's groping hand and the monster's terrified response, his desperate attempt to escape, gave way to at least a suggestion of an actual struggle. The subsequent examination of Grendel's arm with its swordlike claws and apparent invulnerability to edged weapons retrospectively turns the encounter into a monstrous imitation of heroic battle. This suggestive indefiniteness harmonizes with the possible meanings the story creates, with a view of Grendel as a force of darkness, an embodiment of evil, or of chaos and disorder. In contrast, Grendel's mother's attack on Heorot and the underwater battle between the hero and the monster are assimilated to heroic warfare, become increasingly realistic, and make no explicit connection with specifically Christian ideas of good and evil. On her initial entrance into the hall, Grendel's mother seems far less terrifying than her son:

> Wæs se gryre læssa
> efne swa micle,   swa bið mægþa cræft,
> wiggryre wifes   be wæpnedmen,
> þonne heoru bunden,   hamere geþuren,
> sweord swate fah   swin ofer helme
> ecgum dyhtig   andweard scireð.
>   (1282–87)

(The terror was less by just as much as women's strength, a woman's war-terror, is less than that of warriors when the hilted, hammer-forged sword, the blade stained with blood and powerful in its edges, cuts through the defending boar-figure on the helmet.)[21]

The measurement of terror, the comparison of male and female strength, leads to a characteristic image of war in Anglo-Saxon poetry, the poetic capture of that moment at which an edged weapon engages or penetrates protecting armor. Though chilling, the image suggests human warfare, not a cosmological contest.

Grendel's mother's surprise attack takes an even life-for-a-life revenge though the victim seems to have been one of the highest ranking and most valued members of Hrothgar's court, a great warrior and generous giver of gifts. She flees for her life when the warriors in the hall awaken and draw their swords: clearly she has neither the power to bind the Danes in sleep as her son may have had nor is she invulnerable to the bite of swords as he seemed to be. The poem renews the sense of surprise and suspense the appearance of Grendel's mother has created when Beowulf finds himself summoned to Hrothgar's presence without knowing the events of the preceeding night and Hrothgar waits uncertain as to whether the Almighty will ever reverse his misfortunes. To Beowulf's inquiry if the night had gone as Hrothgar wished, the old king responds with an impassioned expression of grief that first makes clear the extent of the loss he and the Danes have suffered in Æschere, then identifies the killer as a murderous monster (1331: "wælgæst"), as female, and as having avenged Grendel's death. The poem's audience shares vicariously in the hero's brief mystification even knowing, as Beowulf did not, what happened in the hall the night before.

Hrothgar's description of the dismal way to the monsters' lair and the horrors of the haunted mere (1357–76) makes one of the poem's most celebrated passages and one frequently discussed almost as a lyric poem.[22] Hrothgar's speech, taken dramatically in the context of the poem's action, challenges and exhorts the hero to undertake another great battle, one in which the place seems more terrible than the antagonist has seemed. The exhortation and geographical detail sketch out the shape of the narrative to come, impose a structure and order on the unanticipated sequel to the Grendel story. One detail in the description of the mere creates at once a particularly powerful expression of the terror of the place and a pointed challenge to Beowulf's courage:

> Ðeah þe hæðstapa   hundum geswenced,
> heorot hornum trum   holtwudu sece,
> feorran geflymed,   ær he feorh seleð,
> aldor on ofre,   ær he in wille
> hafelan beorgan   nis þæt heoru stow!
> (1368–72)

(Even if the heath-walker, the hart powerful with his antlers, enters the wood exhausted by the hounds and pursued from far off, he will give up his very life on the bank before he will plunge in to protect his head—that is no safe place!)

The name of Hrothgar's hall, "Heorot" or "Hart," illustrates that this noble animal had a special significance for the poem's Danish dynasty.

Æschere's Head In remarking that royal animal's willingness to die on the shore rather than seek safety in the haunted pool,

Hrothgar suggests rather openly the necessity that Beowulf plunge into
those waters in search of Æschere's slayer. At the close of Hrothgar's
extended petition and description of the monster's stronghold, Beowulf
promises a pursuit beyond the powers of ordinary men:

> Ic hit þe gehate: no he on helm losaþ,
> ne on foldan fæþm,   ne on fyrgenholt,
> ne on gyfenes grund,   ga þær he wille!
> (1392–94)

(I promise you this: he [a surprising pronoun] will not escape to safety, not in
the depth of the earth, not in the mountain forest, not at the bottom of the
sea, let him go where he will!)

Beowulf's promise leads toward the mere and a mortal combat at the
bottom of a body of water that seems at times to be the ultimate deep,
chaos itself.

A party of Danes following Grendel's bloody track traversed the road
to Grendel's mere and rode back in high spirits along an apparently
well-known path, yet Hrothgar describes the way as secret, terrifying,
and the company of Geats and Danes find their difficult way marked by
the tracks of Grendel's mother as she carried home the corpse of the
king's best retainer. The arrival at Grendel's mere renews the story's
insistent shock, horror, and surprise when the expedition responds to
unexpected proof of Grendel's mother's revenge:

>   Denum eallum wæs,
> winum Scyldinga   weorce on mode
> to geþolianne,   ðegne monegum,
> oncyð eorla gehwæm,   syðþan Æscheres
> on þam holmclife   hafelan metton.
> (1417–21)

(For all the Danes, the friends of the Shieldings, for many a warrior, it was a
heart-wrenching pain to endure, a distress for every nobleman when, on the
seacliff, they found Æschere's head.)

The intricate and chilling sentence runs from the Danes' horrified and
shocked response to the brutal occasion of their grief and compounds the
shock, as modern English could not, introducing first "Æschere's . . ."
and then, after specifying the place, ". . . head." Æschere's severed head

jolts the Danes, and the poem's audience. Grendel's mother fled Heorot taking Æschere and her son's arm, the token and trophy of the hero's victory. Æschere's head, left just at the entrance into the monstrous world, seems an eloquent rebuttal to the claim of victory made by displaying Grendel's arm. The avenging mother challenges her enemy to enter the mere, to venture beyond the reach of ordinary humanity. Hrothgar had assured Beowulf that the mere's depth was beyond any man's knowing, and added that every night fire appeared in its depths, an incomprehensible confounding of the natural order.

The representation of Beowulf's fight with Grendel's mother reverses in texture, tone, and numerous concrete details the story of the battle with Grendel himself. The strategies of narration in the two stories differ strikingly. The telling of Grendel's story combines a retrospective horror and a present irony. A single, gruesome, and appalling event— the monster eating one of Beowulf's followers—abruptly and almost grotesquely makes the reported terrors of Grendel's outrages palpable in a context that has finely represented his terrible, inexorable, and frightening march toward sure destruction. The action moves forward as if in a predetermined course—from the mere to the hall to defeat and mutilation, from the hall to the mere to death. The telling of Grendel's story combines sympathy for the Danes and an almost sardonic, almost guilty pleasure in their discomfiture. The story of Grendel's mother's attack on the Geats and Beowulf's victory over this new and unexpected enemy moves forward by surprises and shocks. Dramatic irony has no significant part in the story of Grendel's mother, but a social drama of human relationships conducted under great stress and in a context of powerful emotions becomes a conspicuous part of the narrative texture in the story of Grendel's mother. In both stories a suggestion of black comedy or of comic contrast, or even a hint of broad humor, becomes a significant part of the story's power and excitement.

The pattern of knowns governing the telling of the first story contrasts the unknowns of the second: extended irony at the expense of the unsuspecting monster modulated by horror, shock, and suggestions of dread characterize the first combat narrative; suspense, surprise, and shock modulated by brief suggestions of irony at the expense of the unsuspecting Danes characterize the second. Even as Grendel approaches the hall, the narrator observes that people know that the monster cannot destroy them if God has not permitted it; the poem's audience (but not Grendel) knows that the monster is approaching a waking hero of incredible strength; God's anger at Grendel (known to the audience [711]) implies Beowulf's inevitable victory. Grendel strides doomed to Heorot, his fate clearly foretold, and enters the hall under the hero's watchful eye. In the second great fight Beowulf enters the unknown uncertain of his victory—which indeed the poem has not promised its audience—and observed by his enemy. In the first battle Beowulf seizes Grendel's outstretched hand and at once the enemy seems to be beaten, but as Beowulf reaches the bottom of the mere, Grendel's mother seizes him like the water itself.

The poem repeatedly points ahead to Beowulf's entry into the abysmal mere, but the expected step is delayed until it comes as a surprise: suspense and unanticipated reversals give the story of Grendel's mother its character. The matter contrasts the hero's victory beneath the mere with the renewed failure of the heroic ideal in Denmark. Though Beowulf's intrusion into the deep, even chaos itself, ends in victory, the restoration of Heorot's morale with poetry and strong drink after the first great victory over the monsters of the mere collapses under the weight of the new assault. At the water's edge the paralysis that gripped the Danes for twelve hapless years claims them again and, save for Beowulf, the Geats as well. The armed troop looks at the blood-stained mere; the horn sounds an eager war song, an audible answer to the monstrous challenge, but anticlimatically the company sits down. The assembled warriors passively observe the mere's teeming population of sea monsters stirred up to fury and violent motion by the sound of the horn; the monsters rush furiously about with no apparent purpose. Then Beowulf kills one of the strange creatures with a shot from a bow. This unanticipated act of violence, a declaration of war, rouses the expedition, the sea monster is speared, dragged ashore, and examined; the warriors become spectators once more. As others view the monster, Beowulf arms himself for his descent into the mere putting on a mail shirt he had earlier identified as an heirloom of Hrethel, the founder of the Geatish dynasty, and as a work of Weland, the great smith of Germanic legend, an ancient helmet, and accepting the loan of Unferth's sword, Hrunting by name.

Beowulf's Will   Armed and ready to enter the mere, Beowulf addresses Hrothgar and, just at the point of plunging into an archetypal battle with a monster of the deep, returns to the social and political context of the human world and to a delicate negotiation of status, public esteem, and responsibility. In calling urgently on Beowulf's help in the renewed catastrophe, indeed in pleading for the hero to save the Danes a second time, Hrothgar implied the hero's responsibility for Grendel's mother's attack: "She avenged that feud in which you violently killed Grendel with hard grips last night" (1333–35). At that point, and without responding to Hrothgar's hint, Beowulf had vowed to pursue Æschere's killer even to the bottom of the sea. At the edge of the mere, Beowulf reminds Hrothgar of an understanding that if the hero should lose his life in the king's cause, Hrothgar would accept a father's responsibilities for the dead hero. The clause "gif ic æt þearfe þinre scolde / aldre linnan . . ." (1477–78; "if I should lose my life in your need . . .") reclaims Beowulf's role as an altruistic defender whose freely offered service places Hrothgar under some obligation, one Beowulf wishes to invoke on behalf of his followers.

The care Beowulf devotes to these arrangements attests to his concern for his followers as well as his real uncertainty about the outcome of this battle; his concerns add to the audience's suspense or apprehension that the narrator neglects to allay. Beowulf asks Hrothgar's protection for his followers (who will be lordless if he falls) and requests that the rewards of his victory over Grendel be sent to Hygelac. The detail and seriousness of Beowulf's orally delivered will contrasts his clear though obliquely stated confidence before defending Heorot against Grendel. Beowulf's will ends with a "beot" acknowledging the coming battle's doubtful issue: "ic me mid Hruntinge / dom gewyrce, oþðe mec deað nimeð!" (1490–92; "I will win fame for myself with Hrunting, or death will take me!"). The narrator reports that Beowulf hastened boldly without waiting for an answer, and abruptly "the surging sea grasped the warrior" (1494–95; "brimwylm onfeng / hilderince"). The long-awaited plunge is not reported; in an instant the water itself grasps him. Beowulf's descent requires only three half-lines in the telling; "Ða wæs hwil dæges, / ær he þone grundwong ongytan mehte" (1495–96; "It was 'hwil dæges' before he could see the bottom"). The phrase "hwil dæges" may specify the time it took Beowulf to reach this depth, the time or space of a day, or, as Fred C. Robinson has argued, may indicate that when Beowulf saw the bottom of the mere, up above the early dawn of his setting out had become broad day.[23]

The Image of Chaos

The abruptness and quick reversals of the narrative of the hero's second battle create a keen sense of desperate violence, danger, and a doubtful outcome to the encounter. The fight itself seems created in largely realistic, perhaps even grossly realistic, terms despite its setting in an underwater hall that almost seems an antiworld, the realm of chaos rendered domestically, a roofed building situated in the plain at the bottom of the mere ("grundwong" 1496) and furnished, like Heorot itself, with treasures and weapons hung on the walls. At the instant Beowulf sees the bottom of the mere, the monster of the deep catches sight of him, seizes him, and carries him into the hall of the monsters, a place roofed against the water of the mere. The fire within the monsters' hall, an awesome indication of the mere's uncanny nature in Hrothgar's description, illuminates the scene and Beowulf immediately strikes at his enemy with the good sword Hrunting. In Heorot Grendel's mother's flight suggested her vulnerability to the weapons of the Danes—the narrator measured her strength and found it inferior—but in the depths of the mere Grendel's mother becomes the archetypal enemy and assumes the powers of the place itself, chaos, the antiworld. Unferth's sword that had cut through the mail shirts and the helmets of many doomed warriors rings harmlessly on the monster's head: "ða wæs forma sið / deorum madme, þæt his dom alæg" (1527–28; "it was then the first time for the precious treasure that its fame fell"). Like sword, like owner: Unferth, too, forfeited some of his reputation when he did not descend into the mere—"þær he dome forleas, / ellenmærðum" (1470–71; "there he lost glory for deeds of valor").

The audience of the poem saw the battle with Grendel only in a few specific details—the monster's footfall on the floor of Heorot, his eyes like fire, his ghastly meal of Hondscioh, his groping hand, his wound, his scream—that did not create an actual battle. The poem indeed leaves the nature of the encounter in doubt, hidden from the poem's audience and the Danes in the darkness of Heorot. In the second battle the Danes—and now Beowulf's followers as well—await the outcome in deepest unknowing, but the audience follows the fight at the bottom of the mere blow by blow. The story's realism and detail become almost unseemly and this hair-raising episode has not received much critical attention partly because of its indelicate realism. When Hrunting proves useless, Beowulf casts it aside and grapples hand to hand with no holds barred:

> Gefeng þa be eaxle   —nalas for fæhðe mearn—
> Guð-Geata leod   Grendles modor;
> brægd þa beadwe heard,   þa he gebolgen wæs,
> feorhgeniðlan,   þæt heo on flet gebeah.
>
> (1537–40)

(Then the prince of the Battle-Geats seized Grendel's mother by the shoulder, he didn't regret that hostile act; when the man hard in battle was enraged, he pulled his mortal enemy so that she fell to the floor).

The first line above lacks alliteration, a metrical fault that the emendation of "eaxle" to "feaxe" would correct. The translation would then run, "the prince . . . seized Grendel's mother by the hair," a better handle than the shoulder; perhaps Grendel's hand (and arm and shoulder) became too strongly fixed in the copyist's imagination. In his revision of A. J. Wyatt's edition of the poem, R. W. Chambers remarked that several editors had adopted this reading and added "To me *feaxe* appears also to give better sense; but this may be disputed. Mr. Wyatt writes: 'William Morris agreed with me that it debased Beowulf's character, turning a wrestle into an Old Bailey brawl. Hair-pulling is a hag's weapon.' "[24]

Wyatt's objection to "feaxe" assumes that the battle beneath the mere should be told with heroic dignity and gravity like a formal duel between gentlemen, but this is another story. The advantage Beowulf gained grasping the enemy's hair proves brief; in countering his attack, she throws and sits on Beowulf (presumably astraddle) whose position is desperate but not dignified. The indecorum of Beowulf's grip on Grendel's mother may have nicely matched the indignity of his position at the moment of his greatest danger: E. G. Stanley has noted that in the Old Frisian laws the offence of "faxfang" (corresponding to Anglo-Saxon "feaxfeng") had "an aggravated form," specified as "faxfang binetha on tha buke," which Stanley translates as "pulling (an opponent's) hair down on to the belly,"[25] raising a question as to whether the hair being pulled is lower than the belly to begin with. Stanley's suggestion might add violent impropriety to the realism of the conflict. Perhaps a hard-pressed Beowulf wisely disregarded the feud the race of Grendel would have had against him for seizing on these particular hairs and threw his enemy down by the most convenient handle.

The Warrior and the Sword   The significance, if not the martial details, of Beowulf's battle with Grendel seemed clear. Grendel bore God's anger, Beowulf seemed God's instrument for delivering Heorot. At the bottom of the mere the physical details of the battle are clear, the metaphysics ambiguous. At the crucial moment, the old master smith's mail coat defends Beowulf's life; he attacks and kills the enemy with an ancient sword made by giants before the flood. The narrator reports that God easily and rightly decided the struggle, but

God's decisive help has no clear function in the story. Beowulf breaks free, stands up, and sees the sword: the crisis has past. The hero's final victory over the monsters of the mere momentarily resolves the suspense that dominates the second great fight. A scene of gruesomely realistic detail closes the monstrous siege of Heorot with savage finality. In desperation and grim determination, Beowulf grasps and draws the giants' sword:

> He gefeng þa fetelhilt,   freca Scyldinga
> hreoh ond heorogrim,   hringmæl gebrægd
> aldres orwena . . .
>
> (1563–65)

(He, the Shieldings' daring warrior, gripped the ring-hilted sword, savage and grim in battle drew the ring-adorned sword despairing of his life . . .)

The adjective "heorogrim" ("grim in battle") could be literally rendered "sword-grim" and makes the mood of Beowulf's mind like the weapon he draws.

The tide of battle has turned when Beowulf perceives the sword, a legacy from the oldest past of history, the age before the flood, but he strikes his enemy in anger, not in expectation of victory or survival:

>   yrringa sloh,
> þæt hire wið halse   heard grapode,
> banhringas bræc;   bil eal ðurhwod
> fægne flæschoman;   heo on flet gecrong,
> sweord wæs swatig,   secg weorce gefeh.
>
> (1565–69)

(he struck angrily so that hard edge gripped her neck, broke through the vertebrae; the sword passed through the doomed body; she fell to the floor, the sword was bloody, the warrior rejoiced in his work)

That last line nicely juxtaposes the bloody sword and rejoicing warrior and, like the adjective "heorogrim," unites the warrior and the weapon. The hero's exultation in the enemy's killing and the sword's bloody stains seem one. In the battle beneath the mere, Beowulf owes life and victory to a coat of mail made by Weland and a still more ancient sword made by giants; legacies of the pagan past become the means of victory.

E. B. Irving acutely observes that as Beowulf arms for his descent, he "takes with him three half-personified comrades. Call them Byrnie, Helm, and the sword named Hrunting."[26] The roles the passage assigns to Beowulf's mail shirt or byrnie and helmet, Irving observes, almost invest those objects with wills or characters. The relationship between Unferth and Hrunting seems even closer still: both fail and fall short of the nearly supernatural standard of heroism set by Beowulf and the great sword at the bottom of the mere; together Hrunting and Unferth suffer a loss of reputation. But in the depths of Grendel's mere, the gigantic sword almost becomes Beowulf's other self, its power, spirit, and mood matching his. The instrument of victory and the victor fuse as the hero's mind acquires the character of the weapon and the weapon seems to exult like its wielder.

The moment of savage exultation, shared by the man and the sword, seems particularly singled out for supernatural, possibly divine, approbation. At the moment of victory the bloody sword and the exulting hero are suddenly illuminated: "Lixte se leoma, leoht inne stod, / efne swa of hefene hadre scineð / rodores candel" (1570–72; "The flame shone, the light within was just like that of the sky's candle shining brightly"). The comparison of the light within Grendel's hall beneath the mere and the sun shining brightly in the heavens suggests divine or supernatural favor, but this brilliance follows Beowulf's triumph and seems a consequence rather than a cause of victory. His way providentially lit, Beowulf stalks the monstrous hall intending to avenge all Grendel's deadly attacks on the Danes:

> He æfter recede wlat;
> hwearf þa be wealle,   wæpen hafenade
> heard be hiltum   Higelaces ðegn
> yrre ond anræd,—   næs seo ecg fracod
> hilderince . . .
>
> (1572–76)

(He looked along the building, went along the wall, angry and determined Hygelac's retainer raised the hard weapon by the hilts—the blade was not worthless to the warrior . . .)

The word "fracod" ('worthless') has a strong sense of moral disapproval not commonly applied to inanimate objects; by a classic understatement the "loyal, excellent" sword becomes a comrade in arms. Beowulf, the "reþe cempa" (1585; "fierce, dire, or savage warrior"), strikes Grendel's corpse a final blow, cutting off the monster's head. The cadaver rebounds at the stroke as the parts of a stick fly up when cut through by a heavy blow, another touch of grisly realism: Grendel's corpse should have still been stiff a day after his mortal wound in Heorot.

From the turning point of the battle with Grendel's mother (the gigantic sword) to the victorious stroke and thence to the unexpected perfection of the war with Grendel, the action moves briskly and powerfully so that suspense aroused by the desperate battle beneath the mere gives way to exultation in sudden, unexpected victory. At the instant Grendel's head comes off, the scene returns to the passive spectators above. Hrothgar's wise old councillors see the surging waves of the mere stained with blood and conclude that Beowulf will not return. At noon the Danes withdraw, the Geats remain behind, sick at heart, hoping for Beowulf's return without expecting to see him again. The enforced passivity and helpless anxiety of Beowulf's companions recaptures the uncertainty and emotional power of the battle in Grendel's hall and reinforces the separation of Beowulf from his companions and the Danes. The geography of the battle dramatically isolates Beowulf from the others: they wait above the surface of the mere, he descends into another world, one apparently never visited by another living man. The battle with Grendel hardly makes a parallel: the Geats remained in Heorot with Beowulf; in the past members of Hrothgar's company had waited in Heorot for Grendel though they died for it. In Grendel's hall, a site no other man could reach, Beowulf defeats the monsters with a weapon no other man could wield.

Changing Places   The reaction of the Danes and Geats to the bloody waves of the mere mark Beowulf's separateness; the Danes depart after seeing graphic evidence that the unseen battle has ended. They have assumed that no man could have won a mortal battle in the depths of the mere. The Geats remain loyally behind—"modes seoce" (1603; "sick in spirit," "heart-sick")—being obliged to avenge their dead lord or to die with him on the field of battle, but the field of that battle lies unthinkably beyond their limits. At exactly the moment that Beowulf's uniqueness and his isolation from the Danes, the Geats, and mankind seems most powerfully indicated, he is on the point of returning to the heroic world. The blade of the gigantic sword begins to melt the instant it has struck off Grendel's head and its melting summons up an almost pastoral simile comparing the dripping steel to icicles and moving from the supernatural or extraordinary event to God's annual unbinding of the bonds of winter. Leaving the treasures of the mere, save for the hilt of the sword, Beowulf swims to the surface and rejoins his companions who, no longer passive spectators, approach him, rejoice in his return, help him from his armor, and struggle back to Heorot with some four of them carrying Grendel's severed head suspended from a pole. Grendel's last harmless appearance in Heorot occasions some stir:

> Þa wæs be feaxe   on flet boren
> Grendles heafod,   þær guman druncon,
> egeslic for eorlum   ond þære idese mid,
> wliteseon wrætlic;   weras on sawon.
>   (1647–50)

(Then Grendel's head was carried by the hair into the hall where the men were drinking, an awesome sight terrible for the men and for the lady with them; men stared.)

The Danes are spectators still. Beowulf reports on the battle the Danes could not watch and assures Hrothgar that at last he has no need to expect harm from the race of Grendel.

Beowulf rejoins his companions at the mere, the Danes in Heorot, and reenters the world of human complications and negotiations he briefly left behind as he entered the world of monsters. The hero's original mission to the Danes made the Danes' failure to deal with Grendel all too explicit—as Unferth's outburst made apparent—but Beowulf's return from the mere to Heorot leaves Hrothgar to reestablish an appropriate relationship between himself, Beowulf, and the heroic world. Hrothgar seems compelled to reassert his quasi-parental role with respect to the hero even as he praises and rewards the man who delivered the Danes from catastrophe. The disturbances Beowulf occasions as he delivers the Danes from their affliction move up the scale of Danish society. Unferth's challenge implicitly acknowledged a rebuke to the Danish warrior-class in Beowulf's journey and purpose and Hrothgar's spokesman seemed to speak for the Danish nobility. The consequences of Grendel's mother's revenge brought the embarrassment directly to King Hrothgar. Beowulf's part in the story of Grendel's mother began when Hrothgar summoned him to a meeting before dawn. That Hrothgar was distraught, even shattered, seems understandable in human terms, though the king's surrender to grief violates the standard of heroic behavior. After schooling himself for years to endure the humiliation and harm of Grendel's campaign, Hrothgar had the curse lifted from his shoulders and rejoiced in freedom and in an end to anguish, then had the wound to his reign and soul reopened in a single, deadly stroke.

At that early morning conference, Hrothgar seems nearly incoherent with grief and anxiety to enlist Beowulf against Grendel's mother. Hrothgar's appeal tumbles out in an order determined by the emotional intensity of the particulars, not their logical connections: he announces that the sorrow of the Danes has been renewed, then that Æschere is dead, then defines and eulogizes that good companion and reveals that Æschere's monstrous killer has escaped with a feast to some unknown retreat. Hrothgar suddenly shifts from that gruesome subject to an implication that Beowulf has brought this trouble on the Danes:

> Heo þa fæhðe wræc,
> þe þu gystran niht   Grendel cwealdest
> þurh hæstne had   heardum clammum,
> forþan he to lange   leode mine
> wanode and wyrde.
>
> (1333–37)

(She avenged that feud in which last night you violently killed Grendel with hard grips because for too long he diminished and destroyed my people.)

Having almost blamed Beowulf for bringing the wrath of Grendel's mother down on the heads of the Danes, Hrothgar promptly justifies Beowulf's violent proceedings with Grendel: the monster had too often slaughtered the king's followers.

Abruptly leaving his powerful description of the haunted mere, Hrothgar appeals directly, almost pathetically, to Beowulf for help no one else can give: "Nu is se ræd gelang / eft æt þe anum" (1376–77; "Now once more help depends on you alone"). The naked admission of renewed helplessness and the direct appeal to Beowulf for help makes the Danes' humiliation painfully explicit. The appeal of royal helplessness to heroic power becomes a challenge to Beowulf's heroic spirit: "Eard git ne const, / frecne stowe, ðær þu findan miht / sinnigne secg; sec gyf þu dyrre!" (1377–79; "You still do not know the homeland, the dangerous place where you can find the guilty warrior; seek it out if you dare!"). Hrothgar's long, almost lyric description of the terrors of the mere, briefly recapitulated in "the dangerous place," becomes part of his rhetorical appeal; the perils of the place and the guilt of the enemy challenge Beowulf to prove the heroic status he won the night before. Hrothgar closes his appeal to Beowulf with an explicit offer of payment as an inducement to action:

> Ic þe þa fæhðe	feo leanige,
> ealdgestreonum,	swa ic ær dyde,
> wundini golde,	gyf þu on weg cymst.[27]
> (1380–82)

(I shall reward you with money, with ancient treasures, with wound gold, for carrying on the feud, as I did before, if you come back.)

Beowulf should not be blamed for the impropriety of this last appeal; he never refers to this offer and makes no effort to discover just how much "wound gold" Hrothgar has in mind.

Hrothgar's offer makes a glaring exception to the aristocratic idealism implicit in the poem's representation of gifts. When he first came to defend Heorot, Beowulf asked for permission to fight Grendel, not for rewards. When Wulfgar first announced Beowulf's arrival, Hrothgar anticipated the hero's purpose and assured the Danes he understood his obligation: "Ic þæm godan sceal / for his modþræce madmas beodan" (384–85; "I shall have to offer the brave man treasures for his daring"). Only after Beowulf has twice vowed to defend the hall against Grendel does Hrothgar mention a material reward for the deed: "Ne bið þe wilna gad, / gif þu þæt ellenweorc aldre gedigest" (660–61; "There will be no lack of precious things for you if you survive that deed of courage"). Even that discreet promise, the close of Hrothgar's brief goodnight, seems part of an almost satiric representation of the king's prompt exit from the hall as nightfall and Grendel approach.

Overwhelming grief compromises Hrothgar's sense of decorum, hence Beowulf finds himself in a socially awkward position. He must comfort and encourage an older, higher-ranking, and conventionally wiser man. Beowulf briefly reasserts the standard of heroic behavior: "Ne sorga, snotor guma! Selre bið æghwæm, / þæt he his freond wrece, þonne he fela murne" (1384–85; "Do not grieve, wise man! It is better for every man that he avenge his friend than that he mourn much"), and promises to pursue the enemy even to the bottom of the sea, a vow of action beyond ordinary heroism. Tacitus reports approvingly that in the

Germanic world men restrained their lamentations for the dead: "A woman may decently express her grief in public; a man should nurse his in his heart." The Latin, "feminis lugere honestum est, viris meminisse" ("it is seemly for women to lament, for men to remember"),[28] fairly expresses the precept Beowulf has in mind. The appropriate remembering for a man is revenge, but Beowulf adds another general truth to this conventional wisdom:

> Ure æghwylc sceal   ende gebidan
> worolde lifes,   wyrce se þe mote
> domes ær deaþe;   þæt bið drihtguman
> unlifgendum   æfter selest.
>
> (1386–89)

(Each of us must come to the end of life in the world, let him who may win fame before his death; that is afterwards best for the departed warrior.)

Beowulf's philosophy offers Hrothgar the comfort that Æschere had indeed won fame before his death and hints that Beowulf's own search for fame will lead him to avenge Æschere's death, the consolation Hrothgar desires. After making his vow, Beowulf calls on Hrothgar to endure for just one day: "Ðys dogor þu geþyld hafa / weana gehwylces, swa ic þe wene to" (1395–96; "For today be patient in every sorrow as I expect of you"). The promise implicit in Beowulf's request has an immediate and dramatic effect on Hrothgar. The old king leaps up, thanks God for Beowulf's speech, and promptly leads the band of Danes and Geats to Grendel's mere. But Beowulf and Hrothgar have exchanged roles: Beowulf has reminded Hrothgar of the truths a heroic world acknowledges. After Beowulf's exhortation Hrothgar recovers and acts as his royal status requires, but that same day, the old king misjudges the outcome of battle, leaves the mere, and returns to Heorot.

Assertions of Wisdom   Beowulf's abrupt and apparently unannounced entrance into Heorot reduces the Danes to their familiar role as spectators, though now they stare at the shocking proof of their deliverance. The hero reports the outcome of the battle at the bottom of Grendel's mere and presents Hrothgar with the trophies of his victory: Grendel's head and the hilt of the gigantic sword. At last, Hrothgar knows the long affliction has been finally and completely ended, but his relationship with Beowulf requires setting in order. Hrothgar's praise of Beowulf asserts and recaptures his own royal dignity:

> Þæt, la, mæg secgan   se þe soð ond riht
> fremeð on folce,   feor eal gemon,
> eald eþelweard,   þæt ðes eorl wære
> geboren betera!
>
> (1700–3)

(Listen, an old ruler who acts according to truth and justice among the people, who remembers everything from long ago, can say that this warrior was very nobly born!)

Hrothgar prefaces his praise of Beowulf with his own qualifications to assess a hero's merit: knowledge reaching back into the distant past, long experience as a ruler and protector of a people and land. From his brief praise of Beowulf (1702–9), Hrothgar moves to his "sermon," the best-known expression of conventional wisdom in *Beowulf.* In one important dramatic function, the speech corrects the anomalous direction of ethical instruction and installs Hrothgar as the sage, Beowulf as the pupil; in another, Hrothgar's wisdom speech, or "sermon," redefines the heroic ideal in terms of wisdom, which he claims, and openhanded generosity, which he promptly and magnificently puts into practice. The speech has been taken as the center of the poem, as the poet's own paraphrase of the meaning of *Beowulf.* Margaret E. Goldsmith claimed that Hrothgar's sermon "was written as a key to the interpretation of the story."[29] The speech can be taken as a dramatic part of the poem's art, part of the social and psychological realism that becomes the context of the monster-fights and the hero's report at home to King Hygelac of the Geats.

Hrothgar examines the hilt of the great sword Beowulf brought back from the mere, then praises the hero's achievement: Beowulf's fame has become known to all nations. The quality in Beowulf that Hrothgar singles out for special approval is wisdom. The young hero governs his strength with "modes snyttrum" (1706; wisdom/prudence of heart/spirit/mind) that will make him an enduring and vital support to his people (a role Hrothgar has assigned to himself at the outset). Hrothgar's wisdom speech draws its historical matter from the Danish poetic tradition. He first contrasts Beowulf with Heremod, a bad king from an older Danish dynasty whom the court poet compared unfavorably with Sigemund, the dragon killer and heroic king. The court poet implies at the same time a complimentary comparison between Sigemund and Beowulf. Hrothgar proceeds from the image of Heremod preserved in the Danish poetic tradition (as understood in *Beowulf*), then generalizes the case of a promising king who went terribly wrong. Hrothgar marvels that a man to whom a gracious God has given much should go astray and explores this wonder, moving from history to a form of allegory suggesting a specifically Christian rhetoric. Within Hrothgar's hypothetical Heremod, almost Everyruler, pride flourishes, the guardian of the soul falls asleep, an enemy, a wicked spirit or demon armed with a bow, shoots iniquitious suggestions until the man is struck with a deadly arrow beneath a figurative helmet. That guardian or keeper of the soul ("se weard . . . sawele hyrde"; 1741–42) who falls asleep seems to be either a figure for conscience or reason, and reflects the language of Christian moralizing. The archer of Hrothgar's allegorized discourse may have been added to the poetic tradition from Christian homilies or adopted from the folklore of the Anglo-Saxons or may represent a fusion of the two traditions.

Hrothgar's sermon is an instance of wisdom literature with an almost Christian rhetoric: iniquitous suggestions corrupt a man whose internal guardian fails to keep good watch, but the violated norms of conduct are specifically heroic. The truths Hrothgar's speech repeats are those of Beowulf's brief exhortation to Hrothgar. The corrupted ruler of the "sermon" grows niggardly: "nallas on gylp seleð / fætte beagas" (1749–50; "he does not dispense ornamented rings as the pursuit of honor requires"). He passes, another takes his place and ungrudgingly dispenses that hoarded wealth, and gains—we guess—the glory, the lasting fame, that the miser forfeited. The ethos of Hrothgar's sermon is not Christian. In specifically Christian contexts, the word "gylp" commonly has the bad sense of "vainglory," or "pride," but in Hrothgar's sermon to act "on gylpe" (as the pursuit of honor requires, honorably, in a way that confers honor on the actor) becomes a moral imperative for the great. On that essential doctrine, that posthumous fame is the reward and goal of noble conduct, the wisdom speeches of Beowulf and Hrothgar agree. After his speech, Hrothgar rewards Beowulf with a generosity that fully exemplifies the virtue the old king recommends so strongly. Hrothgar's speech asserts his dignity, gravity, royal status, and moral authority while recognizing Beowulf's heroic achievement and suggesting that the princely hero, a grandson of the Geatish protomonarch Hrethel on the female side, will eventually become king of the Geats. This becomes one more hint in part I that the poem will include Beowulf's reign as king of the Geats.

The Gift Outright   Hrothgar's brief assessment of Beowulf's heroic achievement recalls the hero's idea of his father's heroic status; the old king announces that Beowulf's fame has travelled far and wide among every nation: "Blæd is aræred / geond widwegas, wine min Beowulf, / ðin ofer þeoda gehwylce" (1703–5; My friend Beowulf your fame is made known to every nation far and wide). When Beowulf first reached the Danish shore, he identified himself as Hygelac's subject and his father's son:

> Wæs min fæder   folcum gecyþed,
> æþele ordfruma,   Ecgþeow haten;
> . . . .
> . . . hine gearwe geman
> witena welhwylc   wide geond eorþan.
> (262–66)

(My father, a noble warrior named Ecgtheow, was famous among nations; . . . all over the world every wise councillor remembers him well.)

Unlike heroes of folktale, Beowulf bears the burden of a famous father, a world-famous father in his own view, and thus has before him a familiar and formidable task in coming to terms with himself and his father's achievement. Shortly after this account of Ecgtheow, Hrothgar gives his followers—and the poem's audience—his own reading of Beowulf's noble descent: Beowulf's father was named Ecgtheow and was married to the only daughter of Hrethel, king of the Geats. The disparity in modes of assessment should catch an audience's attention though the assessments themselves do not necessarily differ. The poem much later reports that King Hygelac of the Geats married his only daughter to Eofor, the hero who struck King Ongentheow of the Swedes a mortal blow. A princess makes a traditional reward for outstanding valor, but when Beowulf enters Heorot, Hrothgar presents still another Ecgtheow for the Danes'—and our—consideration, Ecgtheow as exile. In this account, Hrothgar's power and wealth first protected Ecgtheow from his enemies, then reconciled their feud.

On his return to the Geats, Beowulf has evidently won the struggle to break free of his father's fame and ended that challenge to his sense of himself. Ecgtheow disappears from the poem, and his place is taken by Hygelac, Beowulf's young uncle and king, who claims to have challenged, almost like Unferth, the wisdom of the hero's expedition to the Danes. Hygelac's opening affects not to have noticed that Beowulf's return in itself rebuts the alleged challenge, "Hu lomp eow on lade, leofa Biowulf . . ." (1987; "How did your trip go, dear Beowulf . . ."). Uncle Hygelac may be suspected of warm-hearted teasing, not a suggestion that this nephew took the better part of valor and declined to meet the monster of Hrothgar's meadhall. Beowulf's confident and assured response addresses the intergenerational tensions of part I: he first summarizes the facts of his victory in Denmark, then reports on current Danish diplomacy and Freawaru's engagement to Ingeld. Beowulf predicts the failure of Hrothgar's wisdom. Hrothgar's "sermon" made generosity and wisdom the pillars of greatness in the heroic world. Beowulf's assessment of Hrothgar's diplomacy appropriates to the hero the wisdom the old king claimed; Beowulf's gift to Hygelac, his uncle, his king, of everything he won in Denmark outdoes Hrothgar in generosity unless we think a Geatish prince richer than a Danish king. Hygelac's equally generous part in this gift exchange, an enormous grant of land, makes Beowulf second only to Hygelac among the Geats. Were it not for the many hints of Beowulf's future kingship of the Geats in part I, an audience would think the poem had reached a convincing closure in Hygelac's grant, the final acceptance of Beowulf into the heroic society of his people.

Chapter Five

The Old Kings

The Great Battles: Settings and Origins

W. P. Ker perceptively noted that the "three chief episodes" of *Beowulf* "are well wrought and well diversified . . . there is a change of temper between the wrestling with Grendel in the night at Heorot and the descent under water to encounter Grendel's mother; while the sentiment of the Dragon is different again."[1] Unfortunately, Ker did not attempt to characterize the temper of the main episodes of the poem or trace the specific differences by which the poem's variety becomes discernible. The striking differences in tone and narration between the Grendel story and its continuation in Beowulf's fight with Grendel's mother do not compromise an audience's acceptance of these diverse episodes as parts of one action: the directness with which the second story follows the first, the beginning of the second story where the first ended, in Heorot, and the causal link between Grendel's death and his mother's revenge make the two plots (in a strict Aristotelian analysis) seem one.

In the dragon story, however, the differences of tone and narration, the lapse of fifty years, the change of setting from Denmark to the land of the Geats, and the disassociation of the dragon from Grendel and his mother has made the final episode a crisis for formal criticism. From its abrupt beginning to its powerful close, the second part of *Beowulf* differs dramatically enough from the first to have sustained a prolonged controversy as to whether the poem was conceived as a whole or simply anthologized into a whole from originally separate poems.

The stories of Beowulf's battles with Grendel and Grendel's mother in Denmark involve the hero in a variety of human, social, and political contexts quite strongly contrasting with the human setting of the dragon story. In Denmark, Beowulf rebuts the jealous Unferth openly, assumes the incompatible roles of son and mentor in his delicate relationship with Hrothgar, responds positively but obliquely to Wealhtheow's appeals, and asserts himself unobtrusively but firmly against the teasing possessiveness of his avuncular king, Hygelac. For all the rich clustering of historical allusion and ancient legend created and suggested in the first part of *Beowulf,* the hero appears in the human context of a seemingly historical moment. The chronology, appropriately, seems precisely defined: Beowulf visits the Danes after Freawaru's betrothal to Ingeld of the Heathobards but before her departure for what is to prove an ill-starred marriage. Thus, perhaps more memorably, Beowulf's visit must fall shortly before Ingeld's famous but unsuccessful attack on the Danes. On these considerations alone, a Danish chronicler of a later age could have placed Beowulf's exploits in an immediate context of Danish dynastic history.

The poem separates Beowulf's dragon fight from any close correlation with the legendary history of the Geats. The hero's long tenure as a good king detaches his last battle from the events that brought him to the throne; likewise, Wiglaf's reign puts a temporal barrier of some sort between Beowulf's death and the projected wars and defeat of the Geatish people. The poem isolates King Beowulf from immediate involvement with a Geatish present. Beowulf's long reign separates him from the persons of part I and leaves the old king among a people he loves but whom the poem does not present to its audience. Saving Beowulf and his young kinsman (and designated successor) Wiglaf, no named persons appear in the Geatish present, the time of the dragon. Wiglaf emerges from a shadowy troop of Geatish warriors who accompany Beowulf to the dragon's lair but fail to come to their king's help when the fight against the dragon seems lost. Though he enters the story abruptly, Wiglaf becomes Beowulf's one faithful follower, kinsman, and heir; indeed, Wiglaf joins Beowulf as the last of the Wægmundings. The poem's authentication of Wiglaf's present reality invokes the ever-present past of part II: Wiglaf is identified as a son of that famous warrior Weohstan who played a significant role in the dynastic wars of the Swedes and Geats. In contrast to the dimly perceived present in which Beowulf fights his last battle, a vivid and living past set within other, vaster reaches of time becomes the social, political, and human context of the poem's final section.

The physical setting of action in the dragon story and in the recreated history of the Geatish-Swedish wars contrasts with those of part I. The great events of part II take place out-of-doors and in apparently uninhabited wastelands, the realm of unreclaimed nature, the image of chaos. Throughout part I, both in the Grendel story and in the allusively recreated stories woven into that narration, significant action takes place chiefly in and around the halls, strongholds, or fortresses of great rulers. The halls of Hrothgar, Finn, Ingeld, and Hygelac become sites of the great events of the story's present and its legendary past. The hall indeed has a special, even a symbolic significance, beginning with the poem's first reference to the building of Heorot. In Part I, social and political exchanges within Hrothgar's (and even Hygelac's) royal hall nearly rival the battles with the monsters for the audience's attention. Indeed, Beowulf fights Grendel in Heorot, Hrothgar's hall, and Grendel's mother in a hall or antihall located like Heorot on a plain (though one at the bottom of the mere). In part I, the hall seems both the locus and symbol of the noble life, an analogue of the world's order (and the antihall an analogue of chaos) and the site of the story's most important actions, but in part II all we hear of Beowulf's hall is that the dragon burned it down. The significant scenes are the killing ground between the Swedes and the Geats, the Frisian coast where Hygelac dies, and the wastelands bordering the sea where the dragon guards the last survivor's treasure. Grundtvig's description of the dragon as the "evil spirit of nature"[2] may misrepresent the dragon by making him into a symbol but does place him in the context of "nature," an intriguing insight. The dragon seems to be causeless, to have no known origin; hence he seems to be a "spirit of nature" or of chaos, nature unredeemed. The dragon might be compared to the Geats' other great enemies, the Swedish kings Onela and Ongentheow, who seem almost forces of nature themselves: in victory and defeat, they appear only on the field of battle, never in council with their retainers and companions, nor setting off for bed, like Hrothgar, with their wives. The principle characters of part II are Ongentheow, the dragon, and Beowulf, three old and terrible warriors, rulers of hoards and treasures.

The one external setting important to the story in part I, is, of course, Grendel's mere. In part II, the dragon's barrow and Beowulf's grave mound are the only manmade structures to take a real place in the action. The undescribed and almost featureless scenes of action in the second part of the poem bear names which at least in some cases starkly convey the violence of an age of iron. On King Hrethel's death the warlike sons of the Swedish king Ongentheow frequently committed acts of aggression against the Geats in the neighborhood of Hreosna-beorh (probably "hill of the fallen" or "slaughter-hill").[3] In a place named both Hrefnawudu and Hrefnesholt (with the same meaning, "ravens' wood/forest") King Ongentheow won a brief victory over the Geats, killing Hrethel's son and successor, Hæthcynn, and besieging the remnant of Hrethel's army; that night he vowed to kill some with the sword and leave others on the gallows as sport for (probably) birds,[4] that is, for the carrion-eating ravens for whom the forest was named. Beowulf fought the dragon at or near Earnanæs, "Eagles' Cape"; though that great bird of prey has noble associations for us and for many peoples, it appears in the Anglo-Saxon poetic tradition as one of the eaters of the dead slain on the field of battle, one of the grim figures (raven, wolf, hawk, or eagle) representing violent death. From Eagles' Cape the Geats took their king's body to Hronesnæs, or "Whales' Cape," where Beowulf's funeral cairn was erected. Whales are now rightly in favor, but Anglo-Saxon poetry saw them as hostile monsters like the enemies who in Beowulf's first great adventure, his boyhood contest at sea with Breca, dragged the hero into the depths.

One might say that a poem sets the whole story of Grendel and his avenging mother in motion since the scop's song celebrating the creation of the world (and linking the Creation and the building of Heorot) sets off the monster's outrage and his campaign against Heorot, Hrothgar, and the Danes. In part II tracing the origin of the dragon fight finally ends in two lyric expressions of personal sorrow. If we imagine Beowulf and the dragon asking each other and themselves "why are we here now?," their combined answers would move through every event related in part II and come finally to rest, respectively, in "The Lament of the Last Survivor" and "The Father's Lament." The dragon's answer would begin with the theft of his cup and thence to the origins of the treasure and the tomb. Beowulf's reply would begin with his kingship, his responsibility for the Geats, and tracing his succession to its origins leads to the sorrow that shortened Hrethel's life. The "Lament of the Last Survivor" (2247–66) directly expresses the sorrow of a nobleman of an ancient race who places its entire treasure in a great stone barrow, laments that the precious objects, arms and armor, the rich vessels for feasting and drinking in the hall, must lie now untended and unused in the darkness of earth. The treasure, the dragon's cause, originates in the extinction of a people lost in the poem's antiquity. The dragon, acting as Anglo-Saxon conventional wisdom held he must, becomes the guardian of the hoard, and thus assumes a kingly function. Beowulf creates the "Father's Lament" (2444–62) as an almost Homeric simile comparing King Hrethel's sorrow at his eldest son's death to the grief felt by a hypothetical nobleman whose only son has been hanged. In Hrethel's lifetime, Beowulf's succession would have seemed improbable, but the occasion of Hrethel's sorrow makes the first of the steps leading to Beowulf's kingship.

These lyric-elegiac passages, poignant expressions of the suffering mortal and reasonable beings are inevitably liable to, reflect Beowulf's situation as the last descendant of the line of Hrethel. These lyrics create alienated figures left in inconsolable grief and its solitude, and thus seem in harmony with the concentration of the narrative on the isolated figures of Beowulf, the dragon, and Ongentheow, and part of a consistent artistic design. The poem's final section reports many battles, some with vivid and impressive though brief details; although we hear of the sweep of armies in these great actions, we see only brief scenes of violence enacted by a few individual figures: the Swedish kings Onela and Ongentheow, Weohstan the killer of a rebellious Swedish prince, Wulf and Eofor, two warrior brothers whose atypical names ("wolf" and "boar") suggest their animal power and ferocity and make them part of part II's setting—wastelands named for the beasts of battle or of the monstrous deep. The casts may number thousands, but the story unfolds in close-ups. We find two scenes of combat with three antagonists (Beowulf, Wiglaf, the dragon; Wulf, Eofor, Ongentheow) that close with a single figure, Ongentheow or Beowulf, wounded and dying. Yet for all this lyric concentration, part II creates a powerful narrative action moving inexorably toward its destined end.

Though the buried treasure causes the dragon's coming and the extinction of an ancient race caused the burial of the treasure, the theft of a precious cup from the ancient treasure occasions the dragon's anger and thus sets in motion the present-time action of part II. The story of the theft leaves the offender's name unknown and rank uncertain (at least to modern readers) though the thief's strong motivation seems clear: a refugee from justice or vengeance he sought shelter in the barrow, stole the precious vessel, and cleared himself by giving the cup to his lord (whether Beowulf or a lesser magnate is not clear). After Beowulf has resolved upon his plan of battle with the dragon, the cup comes into his possession by an informer's or informant's means. At this point, Beowulf realizes the cause of the dragon's wrath and his war against the Geats. As Beowulf and his companions set out for the dragon's barrow, the narrator makes clear that at this point Beowulf knows how the crisis has arisen: "hæfde þa gefrunen, hwanan sio fæhð aras, / bealonið biorna; him to bearme cwom / maðþumfæt mære þurh ðæs meldan hond (2403–5; "he had then learned the cause of the [dragon's] enmity, the warriors' cruel distress; the precious vessel had come into his possession by the informer's hand"). The narrator does not clarify the possible identifications (thief as informer, the thief's lord as informer), but the discovery of the cause of the dragon's wrath clarifies a more important matter.

On first hearing of the dragon's attack on the Geats and his burning of the royal hall, Beowulf becomes uncharacteristically melancholy and fears that he has angered God contrary to the "ancient law":

> wende se wisa,   þæt he Wealdende
> ofer ealde riht   ecean Dryhtne
> bitre gebulge;   breost innan weoll
> þeostrum geþoncum,   swa him geþywe ne wæs.
>
> (2329–32)

(the wise one supposed that contrary to the ancient law he had bitterly angered the Ruler, the eternal Lord; his heart surged with dark thoughts as was not his custom.)

A calamity as great as a rampaging dragon might reasonably darken the thoughts of a king seen as the protector of his people and held responsible for their prosperity, but Beowulf's fear that he may have angered God arrests our attention. A recurring sense of guilt seems an inevitable part of the human condition in the modern world, but the poem includes no parallel scene and only Hrothgar's wisdom speech (1724–68) suggests an idea of the conscience. In most contexts *Beowulf*, like the *Song of Roland*, represents a shame culture in which the ethical ideal lies in the public relationship between the individual and society rather than in the "personal and secret tie between man and God."[5] The poem gives no reason for God's anger, but Margaret Goldsmith suggests that Beowulf may have realized that "he had become content to enjoy the *temporalia* that were his in abundance, and, as Hrothgar had foretold, had neglected the service of his Lord," adding that "a Christian poet would not introduce the thought of God's anger without having a cause of that anger in mind." Goldsmith fits Beowulf's self-doubt into her larger argument that Beowulf fails because of his attachment to passing things—most vividly represented by the dragon's hoard—but she most scrupulously notes that "the poem never plainly says" that Beowulf's fears were justified.[6] In fact, the poem seems to say otherwise.

Apparently Beowulf's self-doubts attest to his exemplary life rather than to a moral fault or misconduct. Though troubled with a fear that he might have somehow brought disaster upon his people, Beowulf immediately resolves to undertake the defense of the Geats and gives orders for an iron shield since a wooden one would clearly not serve against the firedragon's chief weapon. After committing himself to the battle and forming his plan for its conduct, Beowulf discovers that the dragon's raids on the Geats originated in the monster's anger at being robbed of a precious cup. The poem's (and the hero's) subsequent silence on the cause (or subject) of God's anger seems entirely reasonable if the hero erred in his scrupulous fears and recognized the truth when he inspected the dragon's cup. For all his strength and courage and wisdom, Beowulf sometimes misjudges, is sometimes deceived by what he does not know (Grendel's invulnerability, the cause of the dragon's anger), but at last by what he hopes. Beowulf believed he could easily defeat Grendel with a sword (but that monster was sword-proof), briefly feared God's anger with him had called up the dragon's wrath, and hoped that the monster's treasure would ensure his people's survival. Beowulf's errors become him: a sense of fair play led him to fight Grendel with a weapon the monster could not withstand, naked strength; a keen sense of responsibility for his people prompted his fears that he had angered God; Beowulf died hoping, even believing, he had won the means of his people's survival. Moreover, in themselves Beowulf's errors confirm his essential humanity—as Stanley Greenfield pointed out in one of his last writings.[7]

The episode in which the thief takes the dragon's cup or drinking vessel and so brings the monster's dreadful wrath down on the Geats illustrates brilliantly the narrative focus in part II on isolated figures seen at brief, crucial moments and the wonderful and startling emphasis the story can give a decisive moment. In the poem's first reference to the event that begins the action of part II, the thief becomes a hand; in the first recapitulation, a foot. In the sequel, reduced to a shadow, a function and emotion, he unwillingly guides Beowulf's company back to the dragon's lair and vanishes from the narrative. The poem dramatically and vividly contrasts the decisive moment of the theft itself and that irrecoverable instant in which Beowulf issues the challenge the dragon assuredly does not refuse and which commits them both to a fatal encounter. The present of part II begins with the dragon's raids, moves swiftly to his lair, a deep stone barrow, the path leading into its depths, and an unknown man's surreptitious entry into the presence of a sleeping dragon. The intruder's desperate need—he is a fugitive, an exile fleeing death—drives him to enter the barrow. The tormented or guilty (2226; "synbysig") fugitive takes refuge in a tomb with a sleeping dragon guarding objects whose value could restore the exile's rights and end the hostility threatening his life.

The manuscript is nearly unreadable in the poem's first telling of the fugitive's story, but the outcome that he takes a precious object and exchanges it for peace (in effect paying a fine or damages and thus satisfying the claims of justice or vengeance) is clear. The moment its terrors come into clear focus (where the manuscript is readable) leave the thief indefinite: he enters the barrow— "þær on innan giong / niða nathwylc . . . . . h gefeng / hæðnum horde hond . . . . / since fahne " (2214-17; "Someone went inside . . . took from the pagan hord . . . his hand . . . the thing adorned with treasure").[8] Some lines later, the poem reports that the dragon found the thief's footprint:

	stearcheort onfand
feondes fotlast;	he to forð gestop
dyrnan cræfte	dracan heafde neah.
	(2288-90)

(the stout-hearted one traced an enemy's footprint; he [the thief] had stealthily stepped very near the dragon's head).

When first introduced into the story, the intruder was simply "some man," then (2223) "þ . . . nathwylces" either "some man's" slave ("þeow") or "some man's" retainer ("þegn"), or perhaps a "þeof" or "thief" who had stolen "something."[9] In any case, the intruder is an isolated man, a fugitive liable to be killed on discovery, and in the dragon's barrow, a solitary man confronting the naked figure of instant death.

Stepping near a sleeping dragon's head, a breathless business, creates a powerful suspense and a heart-crushing awareness that any sound would mean instant annihilation. The fugitive's situation embodies an imperative of silence. The thief's step that carried him near the monstrous head summons up a palpable sense of silence, and of fear. Once committed, the crime is final; to go back would be unthinkable. When Beowulf and his company proceed to the dragon's barrow led unwillingly by the thief, the guide's reluctance attests to the horror of a close encounter with an enormous, destructive force. The thief's unwilling return recalls his stealthy visit, its palpable, enforced silence, and the irreversible consequences of that theft. Beowulf's challenge to the dragon reverses the stealth, the fear, and the silence of the thief's visit. Leaving his companions behind him, Beowulf approaches the entrance to the dragon's barrow and knows that he cannot go down into those burning depths. His peremptory challenge, however, brings the dragon up at once:

> Let ða of breostum,   ða he gebolgen wæs,
> Weder-Geata leod   word ut faran,
> stearcheort styrmde;   stefn in becom
> heaðotorht hlynnan   under harne stan.
>
> (2550–53)

(Then he was enraged, then the prince of the Storm-Geats uttered a word, the stout-hearted one roared; his battle-bright voice went down beneath the grey stone resounding.)

To give silence that is merely privative, the absence of sound, a palpable presence requires a stroke of genius, but just such a stroke marks the thief's visit to the dragon's barrow, a stone built tomb, an appropriate temple of silence. Beowulf's great war cry, the shout resounding down beneath the gray stone and interrupting the silence of centuries, rudely awakens the dragon and the audience's perception of monstrous silence and heroic sound in the poem as a whole. In the darkness of the barrow, Beowulf's "battle-bright" voice finds immediate recognition and his message ("word") an immediate response: "Hete wæs onhrered, hordweard oncniow / mannes reorde" (2554–55; "Enmity was stirred up, the guardian of the hoard recognized a man's voice").

The challenge Beowulf issues to the dragon in his barrow recalls an earlier resounding affront to the monstrous world. When Beowulf, Hrothgar, and their companions reach the haunted mere, a warhorn sounds: "Horn stundum song / fuslic fyrdleoð" (1423–24; "A horn repeatedly sang a ready warsong"). This unaccustomed noise enrages the swarming monsters of the mere: "Hie on weg hruron / bitere ond gebolgne; bearhtm ongeaton, / guðhorn galan" (1430–32; "Furious and enraged they rushed along; they heard the clamor [or 'brightness'], the warhorn singing"). Two Anglo-Saxon words, "bearhtm" (and "breahtm," for both are subject to metathesis or a transposition of sounds), mean 1) "noise, tumult, sound, cry" and 2) "brightness," especially a passing brightness or "twinkle." The imagery of Beowulf's challenge to the dragon recalls the poem's recurrent association of silence and darkness with the monsters, light, brightness, and noise with mankind and particularly with human joy.

History as Context: Ages of Gold and Iron

Assuming that the major events of *Beowulf* join in a single artistic design makes their differences in tone, style, and narration crucial to a reading of the poem. The inevitability of the hero's death darkly distinguishes the final battle from both his earlier encounters; moreover the various narratives of part II concentrate insistently on the theme of death and make the significance of mortality central to the poem. In part I the death of Scyld almost makes the search for meaning in a life bounded by darknesses the poem's subject as his people lament the passing of the great king who delivered them from their kingless distress. The Danes honor Scyld, who had come to them as a sea-borne foundling with a traditional ship burial, but instead of burying the ship laden with Scyld's body and grave goods, arms, armor, and treasures in the earth, it is sent out to sea:

> Men ne cunnon
> secgan to soðe,   selerædende
> hæleð under heofenum,   hwa þæm hlæste onfeng.
> (50–53)

(Men, councillors in the hall, warriors beneath the skies could not truthfully say who received that cargo.)

The mystery of Scyld's origins and destination prepare the poem for the existential questions, but the context of Scyld's mortality defers the accounting for its significance: before Scyld's death, the narrator records his son's fame, generalizes on the rules of conduct by which a young prince can assure himself of loyal followers, and states the rule for a nobleman's success in the heroic world: "lofdædum sceal / in mægþa gehwære man geþeon" (24–25; "in every nation one can prosper only by doing praiseworthy deeds").

Following the moving account of the legendary king's death and his people's sorrow, his passing is restated blandly in the report of his son's succession, success, and long rule: "fader ellor hwearf, / aldor of earde" (55–56; his father, the ruler, departed from the earth"). That son's passing is implied still more blandly by the observation that Scyld's grandson Healfdane ruled the Danes in his own time. The enumeration of Healfdane's four children puts births definitively ahead of deaths; in the next generation Hrothgar's success in war leads to an increase in the band of young retainers: "seo geogoð geweox, / magodriht micel" (66–67; "the company of young warriors, the great band of young retainers, increased"). Growth, success, and an unbroken dynastic succession fill the poem's first history of the Danes. From Scyld to Hrothgar the succession runs unbroken and apparently without complication or challenge, and mortality becomes a painless part of an endless cycle. By the poem's end, Beowulf's death, funeral, and burial within sight of the sea echoes and recalls Scyld's ship burial and restores the long-deferred question, the meaning and the value of a heroic life.

The opening of part II also traces a dynastic history down to the Geatish king of the narrative present, Beowulf himself. The Danish prelude makes the history of Scyld's descendants seem the recital of a golden age, while the history of the Geats tersely sketches an age of iron. Part II begins with Hygelac slain in otherwise unspecified clashes of battle and his son Heardred killed by swords when the hard fighters, the Battle-Swedes, attack the young king in his native country. That grim epitome of Geatish history, and tragedy, occupies a long clause (2200–6); the next (2207–10) records Beowulf's succession and fifty years of good rule. Two more half-lines bring the audience to the narrative present: "wæs ða frod cyning, / eald eþelweard" (2209–10; "then he was an old / wise / experienced king, an old guardian of the people") at which point the dragon's raids begin. The golden age of Geatish history lies in the fifty years of Beowulf's rule sandwiched between the deaths of Kings Hygelac and Heardred and the dragon's raids, a period the poem records without specific detail. The brief history of the Geats opening part II succinctly and darkly introduces the major themes of the narrative: the death of Hygelac, the Geats' wars with the Swedes, and finally the dragon.

The first of these, Hygelac's death, seems a leitmotif shared with part I (hence a positive indication of a narrative design linking parts I and II). Beowulf's fight with the dragon (and his reign) briefly interrupts the long story of the wars of the Swedes and Geats which will resume disastrously for the Geats once the king's death is reported. The concentration and melancholy that mark the prelude to part II also

characterize the narrative as a whole and contrast with the expansiveness and essential optimism, confidence, and buoyancy of part I.

Despite the disjunction of the poem's two parts, the first anticipates
both the melancholy darkness and the insistent matter of the second.
As Beowulf returns from Denmark with Hrothgar's splendid gifts,
symbols of his achievement and status, the narrator moves with Beowulf's company toward Hygelac and characterizes the young hero-king
in honorific terms that anticipate the darker stories part II will tell.
Beowulf and his troop disembark not far from Hygelac's royal hall; the
narrator approvingly adds "Bold was betlic, bregorof cyning, / heah on
healle" (1925–26; "The building was splendid, the royally brave king
exalted in the hall"). The adjective "bregorof" compounds "brego," or
"king, ruler, prince, lord," and "rof," both "strong" and "brave" as if
kings should be, like Hygelac, the bravest of the brave and a standard
of courage. The same assumption appears in the formation of the adjective "cyningbeald" (1634), "royally brave" (said of Beowulf and his
followers returning to Heorot with Grendel's head). In his hall Hygelac
is both "eorla hleo" (1967; "protector of warriors") and "bonan
Ongenþeoes" (1968; "the killer of Ongentheow"). That victory over the
great Swedish king saved a defeated Geatish army from certain annihilation and made Hygelac's greatest triumph as he turned the fortunes of
Geats from defeat to victory. Beowulf himself tells a version of the story
early in part II (2472–89), but the death of Ongentheow becomes a
gloomy leitmotif most fully and vividly presented after Beowulf's death
and as part of the historical background to the messenger's prediction
that wars, defeat, and subjugation await the Geats.

Part II opens with Hygelac's death in battle, another dark leitmotif
part I has anticipated. Among the rewards of Beowulf's victory over
Grendel is a magnificent necklace or torque that, the narrator propheti-
cally reports, Hygelac will wear on a fatal raid against the Frisians
(1197–1214). The poem tells the story of the Frisian raid and King
Hygelac's death four times in all, once in part I, three times in part II.
A royal or royalist audience would remember that in part I the Danes
proclaimed the hero's suitability for kingship, the narrator foretold
Hygelac's fate, and Hrothgar suggested the Geats could choose no
better successor than Beowulf should Hygelac fall in battle (1845–53).
The hero's long speech in part II re-creates Geatish dynastic history
from Hrethel to Hygelac and closes with the battle in which Hygelac
fell though without explicitly mentioning his death. Beowulf names
Herebeald, Hæthcynn, and Hygelac (2434), as the sons of King

Hrethel, Beowulf's grandfather and founder of the first Geatish dynasty. The speech reaches back to Beowulf's seventh year when his, or Hygelac's, succession to the throne would have seemed unlikely. But Prince Hæthcynn's arrow accidently killed his older brother Herebeald. An Anglo-Saxon audience would probably assume a hunting accident; that dangerous and warlike pastime was the sport and sometimes the death of kings and nobles throughout the Middle Ages. King Hrethel died of sorrow, King Hæthcynn in battle with the Swedes. Hygelac rescued the remnant of Hæthcynn's army and succeeded his brother whose reign seems to have been short. Short, too, were the reigns of Hygelac, killed while raiding the Frisians, and his son Heardred, killed for sheltering the rebellious nephews of the Swedish king, Onela.

The essentially optimistic worldview suggested in the story of Grendel arises from the clearly stated axioms that the events of the story ultimately fall under the direction of a single and benevolent God whose partisanship is congenial: Grendel is God's enemy, a figure of evil, a direct lineal descendent of Cain, an archetypal outcast rejected by God; God has the power and inclination to arrest Grendel's violent and wrongful course; Grendel is doomed and Beowulf is God's instrument for the monster's destruction. The story of Grendel's mother challenges what seems the clear meaning of her son's story; she is not a symbol for evil nor is she described as God's enemy. The poem's representation of human affairs in the Danish court, in the history of the Scylding dynasty, and in allusions and episodes recalling the lives of other heroes and histories of other peoples, similarly challenge the reading of the world Grendel's story creates. The tensions between the general vision of human affairs in part I and the apparent meaning of the hero's first great victory seem muted by the powerful narration and excitement of Grendel's career and destruction. But those tensions, like the dragon, seem likely to reawaken at any opportune moment.

Though the Grendel episode as a kind of heroic comedy dominates part I of the poem, the story of Grendel's mother anticipates the darker tone of part II. The dragon story can be described as elegiac and melancholy, but those terms fail to indicate its power and epic grandeur. The force of the dragon's story rises from the inevitable and overwhelming movement of many causes driving toward one great effect. The story of Beowulf's fight with the dragon does not envelope its mighty opposites in an ironic pattern based on unawareness like Grendel's. When Beowulf gives orders for the great iron shield, his protection against the dragon's flames, the narrator comments on the common fate of the hero and his

enemy, joining the opposed champions in rhetorically symmetrical structures as if to preserve narrative objectivity:

> Sceolde lændaga
> æþeling ærgod   ende gebidan,
> worulde lifes,   ond se wyrm somod,
> þeah ðe hordwelan   heolde lange.
> (2341–44)

(The nobleman of long-tested valor was fated to endure the end of his fleeting
days of life in the world, and the dragon too, even though he had ruled the
hoard for a long time.)

The adjective "ærgod" ("good," "brave for a long time") describes the
hero's excellence, the clause "þeah ðe hordwelan heolde lange" ("although he had ruled the hoard for a long time") implies the dragon's
power. The sentence opens announcing Beowulf's fate, the approaching
end of his transitory days, and closes abruptly by adding the dragon's
subjugation to that destiny, the end of another long life. That almost
epigrammatic sentence balances the hero and monster with a surprising
evenhandedness that becomes typical of part II. When the dragon first
advances in its coils to engage Beowulf, the narrator reports that the
monster was hastening to its fate (2570; "to gescipe scyndan") and that
fate had not assigned victory in battle to the hero (2574–75; "him wyrd
ne gescraf / hreð æt hilde"). After the battle, Wiglaf laments Beowulf's
decision to fight the dragon, yet calls the decision Beowulf's destiny,
and regards the event as fated: "Heold on heahgesceap; hord is
gesceawod, / grimme gegongen; wæs þæt gifeðe to swið, / þe ðone
þeodcyning þyder ontyhte" (3084–86; "He kept to his high destiny;
the grimly gained treasure has been revealed; the fate which drew the
great king there was too strong").

The possibilities for an ironic telling of the battle seem evenly divided, but balanced and neutralized rather than developed. At the
conclusion of his first night's raiding, the dragon counted on his prowess and great stone barrow for his defense, but "him seo wen geleah"
(2323; "that expectation deceived him"); as he had the iron shield
made, Beowulf looked ahead to the battle with a confidence based on
his many victories:

> no he him þa sæcce ondred,
> ne him þæs wyrmes wig   for wiht dyde,

eafoð and ellen,   forðon he ær fela
nearo neðende   niða gedigde,
hildehlemma,   syððan he Hroðgares,
sigoreadig secg,   sele fælsode.

(2347–52)

(he had no fear of that battle nor did he consider the dragon's power and strength and courage at all, for, venturing many difficulties, he had survived many hostilities, many pitched battles, after he, a victorious warrior, cleansed Hrothgar's hall.)

The reference to Beowulf's many victories leads to the story of his crushing Dæghrafn, the champion of the Frisians, to death; the context of that exploit was the Viking raid in which Hygelac and many of his followers fell. The narrator promises victories but returns to the defeat and death of Beowulf's uncle and hero-king.

Tolkien misled a generation of readers (and himself) when his poetic gift transformed the dragon of *Beowulf* into a philosophical counter, a symbol for evil that may baffle and terrify the pagan past but not the poem's Christian present and future. Tolkien simply asserted without argument that the conception of the dragon "approaches *draconitas* rather than *draco*" ("dragon-ness" and "dragon"),[10] but the dragon in *Beowulf* is everywhere and always represented in concrete terms as a living being. Tolkien admits that there are "some vivid touches . . . in which this dragon is real worm, with a bestial life and thought of his own."[11] The word "worm" trivializes the poem's realistic representation of the dragon; in ordinary English "worm" designates a trout fisherman's best friend. Like women who justly protest that the word "man" is no longer inclusive ("human being"), the dragon could justly protest that Tolkien's etymologically sound terminology is a dismissive ploy.

The poem makes the dragon's mind and moods thoroughly plausible: the monster feels joy at his discovery of the treasure, pride of ownership, rage at the theft of a precious cup from the hoard, delight in his power of flight, confidence in his defenses, a chill of fear at the sight of Beowulf. The dragon seems most convincing in his initial reaction to the discovery that an item is missing from his treasury. Enraged and baffled, he seeks at times for the thief—

Hordweard sohte
georne æfter grunde,   wolde guman findan,
þone þe him on sweofote   sare geteode;

          hat and hreohmod   hlæw oft ymbehwearf
          ealne utanweardne;   ne ðær ænig mon
          on þære westenne   . . .
                                    (2293–98)

(The guardian of the treasure searched anxiously along the ground, he wanted
to find the man who had caused him an injury in his sleep; burning and
enraged he repeatedly circled the burial mound, but there in the waste land no
man . . .)

—and at times for the missing object—

                              hwilum on beorh æthwearf,
          sincfæt sohte;   he þæt sona onfand,
          ðæt hæfde gumena sum   goldes gefandod,
          heahgestreona.
                                    (2299–2302)

(again and again he returned to the barrow, sought for the precious cup; he
immediately discovered that some man had explored his gold, the ancient
treasures.)

Like many others, he looks for the lost where he did not find it before
and its continued absence increases his rage. That picture of frustration,
of bafflement and rage, of rising anger makes the dragon a memorable
character. The poem does not open up the minds of its characters as an
explicit subject of its art, but the action makes many of those characters
real, and the dragon is one of them.

The poem makes Grendel a symbol of evil and places that conception
of evil within an explicitly Christian scheme. Tracing Grendel's origins
to Cain, that flashpoint between the pagan and Christian traditions,
illuminates the poem's first great battle even as Tolkien claimed,[12] but
the differences between the hero's first and last battles must be crucial
to the poem taken as a whole. Tolkien's reading of Grendel rings true:
the poem indeed begins with a monster who suggests the old Germanic
world's vision of archetypal disorder and joins that vision to a Christian
myth of evil. The narrator of *Beowulf* communicates the truth of Grendel's origin directly to the audience, leaving the Danes, including the
wise monotheist King Hrothgar, unaware of Grendel's descent and
moral significance. The representation of Grendel's mother questions
that vision: the audience of Beowulf understands her no better than
Hrothgar does, but Tolkien ignored her part in the poem. The dragon

cannot be overlooked, but Tolkien disguised him as a "worm," traduced him as an abstraction, yet slandered him as "more evil than any human enemy."[13] In plain fact, no explicit statement in part II identifies the dragon as a symbol of evil and—quite as important—nothing in the poem explains the dragon's origins.

The story of Beowulf's battle with the dragon creates a kind of parity between the great adversaries. When Beowulf's echoing war cry invades the ancient silence of the dragon's tomb, the monster responds at once to the challenge and commits them both to mutual destruction. In their first sight of each other, both Beowulf and the dragon respond with a chill of fear at the sight of an adversary who means death: "æghwæðrum wæs / bealohygendra broga fram oðrum" (2564–65; "both of the murderous enemies felt fear from the other"). This evenhandedness in narrating Beowulf's last battle dramatically contrasts the ironically partisan telling of Grendel's story.

The poem characterizes the dragon more fully than Grendel or Grendel's mother, but does not transform the dragon into a disguised man; he is a brute beast utterly unlike Grendel. The dragon is not joyless or wretched; nor is his solitary state an exile imposed as a divine punishment. He has a more varied and complex inner life than Grendel or his mother. The dragon's first appearance in the poem notes his joy at discovering the last survivor's treasure and entering into the barrow:

> Hordwynne fond
> eald uhtsceaða   opene standan,
> se ðe byrnende   biorgas seceð,
> nacod niðdraca,   nihtes fleogeð
> fyre befangen.
>
> (2270–74)

(The old dawn-enemy who burning seeks out burial mounds, the smooth hostile dragon who enveloped in flames flies by night discovered the joy of the hoard exposed.)

After the fatal battle, the narrator exults in the dragon's fall—

> Nalles æfter lyfte   lacende hwearf
> middelnihtum,   maðmæhta wlonc
> ansyn ywde,   ac he eorðan gefeoll
> for ðæs hildfruman   hondgeweorce.
>
> (2832–35)

(Not at all did he move darting through the air in darkest night and show himself proud of his treasures, but instead he fell to the earth by the war-leader's deed)

—but that ironic contrast between the dragon's sporting in the air and his fatal falling to the earth, powerfully communicates an almost unwilling recognition of the monster's vivid life and reality.

The dragon's almost human self-awareness appears in the pride he takes in his treasures and in his nocturnal displays. This sense of the dragon's inner life also appears as the Geats approach the battlefield. They first discover the dragon's huge body and the narrator comments:

> lyftwynne heold
> nihtes hwilum,   nyðer eft gewat
> dennes niosian,   wæs ða deaðe fæst,
> hæfde eorðscrafa ende genyttod.
>   (3043–46)

(by night he had possessed the joy of flight, and afterwards had descended to seek his den, but then he was motionless in death, had made his last use of caves in the earth.)

The narrator takes grim satisfaction in the dragon's death and in the Geats' casual disposal of the monstrous body (3131–33)—pushed off the cliff into the sea—but though mortal and now extinct, the dragon's vivid reality remains inescapable. The monster had felt the joy of flight (man's long dream) and had taken pleasure in caverns underground. From his pleasures taken in the air and earth, this fiery creature ended at last being given to the sea. A part of nature itself, the dragon has been no symbol of evil but a being so vital the narrator cannot refrain from noting its mighty presence.

The investigation of *Beowulf* analogues in other Germanic literatures convinced G. V. Smithers that at an earlier stage of the story the "last survivor" who placed the treasure in a burial mound entered it and kept watch over his goods in the form of a dragon.[14] We cannot now discover whether any version of the poem transformed the treasure's human owner into its guardian. In *Beowulf,* the dragon has no origin; the Geats, Beowulf, and the poem's audience alike confront the dragon as inexplicable and undefined. The transparent mystery of Grendel's origins separated the uncomprehending pagans (or non-Christian monotheists) of part I and the poem's audience, but that superiority of vision, that possession of a truth denied the poem's actors, disappears in part II. The long-dead Geats and the poem's audience face the dragon with the same knowledge and the same doubt; the separations of time and space and cultural revolution standing between the poem's actors and its audience dissolve. Part I contrasted levels of understanding rising from Grendel's benighted ignorance and the Danes' pagan confusion to the audience's Christian knowledge, but part II decisively reduces such openings for irony. The poem does not make the dragon a symbol of an idea but leaves him as part of nature or things as they are—at once demanding and defying explication. The dragon leaves us all, the poem's actors and audiences, in darkness.

Part II of the poem creates a powerful narrative that moves inevitably to a harsh conclusion, the death of a blameless hero in self-sacrificing battle against an inexplicable enemy. Though Beowulf has lived beyond mankind's allotted span, his courage, suffering, and death joins the poem's audience with the mourning Geats at the poem's close. Every story in part II leads toward the confrontation of Beowulf and the dragon; death is the common theme of these stories. Beowulf's fight with the dragon appears intermingled with parts of the great story of the wars of the Swedes and the Geats (with royal deaths leading relentlessly toward Beowulf's accession) and with restatements on the theme of Hygelac's death creating a continuous movement toward the battle with the dragon and a steady concentration on the deaths of kings, of treasure-givers and holders, of brave heroic spirits. The crucial moments in the dragon story stand out with stark clarity and distinction amid the memories of past triumphs and catastrophes. Like experience and unlike popular philosophy, the story begins with the effect, the dragon's raids and wrath, and subsequently discovers the cause of that wrath from which the present action of part II proceeds.

Beowulf rules well for fifty years until an enemy, a dragon, begins his raids in the darkness of night; the draconian wrath that threatens the Geats' destruction drives the present action of part II; the narrator tracks the dragon to his treasure and a stone burial chamber, a hidden place to which a secret path descends (2210–14) and follows a man's entry into that fearful treasury, his motive and theft, then plunges into the deep past of the treasure's origins in the extinction of an ancient people. History becomes a deadly avalanche. The story returns from the depths to the dragon's present anger, his impatience for nightfall, and the narrator's clipped, chiastic, and epigrammatic summation of the story to come:

Wæs se fruma egeslic
leodum on lande,   swa hyt lungre wearð
on hyra sincgyfan   sare geendod.

(2309–11)

(The beginning was horrible for the people just as for their treasure-giver it quickly and terribly ended.)

The nicely placed antithesis, people and ruler, beginning and end, briskly close the first act of the tragedy and add to the paradoxical impression of a quickly paced narrative reaching into antiquity. The first act of part II runs from an ancient tragedy to the pilfering of the dragon's hoard in Beowulf's fiftieth regnal year.

The second act begins abruptly with the dragon's destructive attack on the Geatish people; he burns down buildings and presumably burns their occupants in: "no ðær aht cwices / lað lyftfloga læfan wolde" (2314–15; "he did not want to leave anything living behind"). The narrator makes the dragon's raids a matter of Geatish survival. A few rapid lines move from Beowulf's melancholy fear that some fault of his might have angered the Almighty and brought this affliction on his people, and his orders for a special shield. That command implies an immediate realization that for this fight a man must be able to hold a large iron shield up against the dragon's flames. Beowulf must fight alone. Beowulf's confidence that he, a man of many battles, can indeed fight a dragon leads to brief sketches of the battles in which Kings Hygelac and Heardred fell, thereby leaving the royal responsibility for the Geats to Beowulf. The narrator notices with satisfaction that Beowulf successively avenged the deaths of Kings Hygelac and Heardred, and observes that the hero survived many battles until that day on which he had to (or was fated to) fight the dragon ("oð ðone anne dæg, / þe he wið þam wyrme gewegan sceolde"; 2399–2400).

As the party reaches the dragon's barrow, the poem returns to Beowulf's preparation for the battle and indeed for death in a long, three-part speech (2426–2537)[15] that the narrator introduces, "Biowulf maþelade bearn Ecgðeowes" (2425; "Beowulf, Ecgtheow's son, spoke") and later interrupts to classify and comment darkly on: "Beowulf maðelode, beotwordum spræc / niehstan siðe" (2510–11; "Beowulf spoke, made a formal vow for the last time"). Though the speech might then seem complete, the narrator's second prophetic interruption— "Gegrette ða gumena gehwylcne, / hwate helmberend hindeman siðe, /

swæse gesiðas" (2516–18; "Then for the last time he saluted each one
of the warriors, the beloved companions")—introduces a fuller statement of Beowulf's heroic vow and his instructions to his companions.
Beowulf's great speech traces the cycle of his life in a few concentrated
images and becomes indeed an act of rather surprising self-definition.
He refers first to his many battles, but at once his memory turns to his
boyhood and a brief golden age in his grandfather's royal household.
The names of his partners in that early happiness, Beowulf's young
uncles Herebeald, Hæthcyn, and Hygelac, the sons of King Hrethel,
lead immediately to the memory of the deaths of those Geatish kings
and princes, the death of the Swedish king Ongentheow, and the death
of the Frisian champion Dæghrefn, whom Beowulf himself slew. Beowulf says nothing of his status as king and transforms the present act
of courage into part of his loyal service as Hygelac's kinsman and
war-leader.

The first section of Beowulf's speech attests to his undimmed love
and still-poignant sorrow for the heroic Hygelac, the young king of
Beowulf's youth. At line 2489 he concludes a brief but grim and vivid
account of King Ongentheow's death (a story the poem will subsequently retell in still greater detail); at line 2490 the hero's memory
leaps from the slain Ongentheow, an enemy of the Geatish people, to
Hygelac whom Beowulf does not now name:

> Ic him þa maðmas,   þe he me sealde,
> geald æt guðe,   swa me gifeðe wæs,
> leohtan sweorde;   he me lond forgeaf,
> eard eðelwyn.
>
> (2490–93)

(With my bright sword I repaid him in battle, as fate allowed me, for the
treasures he gave me; he granted me lands, an estate, the joy of a native
country.")

The next sentence begins "There was no need for him to . . ." where
once more the antecedent of "him" is clearly the unnamed Hygelac.
Early in his speech, Beowulf's memories of his happy boyhood become
a dynastic history of the Geats; at its close, Beowulf's memories return
to a personal vision of the past expressed in a nearly private form. Had
the narrator not insistently reminded his audience of Hygelac's place in
Geatish history and his death in Frisia, an audience might miss Beowulf's reticent references to his beloved, lost king.

The first part of Beowulf's speech (2501–9) closes with him crushing Dæghrefn, the Frisian champion and standard-bearer, to death.
Beowulf omits the circumstances of that act, the vital antecedent fact:
Hygelac's death in battle with the Frisians, the event foretold in part I
and three times told in part II. The memory of his act of heroic loyalty
and savage force returns the hero to the present moment and his resolve
to contest the possession of the hoard with its guardian. Instead of an
immediate movement into action, the narrator reports that Beowulf
"for the last time" (2516–18) addresses his beloved companions; regrets
that because of the dragon's "battle-flames" he cannot fight this enemy
as he did Grendel, without weapons; and vows to gain the dragon's
gold or die in the battle.

Beowulf's decision to fight the dragon, first implied in the hero's
preparations and plan for the battle and thus represented as instinctive
and immediate, has been recreated in the course of an extended and
deeply personal meditation on his membership in the heroic world and
on the heroic history of the Geats. Though Beowulf's recruitment to
that world was inevitable given his royal blood (his mother was King
Hrethel's daughter), the hero's memory fixes on his loyalty to his
grandfather Hrethel, first of the Geatish kings, and to Hrethel's son
and successor, Hygelac. As he affirms his own will and strength to
fight the dragon, Beowulf does not name Hygelac (pronouns without
antecedents refer to Hygelac in lines 2490–97) and makes no direct
reference to Hygelac's death. Beowulf's intention to protect the Geats
seems unchanged from the years of his youthful service to Hygelac in
which he fought in the front rank for his king. The poem identifies the
role of an ideal king as it persistently describes kings as ringgivers,
protectors, and guardians of their peoples. The dragon threatens the
survival of the Geats, yet guards a treasure worthy of a great nation. In
challenging the dragon, Beowulf realizes the traditional language of the
poets and becomes their ideal king. Although the Geats' eulogy on
Beowulf (and the poem's last statement on the hero) praises him as
"lofgeornost" (3182; "most eager for fame, to win or deserve fame"),
Beowulf's long meditation and preparation to oppose a deadly enemy
seems free of egotism or self-aggrandizement. His pursuit of honor
becomes disinterested as he acts heroically and out of loyalty to his
great lord. Though he is the king of the Geats, Beowulf seems ready to
fight "for king and country" and Hygelac is his king.

Though *Beowulf* surrounds the inexorable movement toward the final
battle with explorations and reexplorations of the Geatish past, the

steps toward the encounter that will destroy both Beowulf and the dragon stand out clearly and the battle is created in realistic and specific terms, blow-by-blow as in the encounter with Grendel's mother. In the first of the battle's three distinct stages, the dragon moves to the attack: "Gewat ða byrnende gebogen scriðan, / to gescipe scyndan" (2569–70; "Then he advanced, moving forward burning and coiled, hastening to his fate"); the great iron shield proves an imperfect defense against the heat of the dragon's flames; and Beowulf's sword fails to bite into the monster's head. Enraged at the blow and sensing victory, the dragon continues his attack: "Hyrte hyne hordweard, hreðer æðme weoll, / niwan stefne; nearo ðrowode / fyre befongen se ðe ær folce weold" (2593–95; "The guardian of the treasure took heart, once more his breast swelled with his breathing; enveloped in flames he who had ruled the people suffered distress"). Beowulf's followers run for the woods. The hero's shield, sword, and war band have all failed.

At this moment, the narrator distinguishes one of Beowulf's followers from the anonymous and ignominious band and then gives that loyal follower a name and a father and a family history that merges with the history of the war of the Swedes and Geats. In creating the character of Wiglaf, the narrator retells the story of the Swedish invasion of the Geats that led directly to young King Heardred's death and Beowulf's succession—though without explicitly referring to either of those events. The audience of the poem sees the battle from the other side: Wiglaf's father fought in the army of the great Swedish king Onela and distinguished himself by killing his king's rebellious nephew, Eanmund. Thus identified and realized, Wiglaf comes to Beowulf, encourages his king and kinsman, and promises his support. The second stage of the battle follows immediately on Wiglaf's promise:

> Æfter ðam wordum   wyrm yrre cwom,
> atol inwitgæst   oðre siðe
> fyrwylmum fah   fionda niosian,
> laðra manna.
>
>   (2669–72)

(After those words the dragon, the terrible and malicious enemy, angrily charged for the second time, hostile and with billows of fire to attack his enemies, the hateful men.)

At this moment, Wiglaf joins the fight; the dragon's flames immediately consume the young warrior's wooden shield, thereby approving

Beowulf's preparations for the battle and his decision to fight alone. As Wiglaf takes cover behind the great iron shield, Beowulf strikes the dragon's head with such force that his sword shatters.

The dragon rushes against Beowulf for the third time (2688), closes its jaws around his neck, and bites with venomous teeth. Beowulf is doomed and dying, but Wiglaf strikes the dragon's lower body, its flames cease, and Beowulf fatally slashes the great beast's belly with his short sword. The turning point of the battle and Beowulf's greatest victory come after he has been fatally bitten. His triumph, which wins forever the reward of fame, is also utterly disinterested; Beowulf's last great blow protects the Geats and gains the dragon's treasure for them, not himself. There is nothing in his victory for Beowulf save the fame, his youthful aspiration (1386–89) and his final achievement. He pre- pared for the battle as Hygelac's follower and as if fighting in defense of his king and country, but dying and victorious Beowulf's actions are kingly. He designates his successor, his kinsman Wiglaf (with him the last of the Wægmundings), and makes one final distribution of trea- sures to his people, endowing them with the dragon's immense hoard. A king is the people's protector, their giver of treasures. He enters his last battle as if he had forgotten his youthful maxim that enduring fame is the highest good for a departed warrior; dying, he calls for a barrow to be his memorial; dead, his people describe him as the "most eager for fame" of all kings on earth. The ideal hero's pursuit of fame must be passionate and complete yet disinterested, and such was Beowulf's.

Beowulf: The Last Word

The last word of *Beowulf,* "lofgeornost," literally "most eager for fame," and in this context "most eager to win or deserve fame," stands as both the Geats' last word on their king and the poem's last word on its hero. The word so dramatically and unmistakably emphasized must take a significant place in an audience's attitude toward the hero and understanding of the poem. The last word on Beowulf ends the narra- tor's report of the noblest Geats' eulogy for their dead king. The poem's close, preparing for the last word, includes Beowulf's cremation, a "Geatish woman's" reported lament for the hero and for the hard days to come, the building of Beowulf's barrow, his inhumation with the dragon's treasure, and the final rites in his honor. Twelve warriors ride round his burial mound speaking their sorrow and lamenting their dead king: "eahtodan eorlscipe, ond his ellenweorc / duguðum demdon"

(3173–74; "they praised his manliness and highly valued his deeds of courage").

The narrator commends the Geatish riders for rightly praising their dead lord ("it is fitting that one should praise his lord with words when . . ."; 3174–76), and then reports the sorrow of the Geats and their words of praise for Beowulf:

> Swa begnornodon   Geata leode
> hlafordes hryre,   heorðgeneatas;
> cwædon þæt he wære   wyruldcyninga
> mannum mildust   ond monðwærust,
> leodum liðost   ond lofgeornost.[16]
>
> (3178–82)

The exact tenor of the four superlatives summing up Beowulf's career and character deserves a separate study, but I translate "Thus the princes of the Geats, the hearth companions, lamented their lord's fall; they said that of all the world's kings he was the most generous and loyal to his men, the most protective of his people, the most eager for fame." The values I have given the four great words of praise are heroic; in contrast, Stanley B. Greenfield translated the last lines as "they said that of worldly kings he was / the mildest of men and the gentlest, / most kind to his people, most eager for fame."[17] A reader of Greenfield's translation is likely to feel some tension between the first three words of praise and the last and between those first three words and the story.

In the narrative and dramatic context, the poem's last word is assuredly a word of praise, an honorific, an appropriate conclusion to the Geats' eulogy for Beowulf. Yet some critics have urged that the last of the superlatives on Beowulf faults rather than praises the hero. This critical and philological position sometimes assumes and sometimes argues explicitly that the first three superlatives—"mildust," "monðwærust," and "liðost"—of the Geats' eulogy suggest specifically Christian values, or moral values fully consonant with Christianity, but that the last and sharply contrasting superlative recognizes "the secular Germanic side of the hero's character," and may well mean "ostentatious, boastful."[18]

Since the narrator of the poem explicitly states that one should praise his lord with words ("winedryhten wordum herge"; 3175) at this sad time, the persistent claim that the poem's last word dispraises Beowulf seems perverse.[19] The claim can be traced back to Tolkien, who called

the poem's close a "dirge," its first 3,136 lines a "prelude," and the last
word "the summit of the praise of the dead hero."[20] From that point, he
traced the later Christian meanings of "lof" to praises sung by angelic
choirs in other Anglo-Saxon poems and contrasted *Beowulf* in which
"there is *hell*, justly the poet said of the people he depicted, *helle
gemundon on modsefan*" ("they were mindful of hell in their hearts").[21]
This leap from heaven to hell found some clarification in Tokien's 1953
essay on *The Battle of Maldon*, where he asserted that the last word in
Beowulf sounded "an ominous note," and made "ofermod" in *The Battle
of Maldon* and "lofgeornost" in *Beowulf* central to his claim that these
poems disapprove of traditional heroism.[22] In 1964 Robinson doubted
the existence of an approving sense of "lofgeornost," but in 1982 asked
"Even if there were a positive, Christian sense of *lofgeorn*, would a
contemporary of the poet's have thought such a meaning available to
the poem's pagan mourners?" The unexpressed possibility that the
audience knew a positive, pagan sense of "lofgeornost" beckons, Robinson's thesis that the poem schools its audience in "discriminating between pagan and Christian senses of words"[23] suggests that at the
poem's end he would argue that the Geats intend to praise the hero as
"lofgeornost" (their meaning: "most eager to deserve praise"), but the
Christian audience would perceive that pagan virtue as a vice and
correct the Geats' sense of the word to Robinson's, "the most eager for
praise" or "most vainglorious." In fact, Robinson's reading of the
poem's close apparently rests on the contrast between the three "Christian" and honorific superlatives of the Geats' eulogy and "lofgeornost"
as a term of disapprobation,[24] and thus does not counter the argument
that the Geats, on the narrator's authority, praise rather than blame
Beowulf in his eulogy.

The claim that all the other appearances of "lofgeorn" in Anglo-
Saxon have a disapproving sense and that therefore we should doubt
that the sense in *Beowulf* 3182 can be honorific has almost no merit.
The meaning of a word in a religious (and professionally religious)
context has very little weight in assessing its meaning in a secular
context. Moreover, when the religious contexts are scrutinized, the
sense of "lofgeorn" frequently seems neutral rather than disapproving as
Greenfield argued.[25]

Robinson argues that "mildust," "monðwærost," and "liðost" attribute to Beowulf virtues Christian and pagan cultures shared, but takes
the final adjective as qualifying or negating the effect of the first three
at the close of *Beowulf*.[26] In contrast, Mary P. Richards documents still

more fully the specifically Christian contexts of "milde and man-
þwære," even pointing out an instance in which this collocation refers
to Christ, but concludes that "The ending of the poem does not reveal a
blend of Christian and pagan Germanic ideals. Rather, the poem concludes with the suggestion that Beowulf was as excellent a Christian as
possible here on earth."[27] In this view the first three superlatives mod-
ify or shape the audience's reception of the last. A.D. Horgan indicates
that a Christian audience could readily impose a Christian and approving meaning on "lofgeornost."[28] Assuming a radical split in meanings
for the four superlatives does not establish our reading of the poem's
closing lines. But whatever meanings the four adjectives of Beowulf's
eulogy may have gained after the conversion, we should guess these
were honorifics before the introduction of Christianity and probably
had specifically secular and even heroic meanings.

The text of *Beowulf* itself contains fairly clear evidence for secular and
heroic meanings of the superlatives that combine to make the hero's
eulogy. Comparative evidence supports the implications of the other
contexts of these adjectives in the poem. When we reflect that the
collocation "milde and mannþwære" once describes Christ, the influence of the familiar "meek and mild" can easily suggest a powerful
contrastive resonance in Beowulf's eulogy. When Wealhtheow characterizes the harmony of Danish royal society, her praise of Heorot's
heroes anticipates the words with which Beowulf's people praised their
late lord. The Danish queen describes Heorot as a harmonious and
heroic world: "Her is æghwylc eorl oþrum getrywe, / modes milde,
mandrihtne hold, / þegnas syndon geþwære" (1228–30; "Here every
nobleman is true to the other, 'milde' of spirit, loyal to their liege lord,
the thegns are 'geþwære' "). The adjective "geþwære" (essentially
"agreeable," "harmonious," or "in good accord,") strongly suggests that
the closing eulogy's superlative "monþwærust" describes Beowulf as
being agreeable and in good accord with his followers, and contrasts his
benevolent kingship with destructive reigns like that of Heremod, a
bad king of the distant Danish past (see 901–15, 1707–24). Since
Wealhtheow's honorific "milde" can hardly compare the Danish courtiers with Christ, the closing "mildust" may attribute to Beowulf a
virtue suitable for heroes in a royal hall. Wealhtheow can hardly say the
warriors in Heorot are "mild," as in "meek and mild," but she can
praise them as magnanimous of spirit, liberal, or generous. Somewhat
earlier, Wealhtheow prompts Hrothgar "to Geatum spræc / mildum
wordum, swa sceal man don" (1171–72; "speak to the Geats with

'milde' words as a man ought to do") and to be mindful of gifts for the Geats (1173). Hrothgar thereupon extends words of friendship and fabulously rich gifts to Beowulf (1192–1201), hence the variety of kindness "milde" suggests in a heroic context is openhanded.

One might wonder if a generous king's followers would be praised for their own liberality, but Hrothgar's eulogy for Æschere implies that nobleman's generosity. The Old Norse-Icelandic cognates, the adjective "mildr" and noun "mildi," regularly mean "generous" and "generosity," and the Old Norse noun "mildingr" means "a generous man" or frequently "a prince," suggesting that the virtue of liberality is a princely quality, a mark of nobility.[29] Beowulf intended to win the dragon's treasure for his people and dying bequeathed it to them, surely an act of superlative generosity. The eulogy for Beowulf describes him as having been "leodum liðost," "most gracious to his people" or "most protective of his people." The adjective "liðe" often describes the Almighty and lesser figures of authority in their most benevolent aspects, hence "gracious" seems an appropriate translation. But "liðe" has an aristocratic and heroic flavor in *Beowulf*: Wealhtheow urges Beowulf to be "lara liðe" (1220; "gracious in councils") to her sons and clearly hoped that Beowulf's graciousness would take a heroic and protective form. His parting promise to bring an army to the aid of the Danes should need arise and his assurance that the Danish prince, Hrethric, would find a welcome among the Geats if he came to them, indicate that Beowulf and Wealhtheow gave "gracious" a heroic gloss, understood that the term implied benevolent protection. Beowulf's protection of the Geats through an extraordinarily long reign and finally his successful defense of them from a seemingly invincible enemy fully justifies the claim that of all kings on earth he was the most gracious, the most protective of his people.

At the poem's close, Beowulf's burial on a headland overlooking the sea and the treasures heaped up on the hero's pyre and those committed to the earth with his ashes in the great barrow summon up the audience's memory of Scyld Scefing's unique and mysterious ship burial and that great king's final voyage to an unknown destination in the midst of his arms and armor and treasure. Scyld's death posed the question the triumphant history of the Danish golden age deferred: What is the significance of a life bounded by darknesses? *Beowulf* asks the significance of a life lived in the context and according to the ideals of a heroic and aristocratic culture. The poem's closing scene allows only brief and uncertain marks or hints of divine favor to attend Beowulf's departure, but the last poem's last word affirms the reality and enduring validity of the hero's success. The memory of Scyld's passing revived in Beowulf's funeral recalls the aphorism the narrator drew from the history of the Danes, that universal truth that praiseworthy deeds ("lofdædum") alone assure a man's success.

The poem's last word recalls Beowulf's answer to Hrothgar's grief at Æschere's death and the hero's concise articulation of value in a life that must end:

> Ure æghwylc sceal   ende gebidan
> worolde lifes,   wyrce se þe mote
> domes ær deaþe;   þæt bið drihtguman
> unlifgendum   æfter selest.
>
> (1386–89)

(All of us must experience the end of life in the world, let him who can achieve fame before his death; that will afterwards be best for the dead nobleman.)

The narrator marks the precise moment of Beowulf's death; it comes just as the hero declares that fate had swept all his kinsmen off and "ic him æfter sceal" (2816; "I must follow them"). The narrator observes at that moment "him of hræðre gewat / sawol secan soðfæstra dom" (2819–20; "his soul abruptly departed seeking the 'soðfæstra dom' "). In that last phrase, "dom" is the "judgment/reputation/glory" of the "soðfæstra," that is "of those confirmed in truth," the "true-judging," "true," "just." Beowulf may be one of those "confirmed in truth" or they may award him the "dom" due a hero. Whatever the meaning of this intriguing passage, lines 2815–20 have a positive resonance, a note of triumph, as they record the moment of the hero's death. We cannot know what Beowulf's soul seeks, yet we cannot suppose that search fails. For all the bleakness of the projected Geatish future, Beowulf's funeral restates that suggestion of triumph. At his cremation the elements themselves seem to honor the hero; as the great pyre burns

>   wudurec astah
> sweart ofer swioðole,   swogende leg
> wope bewunden   —windblond gelæg—,
> oð þæt he ða banhus   gebrocen hæfde
> hat on hreðre.
>
> (3144–48)

(the smoke rose black above the fire, the roaring flame surrounded by weeping—the tumultous winds subsided—until the fire had destroyed the body, hot to the heart)

After a few lines creating the weeping that surrounded the funeral pyre, the narrator observes that "Heofon rece swealg" (3155; "Heaven swallowed up the smoke"). The sudden stilling of the "wind-blond" ("wind-tumult") suggests that the tower of smoke rising above Beowulf's pyre rose unbroken to the clouds, a sign of divine favor.[30]

The poem's last word describes Beowulf as "lofgeornost," or "most eager for fame" and praises the hero for his lifelong pursuit of the goal of well-earned fame, "dom" or "lof." But when Beowulf prepared himself for the greatest triumph of his career, his long speech—history, memory, self-definition—made loyalty and duty and not self-aggrandizement the wellspring of his great resolve. The poem itself witnesses the success of Beowulf's quest; the "soðfæstra dom," the smoke of the funeral pyre, the poem's closing eulogy for the hero announce the fame Beowulf sought and assert the significance of a life bounded by the unknown. The hero's lasting fame, more enduring than monuments, confirms the value of a heroic life.

Afterword

In the coming decades, *Beowulf* scholarship will almost surely be deeply influenced by the findings of archaeological research and especially by the excavation at Sutton Hoo. Students of the poem have hardly digested the importance of the original Sutton Hoo excavation of 1939, definitively published in a massive study by Rupert Bruce-Mitford and others (1975–83). Already the new excavations at Sutton Hoo have offered some surprises. While archaeologists extend our knowledge of the material culture of the Anglo-Saxon world, lexicographers are doing the same for the word-hoard of the Anglo-Saxons. *The Dictionary of Old English* project at the University of Toronto has already produced a microfiche concordance of the corpus of Anglo-Saxon texts, an immensely valuable tool for the study of *Beowulf.* The project has published the letters C and D in microfiche and at some point in the twenty-first century we will have a better dictionary of the Old English or Anglo-Saxon language than most of us dreamed possible when the late Angus Cameron began the work.

The study of the poem itself will surely develop in some directions already partially mapped out. The poem's psychological and social realism has already become a topic of critical inquiry that will continue to prosper in an age that can accept or even value mixtures of realism and fantasy. A renewed effort to reconstruct the poem's social and cultural milieu seems likely: reader-response criticism and the new historicism alike will demand a vigorous inquiry into the poem's origins and attempt to discover what the poem meant to its earliest audiences and what the place of poetry was in the Anglo-Saxon world. The poem's idea of the basic social institutions needs a deeper reading against what we know of those institutions in the Anglo-Saxon age. The questions of the poem's date and place of origin will burn strongly for some decades to come. We are likely to find too many rather than too few answers, and the profusion of seemingly contradictory solutions may strengthen the case for the poem's oral transmission and for its susceptibility to at least some reworking even after being committed to parchment.

The poststructuralist new criticisms and formalist approaches to narrative texts will try (and have tried already) their strength with *Beowulf.*

The possibility of a deconstructive reading of *Beowulf* may fill some philologists with horror, but such a reading may be illuminating. The concentration of the newer critical schools on narrative will almost surely benefit the study of the greatest poem in English before the *Canterbury Tales*.

Notes and References

Chronologies

1. I have benefited from Marijane Osborn's chronological chart that systematizes the information contained in Klaeber's genealogical tables and chronological note. See Jess B. Bessinger, Jr., and Robert F. Yeager, eds., *Approaches to Teaching "Beowulf"* (New York: Modern Language Association, 1984), 100–2.

Chapter One

1. John Gardner, *Grendel* (New York: Knopf, 1972). See Jess B. Bessinger, Jr., and Robert F. Yeager, *Approaches to Teaching "Beowulf,"* 16, for a brief list of "Derivative Works" to which Michael Crichton's *Eaters of the Dead* (New York: Alfred Knopf, 1976; reprint, New York: Bantam Books, 1977) should be added. For the poem's influence on several modern works of art, see Andreas Haarder, *"Beowulf": The Appeal of a Poem* (Copenhagen: Akademisk Forlag, 1975), 243–66.

2. N. R. Ker, *Catalogue of Manuscripts Containing Anglo-Saxon* (Oxford: Clarendon Press, 1957), 281–82.

3. R. W. Chambers, *"Beowulf": An Introduction to the Study of the Poem,* 2d ed. (Cambridge: Cambridge University Press, 1932), 304–8.

4. John D. Niles, *"Beowulf": The Poem and Its Tradition* (Cambridge: Harvard University Press, 1983), 17–19 and note 29.

5. Chambers, *Introduction,* 367 and note 1.

6. For a good account of the fire and the damage to the manuscript, see Kevin Kiernan, *"Beowulf" and the "Beowulf" Manuscript* (New Brunswick, N.J.: Rutgers University Press, 1981), 67–71.

7. Daniel G. Calder, "Histories and Surveys of Old English Literature: A Chronological Review," *Anglo-Saxon England* 10 (1982):201.

8. Kenneth Sisam, "The *Beowulf* Manuscript," in *Studies in the History of Old English Literature* (Oxford: Clarendon Press, 1953), 62.

9. Ker, *Catalogue,* 282.

10. For an excellent brief discussion of the manuscript, see Elliott Van Kirk Dobbie, ed., *Beowulf and Judith* (New York: Columbia University Press, 1953), ix–xx.

11. Albert H. Marckwardt, ed., *Laurence Nowell's Vocabularium Saxonicum* (Ann Arbor: University of Michigan Press, 1952), 6, identifies William Camden as the first to give Nowell this title.

12. Marckwardt briefly indicates the extent of Nowell's reading in Anglo-Saxon (*Vocabularium,* 7–8). Michael Murphy, "Antiquary to Academic: The Progress of Anglo-Saxon Scholarship," in *Anglo-Saxon Scholarship: The First Three Centuries,* ed. Carl T. Berkhout and Milton McC. Gatch (Boston: G. K. Hall, 1982), discusses Nowell's work with Lambarde and others, 4–5. See also Carl T. Berkhout, "In Search of Laurence Nowell," *Old English Newsletter* 20, no. 2 (1987): A31–32.

13. C. E. Wright, "The Elizabethan Society of Antiquaries and the Formation of the Cottonian Library," in *The English Library Before 1700,* ed. Francis Wormald and C. E. Wright (London: Athlone Press, 1958), 176–208.

14. This is the generally accepted view; see Sisam, *Studies,* 61–62. For an argument that *Beowulf* was first bound together with the Nowell codex and other manuscripts in the time of Sir Robert Cotton, see Kiernan, *"Beowulf" Manuscript,* 71, 132, 133–34.

15. Roland Torkar, "Cotton Vitellius A. xv (pt. 1) and the Legend of St. Thomas," *English Studies* 67 (1986):290–303.

16. Humfrey Wanley, *Antiquae literaturae septentrionalis . . . Catalogus historico-criticus . . .* (Oxford: 1705), 218–19. Wanley's description can be translated so that he seems confident in error rather than careful in labelling a guess.

17. Sharon Turner, *History of the Manners, Landed Property, Laws, Poetry, Literature, Religion, and Language of the Anglo-Saxons,* eds. 1–6 (London, 1805–36).

18. Franklin Cooley, "Early Danish Criticism of *Beowulf,*" *English Literary History* 7 (1940):45.

19. Kevin Kiernan, "Thorkelin's Trip to Great Britain and Ireland, 1786–1791," *Library,* 6th ser., 5 (1983):1–21, gives a fascinating account of Thorkelin's research.

20. Grímur J. Thorkelin, ed., *De Danorum Rebus Gestis Secul. III et IV. Poema Danicum Dialecto Anglo-Saxonica Ex Bibliotheca Cottoniana Musaei Britannici* (Copenhagen: 1815).

21. Haarder, *Appeal,* chapters 2–4, characterizes early responses to *Beowulf* in illuminating detail, giving a particularly informative account of Grundtvig's criticism from 1815 to 1861. Kemp Malone, "Grundtvig as *Beowulf* Critic," *Review of English Studies* 17 (1941):129–38, provides long excerpts (in English translation) to support his thesis that Grundtvig was "the first and greatest of *Beowulf* scholars" (129), and that Grundtvig's views "have more meat in them, for us, than any other nineteenth-century student of the poem" (138). See also Cooley, "Early Danish Criticism," 45, 54–55, 64–67, and David J. Savage, "Grundtvig: A Stimulus to Old English Scholarship," in *Philologica,* ed. Thomas A. Kirby and Henry Bosley Woolf (Baltimore: Johns Hopkins Press, 1949), 275–80.

22. Malone, "Grundtvig," 134, 136; Haarder, *Appeal,* 72–73.

23. Malone, "Grundtvig," 132.

24. Malone, "Grundtvig," 132; Haarder, *Appeal*, 75.

25. Haarder, *Appeal*, 67.

26. Haarder, *Appeal*, 72; Malone, "Grundtvig," 132–36.

27. Malone, "Grundtvig," 134.

28. For a brief sketch of some of these myths, see William Witherle Lawrence, *"Beowulf" and Epic Tradition* (Cambridge: Harvard University Press, 1928), 145–50.

29. Malone, "Grundtvig," 130. William Paton Ker, *Epic and Romance*, 2d ed. (London: Macmillan, 1908), 158–75.

30. Malone, "Grundtvig," 130; William Paton Ker, *The Dark Ages* (1904; reprint, London: Thomas Nelson, 1955), 253.

31. D. H. Lawrence, *The Rainbow* (London: Heineman, 1955), chap. 15, 435. First published in 1915.

32. Robert Graves, *Goodbye to All That* (London: Jonathan Cape, 1929), 362. I have cited the first edition, published a decade after Graves's first encounter with *Beowulf.*

33. J. R. R. Tolkien, *"Beowulf:* The Monsters and the Critics," *Proceedings of the British Academy* 22 (1936):245–95. Separately printed by Oxford University Press in 1958 and 1960, and often reprinted.

34. R. E. Kaske, *"Beowulf,"* in *Critical Approaches to Six Major English Works*, ed. R. M. Lumiansky and Hershel Baker (Philadelphia: University of Pennsylvania Press, 1968), 3–5.

35. Michael Alexander, *Old English Literature* (London: Macmillan, 1983), 59.

36. Niles, *Tradition*, 4.

37. Bessinger, *Approaches*, 25.

38. Tolkien, "Monsters," 258.

39. Ibid., 246–47, 253.

40. Humphrey Carpenter, *Tolkien: A Biography* (Boston: Houghton Mifflin, 1977), 213–18.

41. J. R. R. Tolkien, "The Homecoming of Beorhtnoth, Beorhthelm's Son," *Essays and Studies*, n.s., 6 (1953):1–18.

42. Tolkien, "Monsters," 275, 271.

43. Ibid., 271–72.

44. Ibid., 261–62.

45. Ibid., 246; cf. 259.

46. Ibid., 280.

47. Ibid., 258–59.

48. Ibid., 265.

49. Ibid., 263, 269, the poet as writer; 269–70, the poet's learning.

50. Ibid., 265.

51. Ibid., 262–63, 267. "Chaos and Unreason" taken from Ker.

52. Ibid., 269–70.

53. Fr. Klaeber, "Review: J. R. R. Tolkien, *Beowulf:* The Monsters and the Critics," *Beiblatt zur Anglia* 48 (1937): 323.

54. Tolkien, "Monsters," 262–63, 270, and note 25.

55. Nordal's edition of *Völuspá* first appeared in 1923, a partial German translation in 1924, and a Danish translation in 1927. I cite the English translation of Nordal's second edition (1952) published as Sigurður Nordal, "Three Essays on *Völuspá*," trans. B. S. Benedikz and J. S. McKinnell, *Saga-Book of the Viking Society* 18 (1970–71):79–135. Quotation from page 79.

56. Ibid., 120. Nordal identifies the author of the *Völuspá* as Völu-Steinn, a historical Icelander whose biography seems appropriate for the author of the *Völuspá* as Nordal reads it. See Sigurður Nordal, "The Author of the *Völuspá*," trans. B. S. Benedikz, *Saga-Book of the Viking Society* 20 (1978–79): 114–30.

57. Nordal, "Essays," 120.

58. John C. Pope, ed., *Seven Old English Poems* (Indianapolis: Bobbs-Merrill, 1966), 73.

59. J. R. R. Tolkien, *The Return of the King* (London: George Allen and Unwin, 1955), 177.

60. Tolkien, "Homecoming," 14.

61. Tolkien, "Monsters," 281, and "Homecoming," 16.

62. Tolkien, "Monsters," 266.

63. Ibid., 283–84, 287.

64. Ibid., 287–88 and note 38.

65. Charles Donahue, "*Beowulf,* Ireland and the Natural Good," *Traditio* 7 (1949–51):263.

66. Martin Camargo, "The Finn Episode in *Beowulf* and the Tragedy of Revenge," *Studies in Philology* 78 (1981):134.

67. Tolkien, "Monsters," 268.

68. Ibid., 268–69.

69. Fr. Klaeber, "Die christlichen Elemente im Beowulf," *Anglia* 35, n.s., 23 (1912):111–36, 249–70, 453–82 and *Anglia* 36, n.s., 24 (1912): 169–99. For "The Christian Coloring," see Klaeber's edition, xlviii–li, and especially li and note 2.

70. M. B. McNamee, "*Beowulf*—An Allegory of Salvation?," *Journal of English and Germanic Philology* 59 (1960):190–207.

71. Alan Cabaniss anticipated McNamee on baptism; see "*Beowulf* and the Liturgy," *Journal of English and Germanic Philology* 54 (1955):195–201.

72. William Whallon, *Formula, Character, Context* (Washington, D. C.: Center for Hellenic Studies, 1969), 117–38. See also Whallon, "The Idea of God in *Beowulf*," *PMLA* 80 (1965):19–23.

73. Dorothy Whitelock, *The Audience of "Beowulf"* (Oxford: Clarendon Press, 1951), 3–7, 12, 21; quotation, 6.

74. Kenneth Sisam, *The Structure of "Beowulf"* (Oxford: Clarendon Press, 1965), 72–78; quotation, 78.

75. E. G. Stanley, "Hæthenra Hyht in *Beowulf*," in *Studies in Old English Literature,* ed. Stanley B. Greenfield (Eugene: University of Oregon Press, 1963):136.

76. Tolkien, "Homecoming," 16.

77. Stanley, "Hyht," 147.

78. Ibid., 137.

79. For despair in Tolkien's "Monsters," see "heathen, noble, and hopeless" (264), "despair" (265, twice), "hopeless" (278), "hopeless sorrow" (284), "pagan and hopeless" (286), but for all this, Tolkien seems to hope that Beowulf was not utterly lost (283).

80. Stanley, "Hyht," 147–49, 149–51, 143–47. A. J. Bliss argues for Beowulf's damnation in *"Beowulf,* Lines 3074–3075," in *J. R. R. Tolkien: Scholar and Storyteller,* ed. Mary Salu and Robert T. Farrell (Ithaca: Cornell University Press, 1979), 41–63. For the defense, see Bruce Mitchell, *"Beowulf,* Lines 3074–3075: The Damnation of Beowulf?," *Poetica* 13 (1982 for 1980): 15–26.

81. Roberta Frank, "Old Norse Memorial Eulogies and the Ending of *Beowulf,*" *Acta* 6 (1979):12–13.

82. A. D. Horgan, "Religious Attitudes in *Beowulf,*" in *Essays and Poems Presented to Lord David Cecil* [ed. W. W. Robson] (London: Constable, 1970), 9–17; see especially 10–11.

83. William Whallon, "The Christianity of *Beowulf,*" *Modern Philology* 60 (1962):86–87.

84. Donahue, "Natural Good," 264–65. Klaeber, edition, cxxiii.

85. Charles Donahue, *"Beowulf* and Christian Tradition: A Reconsideration from a Celtic Stance," *Traditio* 21 (1965):74, 81.

86. Ibid., 116.

87. Margaret Goldsmith, *The Mode and Meaning of "Beowulf"* (London: Athlone Press, 1970), 254–56.

88. Ibid., 13, 72–73, 146.

89. Ibid., 269.

90. Robert E. Kaske, *"Sapienta et Fortitudo* as the Controlling Theme of *Beowulf,*" *Studies in Philology* 55 (1958): 423–56.

91. Ibid., 427–31, 431–37, 448–50.

92. Ibid., 440–45.

93. Ibid., 455–56.

94. Tolkien, "Homecoming," 15.

95. John Leyerle, "Beowulf the Hero and the King," *Medium Ævum* 34 (1965):89, 97, 101–2.

96. John Halverson, "The World of *Beowulf,*" *English Literary History* 36 (1969):608.

97. Stanley, "Hyht," 136.

98. David Williams, *Cain and Beowulf: A Study in Secular Allegory* (Toronto: University of Toronto Press, 1982), 67, 96.

99. Harry Berger, Jr., and H. Marshall Leicester, Jr., "Social Structure as Doom: The Limits of Heroism in *Beowulf*," in *Old English Studies in Honor of John C. Pope*, ed. Robert B. Burlin and Edward B. Irving, Jr. (Toronto: University of Toronto Press, 1974), 56, 58, 65, 68.

100. For a good brief account of the *Liedertheorie*, see Chambers, *Introduction*, 112–17, and Klaeber, edition, cii–cvii.

101. Klaeber, edition, li–lii.

102. Ibid., cxiv, cxvi–cxviii.

103. Ibid., cxvii–cxviii.

104. Francis Peabody Magoun, Jr., trans., *The "Old Kalevala" and Certain Antecedents Compiled by Elias Lönnrot* (Cambridge: Harvard University Press, 1969), xiii–xix; comparison of the *Kalevala* and *Beowulf*, xiv and note 2.

105. Tolkien, "Monsters," 271, 272, 274, 248–49.

106. John Leyerle, "The Interlace Structure of *Beowulf*," *University of Toronto Quarterly* 37 (1967):1–17. For the technique of "interlace," see Eugene Vinaver, *The Rise of Romance* (Oxford: Clarendon Press, 1971), 72–98, and for a critique, see Morton W. Bloomfield, " 'Interlace' as a Medieval Narrative Technique with Special Reference to *Beowulf*," in *Magister Regis: Studies in Honor of Robert Earl Kaske*, ed. Arthur Groos (New York: Fordham University Press, 1986), 49–68.

107. Joan Blomfield, "The Style and Structure of *Beowulf*," *Review of English Studies* 14 (1938):396–403.

108. Clare Kinney, "The Needs of the Moment: Poetic Foregrounding as a Narrative Device in *Beowulf*," *Studies in Philology* 82 (1985):297,314.

109. Gwyn Jones, *Kings, Beasts, and Heroes* (London: Oxford University Press, 1972), 16 note 1, 28, 55–61.

110. T. A. Shippey, *Beowulf* (London: Edward Arnold, 1978), 7–11.

Chapter Two

1. William Witherle Lawrence, *"Beowulf" and Epic Tradition* (Cambridge: Harvard University Press, 1928), 19–20.

2. Friedrich Panzer, *Studien zur germanischen Sagengeschichte*, vol. 1: *Beowulf* (Munich: Beck, 1910), especially 95–108 and 249–313. The book is somewhat rare, but useful summaries appear in Chambers, *Introduction*, 365–81; G. V. Smithers, *The Making of "Beowulf"* (Durham, England: University of Durham, 1961), 7; and Klaeber's edition, xiii–xxi.

3. Antti Aarne and Stith Thompson, *The Types of the Folktale*, Folklore Fellows Communications no. 184, 2d revision (Helsinki: Academia Scientiarum Fennica, 1964), 90–92, 225–26.

4. Chambers, *Introduction*, 381; (so, too, the first edition of 1921) and

Douglas D. Short, *"Beowulf* and Modern Critical Tradition," in *A Fair Day in the Affections,* ed. Jack D. Durrant and M. Thomas Hester (Raleigh, N.C.: Winston Press, 1980), 8.

5. *Edda Snorra Sturlusonar,* ed. Guðni Jónsson (Reykjavík: Islendin-gasagnaútgávan, 1949), 118. See Snorri Sturluson, *Edda,* trans. Anthony Faulkes (London: Dent, 1987), 72.

6. George Clark, "Beowulf and Bear's Son in the *Vishnu Purana," Philological Quarterly* 43 (1964):125–30; and Joseph Fontenrose, *Python: A Study of Delphic Myth and Its Origins* (Berkeley and Los Angeles: University of California Press, 1959), 524–34.

7. For the translation, see *Religions of the Ancient Near East: Sumero-Akkadian Religious Texts and Ugaritic Epics,* ed. Isaac Mendelsohn (New York: Liberal Arts Press, 1955), 19 (Tablet I).

8. Nora K. Chadwick, "The Monsters and Beowulf," in *The Anglo-Saxons,* ed. Peter Clemoes (London: Bowes and Bowes, 1959), 186, 192, 200.

9. For the text (here slightly modernized) of *Gylfaginning,* I have cited the edition of Anthony Faulkes, ed., *Snorri Sturluson: Edda* (Oxford: Clarendon Press, 1982), 4–5; my translation.

10. *Njal's Saga,* trans. Magnus Magnusson and Hermann Pálsson (Harmondsworth, England: Penguin, 1960), 247–48.

11. *Brennu-Njáls saga,* ed. Einar Ol. Sveinsson (Reykjavík: Hið Islenzka fornritafélag, 1954), 303 note 1.

12. *Örvar-Odds Saga,* chapter 19; see *Fornaldar sögur Norðurlanda,* vol. 2, ed. Guðni Jónsson (Reykjavík: Islendingasagnaútgáfan, 1950), 282. The saga is now available in English: *Arrow-Odd: A Medieval Novel,* trans. Paul Edwards and Hermann Pálsson (New York: New York University Press, 1970).

13. For a fuller discussion of the theme, see George Clark, *"Beowulf* and *Njálssaga,"* in *Proceedings of the First International Saga Conference, University of Edinborough, 1971,* ed. Peter Foote, Hermann Pálsson, and Desmond Slay (London: Viking Society, 1973), 66–87. The paper is published as read in August 1971. Jeff Opland independently identified the episode in chapter 119 as a *Beowulf* analogue; see "A *Beowulf* Analogue in *Njálssaga," Scandinavian Studies* 45 (1973):54–58.

14. See Smithers, "Making," 12, for a strong statement of this point.

15. R. D. Fulk, "Review Article: Dating *Beowulf* to the Viking Age," *Philological Quarterly* 61 (1982):343–44.

16. Rupert Bruce-Mitford, *The Sutton Hoo Ship-Burial: A Handbook,* 2d ed. (London: British Museum, 1972), 18.

17. Ibid., 64. Alan M. Stahl presented his findings in a paper, "The Date of the Sutton Hoo Coins," read at the Twenty-fourth International Conference on Medieval Studies in Kalamazoo, Michigan, 4–7 May 1989.

18. Rupert Bruce-Mitford, *The Sutton Hoo Ship-Burial,* 3 vols. (London: British Museum, 1975–83), 2:91–94; 2:220–25.

19. Robert T. Farrell, *"Beowulf:* Swedes and Geats," *Saga-Book of the Viking Society* 18, no. 3 (1972):271–73.

20. Bruce-Mitford, *Sutton Hoo,* 1:422–23; for the number of oars, see 1:350–51.

21. Bruce-Mitford, *Sutton Hoo,* 2:360–75; 2:428–31.

22. Ibid., 2:375–77.

23. Paul Beekman Taylor, "Heorot, Earth, and Asgard: Christian Poetry and Pagan Myth," *Tennessee Studies in Literature* 11 (1966):127–28, illustrates early attitudes toward the hart and compares the hart in Hrothgar's description of Grendel's mere to the old king himself.

24. Chambers, *Introduction,* 16–20.

25. Martin Carver and Jenny Glazebrook, "Sutton Hoo 1987:Excavation Report," *Saxon* 7 (1988):1–2. At the Twenty-fourth International Conference on Medieval Studies in Kalamazoo, Michigan, 4–7 May 1989, Professor Carver kindly screened a recent videotape dealing with the excavation of Mound Two, suggested some corrections, and brought the audience up to date on the excavation. Martin Carver and Angela Evans have reported on the excavations of 1987–88 in the *Bulletin of the Sutton Hoo Research Committee* 6 (April 1989):4–15.

26. Howell D. Chickering, ed. and trans. *"Beowulf:" A Dual Language Edition* (Garden City, N.Y.: Anchor Books, 1977), 248–49, notes the poem's possible origin in the East Anglian culture Sutton Hoo represents, and Kevin Crossley-Holland, trans., *Beowulf* (Woodbridge: Boydell Press, 1987), 29, accepts the suggestion warmly. My colleague Elizabeth Greene has long argued (in private communications) that the poem's form and matter suggest that it is in part a family album and scrapbook preserving the memory of the race for the East Anglian royal house.

27. Martin Carver, *Bulletin of the Sutton Hoo Committee* no. 4 (July 1986):45–47.

28. For a different view of the oral tradition behind the poem, see Jeff Opland, *Anglo-Saxon Oral Poetry* (New Haven: Yale University Press, 1980), especially 257–66. I am not convinced, but the argument deserves consideration.

29. Winfred P. Lehmann, *The Development of Germanic Verse Form* (Austin: University of Texas Press, 1956), 23–63, traces the Germanic alliterative line from the early inscriptions onward. The cardinal rule of Germanic verse is that the first stress of the *second* half-line must alliterate with one (or both) of the stresses of the first.

30. M. Mattingly, trans., *Tacitus: On Britain and Germany* (Harmondsworth, England: Penguin, 1948), 102–3.

31. Francis Peabody Magoun, trans., *The "Old Kalevala" and Certain Antecedents Compiled by Elias Lönnrot* (Cambridge: Harvard University Press, 1969), xiii and note 1.

32. For an excellent brief discussion of literary criticism and traditional

poetry, see Frederick Goldin, trans., *The Song of Roland* (New York: Norton, 1978), 32–43. Albert B. Lord, *The Singer of Tales* (Cambridge: Harvard University Press, 1960), 13–29, characterizes the role and training of oral poets or singers in Yugoslavia, noting especially that singers do not memorize texts but recreate songs.

33. Lord, *Singer,* 26–29. An intensive study of all surviving texts of Cædmon's hymn has shown that the hymn did not acquire a fixed text in copies of the Alfredian translation of Bede but did when it was attached to Bede's Latin text. That is, even as a written document the hymn remains partly in an oral tradition when it accompanies the vernacular text of Bede. See Katherine O'Brien O'Keeffe, "Orality and the Developing Text of Caedmon's *Hymn,*" *Speculum* 62 (1987):1–20.

34. For the Latin and Anglo-Saxon versions of this story, see the admirable edition in F. G. Cassidy and Richard N. Ringler, eds., *Bright's Old English Grammar and Reader,* 3d ed. (New York: Holt, Rinehart, and Winston, 1971), 125–34.

35. Simon Keynes and Michael Lapidge, trans., *Alfred the Great: Asser's "Life of King Alfred" and Other Contemporary Sources* (Harmondsworth, England: Penguin Books, 1983), 75, 91.

36. *The Saga of the Volsungs,* ed. and trans. R. G. Finch (London: Thomas Nelson, 1965), 14. My translation.

Chapter Three

1. The story was often told. See Bede's *Ecclesiastical History of the English People,* ed. Bertram Colgrave and R. A. B. Mynors (Oxford: Clarendon Press, 1969), 40–45, 47–53, and *The Anglo-Saxon Chronicle* for the year 449, in *English Historical Documents,* vol. 1, 2 ed., ed. Dorothy Whitelock (London: Eyre Methuen, 1979):153–54.

2. I accept Wrenn's interpretation and translation of line 1142— Hengest "did not refuse the universally acknowledged duty"—rather than Klaeber's emendation of the manuscript reading. See C. L. Wrenn, ed., *Beowulf,* 2d ed. (London: George G. Harrap, 1958), 207.

3. See Colin Chase, "Opinions on the Date of *Beowulf* 1815–1980," in *The Dating of "Beowulf,"* 3. For Hygelac's raid, see Gregory of Tours, *The History of the Franks,* trans. Lewis Thorpe (Harmondsworth, England: Penguin, 1974), 163–64, and the *Liber Historiae Francorum,* trans. Bernard S. Bachrach (Lawrence, Kansas: Coronado Press, 1973), 56–57.

4. See Bessinger and Yeager, *Approaches to Teaching "Beowulf,"* 99.

5. Faulkes, trans., *Snorri Sturluson: The Prose Edda,* 1–2.

6. See *The Old English Version of the Heptateuch,* ed. S. J. Crawford, Early English Text Society, o.s., 160 (London: Oxford University Press, 1922):22–23.

7. Ibid., 76.

8. E. V. K. Dobbie, ed., *Beowulf* (New York: Columbia University Press, 1953), 189.

9. For the argument that *Beowulf* may have been composed during the first Viking age, see Nicolas Jacobs, "Anglo-Danish Relations, Poetic Archaism, and the Date of *Beowulf,*" *Poetica* 8 (1977):35–43.

10. Roberta Frank, "Skaldic Verse and the Date of *Beowulf,*" in Chase, *"The Date of "Beowulf,*" 129–30.

11. For the names of Scyld and Beowulf, see Chambers, *Introduction,* 421–22; 356–69.

12. E. G. Stanley, *"Beowulf,"* in *Continuations and Beginnings,* ed. E. G. Stanley (London: Thomas Nelson, 1966), 139.

13. Ibid., 139.

14. See Gerd Wolfgang Weber, "Irreligiosität und Heldenzeitalter: Zum Mythencharakter der altisländischen Literatur," in *Speculum Norroenum,* ed. Ursula Dronke (Odense University Press, 1981), 474–505.

15. *The Book of Settlements,* trans. Hermann Pálsson and Paul Edwards (Winnipeg: University of Manitoba Press, 1972), 21–22.

16. Gwyn Jones, trans. *"Eric the Red" and Other Sagas* (London: Oxford University Press, 1961), 115.

17. Save the Wealhtheow, Heorot seems a men's hall. The legendary laws of the Jómborg Vikings excluded all women from their fortress and limited members to three-day leaves. See N. F. Blake, ed. and trans., *The Saga of the Jomvikings* (London: Thomas Nelson, 1962), 17–18.

18. Ælfric, *De auguriis,* lines 75–91; see W. W. Skeat, ed., *Ælfric's Lives of the Saints,* Early English Text Society, o.s., 82 (1885; reprint, London: Oxford University Press, 1966), 368–71.

19. The text follows the manuscript's "næfre" rather than Klaeber's emendation to "næfne." Fred C. Robinson, "Two Non-Cruces in *Beowulf,*" *Tennessee Studies in Literature* 11 (1966):155–58, first defended the manuscript reading that is now generally favored.

20. For the conversation and its tensions, see George Clark, "Beowulf's Armor," *English Literary History* 32 (1965):416–17, and T. A. Shippey, *Beowulf* (London: Edward Arnold, 1978), 12–15.

21. Edward B. Irving, Jr., *A Reading of "Beowulf"* (New Haven: Yale University Press, 1968), 68–77, first hinted at this tension in the Danish court.

22. Wrenn, edition, 195.

23. G. N. Garmonsway, "Anglo-Saxon Heroic Attitudes," in *Franciplegius,* ed. Jess B. Bessinger, Jr., and Robert P. Creed (New York: New York University Press, 1965), 142. I have borrowed Garmonsway's memorable phrase from another context.

24. For the text of *Maldon,* see *The Anglo-Saxon Minor Poems,* ed. Elliott

Van Kirk Dobbie (New York: Columbia University Press, 1942), 7–16; for a translation, see S. A. J. Bradley, *Anglo-Saxon Poetry* (London: J. M. Dent, 1982), 519–28.

25. Barbara Nolan and Morton W. Bloomfield, *"Beotword, gilpcwidas,* and the *gilphlæden* Scop of *Beowulf,"Journal of English and Germanic Philology* 79 (1980):499–516; see especially 508–11.

26. See M. W. Bloomfield, *"Beowulf* and Christian Allegory: An Interpretation of Unferth," *Traditio* 7 (1949–51):410–15, and Whitney F. Bolton, *Alcuin and "Beowulf"* (London: Edward Arnold, 1979), 117–24.

27. Arthur G. Brodeur, *The Art of "Beowulf"* (Berkeley and Los Angeles: University of California Press, 1960), 151–55.

28. E. O. G. Turville-Petre, *Myth and Religion of the North* (London: Weidenfeld and Nicolson, 1964), 34–74 and especially 71–74.

29. Carol J. Clover, "The Germanic Context of the Unferth Episode," *Speculum* 55 (1980):444–68, especially 452–53, 459.

30. The seminal article in this vein, Bloomfield's "Beowulf and Christian Allegory," was published in 1951.

31. For the image of Cain as the controlling theme of the poem, see Williams, *Cain and Beowulf.*

32. Norman E. Eliason, "The þyle and Scop in *Beowulf,"* *Speculum* 38 (1963):267–84, argues that we should regard Unferth as a court jester or buffoon; F. C. Robinson has supported and developed the suggestion; see "Elements of the Marvellous in the Characterization of Beowulf," in *Old English Studies in Honor of John C. Pope,* ed. Robert B. Burlin and Edward B. Irving, Jr. (Toronto: University of Toronto Press, 1974), 127–32.

33. R. D. Fulk, "Unferth and His Name," *Modern Philology* 85 (1987): 113–27. I am grateful to Professor Fulk for allowing me to read this convincing and learned paper before its publication.

34. Robinson, "Elements," 129–30.

35. In the last line I have retained the manuscript "gehedde" in place of Klaeber's emendation "gehede"; here I follow Robinson, "Elements," 128–29. For a detailed study of this word, the passage, and interpretations of Unferth, see John C. Pope, *"Beowulf* 505, 'gehedde,' and the Pretensions of Unferth," in *Modes of Interpretation in Old English Literature,* ed. Phyllis Rugg Brown et al. (Toronto: University of Toronto Press, 1986), 173–87; I accept Pope's argument on the meaning of "gehedde"; see 174–79.

36. On "dollic," see Stanley B. Greenfield, "Beowulf and the Judgement of the Righteous," in *Learning and Literature in Anglo-Saxon England,* ed. Michael Lapidge and Helmut Gneuss (Cambridge: Cambridge University Press, 1985), 399–400.

37. Fred C. Robinson, *"Beowulf" and the Appositive Style* (Knoxville: University of Tennessee Press, 1985), 74–79, makes and supports this suggestion.

38. We cannot be quite sure the poem states Breca and Beowulf were

swimming instead of rowing; see Robinson, "Elements," 126–27; for an
ingenious suggestion that Unferth is playing with words that may mean
swimming or rowing, see Roberta Frank, " 'Mere' and 'Sund': Two Sea-
Changes in *Beowulf*," in Brown, *Modes of Interpretation*, 158–65.

39. See Whitelock, *Documents*, 175–77, for the heroic events of 786
reported in *The Anglo-Saxon Chronicle* under the year 755 (for 757).

40. Vows spoken over the mead or other strong drink seem common in
the literature of the old Germanic world. Robinson, *Style*, 76, quotes Snorri
Sturluson's brief description of the ceremony in which the speaker of the vow
must "stand up, take the *Brage*-beaker, make solemn vows to be afterward
fulfilled, and thereupon empty the beaker."

41. Richard N. Ringler, "*Him seo wen geleah:* The Design for Irony in
Grendel's Last Visit to Heorot," *Speculum* 41 (1966): 65 and note 47.

Chapter Four

1. For the terror, see Brodeur, *The Art of "Beowulf*," 88–94; for the
irony, see Ringler, "*Him seo wen geleah:* The Design for Irony," 49–67.

2. Ringler, "Irony," 59–64.

3. George Clark, "The Traveler Recognizes His Goal: A Theme in
Anglo-Saxon Poetry," *Journal of English and Germanic Philology* 64 (1965):657–
58.

4. For the suggestion and a brief account of earlier views, see Stanley B.
Greenfield, "Three *Beowulf* Notes," in *Medieval Studies*, ed. Jess B. Bessinger,
Jr., and Robert R. Raymo (New York: New York University Press, 1976),
169–70.

5. Ringler, "Irony," 50–59.

6. C. J. E. Ball, "*Beowulf* 987," *Archiv* 201 (1964):45–46.

7. In his text Klaeber emends the manuscript "sendeþ" to "snedeþ," but
his later note on line 600 decides in favor of the manuscript reading; see his
edition, 454.

8. Grendel's power to dull weapons by a spell has been denied; see H.
L. Rogers, "*Beowulf*, Line 804," *Notes & Queries* 229 (1984):289–92.

9. Kenneth Sisam, *The Structure of "Beowulf*" (Oxford: Clarendon Press,
1965), 29–32, first observed that lines 917–18 return the action to the dawn
reported in line 837.

10. See Bruce Moore, "The Relevance of the Finnsburh Episode," *Journal
of English and Germanic Philology* 75 (1976):317–29, and Martin Camargo,
"The Finn Episode and the Tragedy of Revenge in *Beowulf*," *Studies in Philology*
78 (1981):120–34.

11. Camargo, "Finn Episode," 125–30, and Edward B. Irving, Jr., *A
Reading of "Beowulf*" (New Haven: Yale University Press, 1968), 133–34,
136–37.

12. Alcuin, no friend of secular poetry, attests indignantly to the popularity (in a monastic setting) of stories about Ingeld. For an acute reading of Alcuin's remarks, see Alain Renoir, "*Beowulf:* A Contextual Introduction to Its Contents and Techniques," in *Heroic Epic and Saga,* ed. Felix J. Oinas (Bloomington: Indiana University Press, 1978), 99–100; and for the intellectual background of Alcuin's rhetoric, see Robinson, "*Beowulf*" *and the Appositive Style,* 8–9. A translation of the relevant portions of Alcuin's letter appears in Garmonsway, Simpson, and Davidson, "*Beowulf*" *and Its Analogues,* 242.

13. For the story, see Saxo Grammaticus, *The History of the Danes,* 2 vols., trans. Peter Fisher, ed. Hilda Ellis Davidson (Cambridge, England: D. S. Brewer, 1979–80), 1:184–95 and 2:103–7.

14. Lines 45–49; for a translation, see Bradley, *Anglo-Saxon Poetry* 338. For the original, see George Phillip Krapp and Elliott Van Kirk Dobbie, *The Exeter Book* (New York: Columbia University Press, 1936), 150–51.

15. Sisam, *Structure,* 34–40; quotation, 40.

16. Shippey, *Beowulf,* 9.

17. Robinson, *Style,* 77–78. For the drinking ceremony and its meaning, see also 74–76.

18. Peter Sawyer's careful examination of the evidence indicates that the Viking armies of the 900s numbered in the hundreds not thousands; see his *The Age of the Vikings* (London: Edward Arnold, 1971), 120–31.

19. Tolkien, "Monsters," 278–80.

20. Ibid., 280.

21. The meaning of "bunden" is not clear; I have guessed it refers to the means of fastening the grip to the hilt. I have accepted the manuscript reading "geþuren" rather than Klaeber's emendation.

22. For an excellent discussion of the passage, see Irving, *A Reading,* 115–17.

23. Robinson, "Elements of the Marvellous, 121–24 and 134 note 13.

24. A. J. Wyatt, ed., *Beowulf,* revised by R. W. Chambers (Cambridge: Cambridge University Press, 1948), 76.

25. E. G. Stanley, "Did Beowulf Commit *Feaxfang* against Grendel's Mother?" *Notes & Queries* 221 (1976):339–340.

26. Irving, *A Reading,* 118–19.

27. Klaeber's text reads "wundnum," but in the third supplement to his edition (467, 470) he preferred the present reading, "wundini."

28. H. Mattingly, trans., *Tacitus: On Britain and Germany* (Harmondsworth, England: Penguin, 1948), 122–23; Cornelii Taciti, *De origine et situ Germanorum,* ed. J. G. C. Anderson (Oxford: Clarendon Press, 1938), 27.2.

29. Goldsmith, *The Mode and Meaning of "Beowulf,"* 183. Goldsmith begins this study with some reflections on Hrothgar's sermon and the "curiously ambivalent treatment of the treasure hoard" in the poem (vii).

Chapter Five

1. William Paton Ker, *The Dark Ages,* cited in Tolkien, "Monsters," 251; the passage appears on page 253 of the centenary reprint (London: Thomas Nelson, 1955) of Ker's work.

2. Haarder, *"Beowulf": The Appeal of a Poem,* 75.

3. I am indebted to H. D. Chickering for a helpful and learned letter on the etymology of this place-name.

4. The line is defective, but most editors supply "fuglum," which we may translate "for birds."

5. For "shame culture" and the *Song of Roland,* see George Fenwick Jones, *The Ethos of the "Song of Roland"* (Baltimore: Johns Hopkins Press, 1963), 96–158; for an account of cultural changes which in Europe eventually displaced the shame culture and heroic sense of life, see R. W. Southern, *The Making of the Middle Ages* (London: Hutchinson, 1953; often reprinted), 219–57, whom I have quoted (224) for the "personal and secret tie."

6. Goldsmith, *The Mode and Meaning of "Beowulf,"* 154–56 (quotations, 155) and 254–56.

7. Stanley B. Greenfield, "Beowulf and the Judgement of the Righteous," in *Learning and Literature in Anglo-Saxon England,* ed. Michael Lapidge and Helmut Gneuss (Cambridge: Cambridge University Press, 1985), 393–407. I do not endorse Greenfield's view that the Geats will fall because of their weakness (405); the poem does not assume the operation of poetic justice.

8. For lines 2214–17 I have followed the very conservative text of Else von Schaubert, 18th ed. (Paderborn, Germany: Ferdinand Schöningh, 1963). The number of dots between words represents the probable number of missing or illegible letters.

9. See Theodore M. Andersson, "The Thief in *Beowulf,*" *Speculum* 59 (1984):493–508, for a thorough discussion of the episode and a very learned argument that the intruder in the dragon's barrow was a fugitive from punishment as a thief.

10. Tolkien, "Monsters," 259.

11. Ibid., 258–59.

12. Ibid., 269.

13. Ibid., 259.

14. Smithers, *The Making of "Beowulf,"* 12–16.

15. See John C. Pope, "Beowulf's Old Age," in *Philological Essays,* ed. James L. Rosier (The Hague: Mouton, 1970), 55–64 and especially 60–64, for a profound study of this speech.

16. The text for *Beowulf* 3178–82 follows Klaeber in emending the manuscript's "wyruldcyning" to "wyruldcyninga" and further accepts Malone's reading of "mannum" (to men) rather than the probable manuscript reading "manna" (of men); see Kemp Malone, "A Reading of *Beowulf* 3169–82," in

Medieval Literature and Folklore Studies, ed. Jerome Mandel and Bruce A. Rosenberg (New Brunswick, N.J.: Rutgers University Press, 1970), 37, 348 note 6.

17. Stanley B. Greenfield, *A Readable "Beowulf"* (Carbondale: Southern Illinois University Press, 1982), 114.

18. Fred C. Robinson, "Lexicography and Literary Criticism," in Rosier, ed., *Philological Essays,* 101–2. See also Robinson's *"Beowulf" and the Appositive Style,* 80–82.

19. Roberta Frank accurately observes that the Geatish riders "clearly intend to praise" and that the *"Beowulf* poet makes sure that sixth-century pagan Geats and not he describe their fallen king as *lofgeorn* . . . forcing his audience to take the word in its secular, heroic sense." Frank compares that sense of *lofgeorn* and its Old Norse cognate *lofgjarn* which has a clearly honorific force in its one appearance in the *Poetic Edda.* See her papers "Skaldic Verse and the Date of *Beowulf,"* in Chase, *The Dating of Beowulf,* 135 (first quotation); and "Old Norse Memorial Eulogies and the Ending of *Beowulf,"* *Acta* 6 (1979):12–13 (second quotation).

20. Tolkien, "Monsters," 275, 281.

21. Ibid., 281–82.

22. Tolkien, "Homecoming," 16.

23. Robinson, *Style,* 81.

24. Robinson, "Lexicography," 101, and *Style,* 81–82.

25. Stanley B. Greenfield, *The Interpretation of Old English Poems* (London: Routledge and Kegan Paul, 1972), 40–43.

26. Robinson, *Style,* 81.

27. Mary P. Richards, "A Reexamination of *Beowulf* 3180–3182," *English Language Notes* 10 (1973):165–67.

28. A. D. Horgan, "Religious Attitudes in *Beowulf,"* in *Essays and Poems Presented to Lord David Cecil,* 10–11.

29. Richard Cleasby and Gudbrand Vigfusson, *An Icelandic-English Dictionary,* 2d ed. (Oxford: Clarendon Press, 1957), 428; Finnur Jónsson, *Ordbog over det Norsk-Islandske Skjaldesprog,* 2d ed. (Copenhagen, 1931; reprint, 1966), 406.

30. See Smithers, *Making,* 18, and Paul Beekman Taylor, *"Heofon riece swealg:* A Sign of Beowulf's State of Grace," *Philological Quarterly* 42 (1963): 257–59.

Selected Bibliography

The bibliography is necessarily selective; see the notes to the several chapters for items of more specialized interest.

Primary Works

Editions

Dobbie, Elliott Van Kirk, ed. *"Beowulf" and "Judith."* New York: Columbia University Press, 1953. The scholar's best choice. No glossary; the notes and introduction aim chiefly at establishing the text.

Klaeber, Fr., ed. *Beowulf.* 3d ed., with 1st and 2d supplements. Boston: D. C. Heath, 1950. Old, but still the student's best choice. The notes, glossary, and introduction set an inspiring standard of scholarship.

von Schaubert, Else, ed. *Heyne-Schückings "Beowulf."* 18th ed. 3 vols. Paderborn, Germany: Verlag Ferdinand Schöningh, 1963. Reprints 17th edition (text, 1958; notes and glossary, 1961). Splendid, but with German apparatus.

Wrenn, C. L., ed. *"Beowulf" with the "Finnsburg Fragment."* 2d ed. London: George Harrap, 1958. 3d ed. Revised by W. F. Bolton. 1973. Wrenn introduced some interesting and valuable new readings and annotations to the text; Bolton's revisions occasionally seem incompatible with Wrenn's original, but the new version gives a sympathetic account of modern Christian readings of *Beowulf.*

Editions with Translations

Chickering, Howell D., ed. *"Beowulf": A Dual-Language Edition.* Garden City, N.Y.: Anchor Books, 1977. Excellent introduction and annotation, verse translation, a modern treatment of the text.

Swanton, Michael, ed. *Beowulf.* Manchester, England: Manchester University Press, 1978. Accurate prose translation, sparse but good commentary.

Translations

Alfred, William. *Beowulf.* In *Medieval Epics.* New York: Modern Library, 1963. Though set as prose, this sometimes seems a poetic translation and perhaps the best of them.

Crossley-Holland, Kevin. *Beowulf.* Woodbridge, England: Boydell Press, 1987. Too free perhaps, but a magnificent example of book-design and readable.

Garmonsway, G. N., Jacqueline Simpson, and Hilda Ellis Davidson. *"Beowulf" and Its Analogues.* London: J. M. Dent, 1968. A reliable translation made extremely valuable by the addition of translations of a wide range of illustrative materials.

Greenfield, Stanley B. *A Readable "Beowulf."* Carbondale: Southern Illinois University Press, 1982. A good, readable translation of the poem.

Secondary Works

Bibliographies

Anglo-Saxon England. Edited by Peter Clemoes. Cambridge: Cambridge University Press, 1972–. Annual publication with an excellent bibliography of the preceding year's work.

Bessinger, Jess B., and Robert F. Yeager. *Approaches to Teaching "Beowulf."* New York: Modern Language Association, 1984. Pages 3–30 briefly survey scholarship and criticism devoted to the poem; the "List of Works Cited" is selective but includes much useful background material.

Greenfield, Stanley B., and Fred C. Robinson. *A Bibliography of Publications on Old English Literature to the End of 1972.* Toronto: University of Toronto Press, 1980. Items 89–91, 191–205, 1628–3196A, and various items under "General Studies" deal with *Beowulf.* An extraordinarily thorough and careful bibliography.

Old English Newsletter. Edited by Paul Szarmach. Binghamton, N.Y.: Center for Medieval and Early Renaissance Studies. Issued twice yearly; an excellent annual bibliography and review of Anglo-Saxon and *Beowulf* studies.

Short, Douglas D. *"Beowulf" Scholarship: An Annotated Bibliography.* New York: Garland, 1980. The annotations make this indispensible. Useful indices.

Essay Collections on Beowulf

Chase, Colin, ed. *The Dating of "Beowulf."* Toronto: University of Toronto Press, 1981. Multiple perspectives on the problem but no conclusion on the date.

Fry, Donald K., ed. *The "Beowulf" Poet: A Collection of Essays.* Englewood Cliffs, N.J.: Prentice-Hall, 1968. A small collection with some very good choices.

Nicholson, Lewis E., ed. *An Anthology of "Beowulf" Criticism.* Notre Dame, Ind.: University of Notre Dame Press, 1963. Heavy on Christian interpretations of the poem but useful.

Books

Bonjour, Adrien. *The Digressions in "Beowulf."* Oxford: Basil Blackwell, 1950. Sometimes doctrinaire but often stimulating and acute.

Brodeur, Arthur Gilchrist. *The Art of "Beowulf."* Berkeley and Los Angeles: University of California Press, 1960. Warmly defends the poet's conscious artistry from a mechanistic reading of the oral theory and makes many good observations on the poem.

Chambers, R. W. *"Beowulf": An Introduction to the Study of the Poem.* 2d ed. Cambridge: Cambridge University Press, 1932. A classic. The third edition (1959) includes materials now out-of-date and omits some splendid plates; the second should be consulted if available.

Evans, Angela Case. *The Sutton Hoo Ship-Burial.* 2d ed. London: British Museum, 1986. A brief but up-to-date and authoritative introduction to the most important archaeological find in the history of Anglo-Saxon studies.

Goldsmith, Margaret. *The Mode and Meaning of "Beowulf."* London: Athlone Press, 1970. The most consistent and powerful of the Christian readings of the poem.

Haarder, Andreas. *"Beowulf": The Appeal of a Poem.* Copenhagen: Akademisk Forlag, 1975. Excellent introduction to the early criticism of the poem.

Irving, Edward B. *A Reading of "Beowulf."* New Haven: Yale University Press, 1968. The best modern reading of the poem as a work of art.

―――. *Rereading "Beowulf".* Philadelphia: University of Pennsylvania Press, 1989. A sensitive and acute reading of the poem as a work of traditional, essentially oral-formulaic art. This book was published after the present study was completed (in July 1988), but *Rereading "Beowulf"* is clearly an important work.

Kiernan, Kevin. *"Beowulf" and the "Beowulf" Manuscript.* Lexington: University of Kentucky Press, 1981. The central thesis is very controversial and indeed doubtful, but the book contains much useful information on the manuscript.

Niles, John N. *"Beowulf:" The Poem and Its Tradition.* Cambridge: Harvard University Press, 1983. Interesting chapters on elements of style and narration.

Robinson, Fred C. *"Beowulf" and the Appositive Style.* Knoxville: University of Tennessee Press, 1985. Promotes a stylistic feature (apposition or variation) to a theoretical model for reading the poem. The asides (especially on vows and drinking) are particularly valuable.

Shippey, T. A. *Beowulf.* London: Edward Arnold, 1978. Sprightly and original though brief. A stimulating study.

Sisam, Kenneth. *The Structure of "Beowulf."* Oxford: Clarendon Press, 1965. A misleading title, but the book contains much learning and common sense.

Smithers, G. V. *The Making of "Beowulf."* Durham, England: University of Durham, 1961. Valuable comments on the origins of *Beowulf.*

Whitelock, Dorothy. *The Audience of "Beowulf."* 2d ed. Oxford: Clarendon Press, 1958. A classic. Places the poem in the context of the Anglo-Saxon age and illuminates the age and the poem.

Parts of Books

Benson, Larry D. "The Pagan Coloring of *Beowulf.*" In *Old English Poetry: Fifteen Essays,* edited by Robert P. Creed, 193–248. Providence, R.I.: Brown University Press, 1967. A witty conjecture coupled with careful historical research, a window into the age of *Beowulf.*

Berger, Harry, Jr., and Marshall Leicester, Jr. "Social Structure as Doom: The Limits of Heroism in *Beowulf.*" In *Old English Studies in Honor of John C. Pope,* edited by Robert B. Burlin and Edward B. Irving, Jr., 37–79. Toronto: University of Toronto Press, 1974. An intriguing search for the contradictions of the heroic society.

Chadwick, Nora K. "The Monsters and Beowulf." In *The Anglo-Saxon,* edited by Peter Clemoes, 171–203. London: Bowes and Bowes, 1959. Much neglected, hard to read, deeply learned, and potentially very important. Postmodern readings of *Beowulf* will probably be much in Chadwick's debt.

Fontenrose, Joseph. "Appendix 5: The Combat in Germanic Myth and Legend." In *Python: A Study of Delphic Myth and Its Origins,* 521–44. Berkeley and Los Angeles: University of California Press, 1959. Speculative but fascinating suggestions connecting the poem and the "combat myth."

Greenfield, Stanley B. "Beowulf and the Judgement of the Righteous." In *Learning and Literature in Anglo-Saxon England,* edited by Michael Lapidge and Helmut Gneuss, 393–407. Cambridge: Cambridge University Press, 1985. A careful study of the evidence for the poem's attitude toward Beowulf in the final episode.

Pope, John C. "Beowulf's Old Age." In *Philological Essays,* edited by James L. Rosier, 55–64. The Hague: Mouton, 1970. A brilliant study of the poem's, and the hero's, close.

Robinson, Fred C. "Lexicography and Literary Criticism: A Caveat." In *Philological Essays,* edited by James L. Rosier, 99–110. The Hague: Mouton, 1970. An important comment on the poem's last word.

———. "Elements of the Marvellous in the Characterization of Beowulf: A Reconsideration of the Textual Evidence." In *Old English Studies in Honour of John C. Pope,* edited by Robert B. Burlin and Edward B. Irving, Jr., 119–37. Toronto: University of Toronto Press, 1974. An intriguing argument tending to reduce the element of the wonder-tale in *Beowulf.*

Short, Douglas D. *"Beowulf* and Modern Critical Tradition." In *A Fair Day in the Affections,* edited by Jack D. Durrant and M. Thomas Hester, 1–23. Raleigh, N.C.: Winston Press, 1980. A useful account of *Beowulf* criticism.

Stanley, E. G. "Hæthenra Hyht in *Beowulf."* In *Studies in Old English Literature,* edited by Stanley B. Greenfield, 136–51. Eugene: University of Oregon Press, 1963. A deeply learned argument hinting at Beowulf's eternal damnation.

―――. *"Beowulf."* In *Continuations and Beginnings,* edited by E. G. Stanley, 104–41. London: Nelson, 1966. A learned meditation on the appeal and excellence of the poem.

Wormald, Patrick. "Bede, *Beowulf* and the Conversion of the Anglo-Saxon Aristocracy." In *Bede and Anglo-Saxon England,* edited by R. T. Farrell, 32–89. Oxford: Basil Blackwell, 1978. A brilliant study of the age and culture that may have produced *Beowulf.*

Articles

Blomfield, Joan. "The Style and Structure of *Beowulf." Review of English Studies* 14 (1938): 396–403. An interesting attempt to define the narrative style of the poem.

Clark, George. "Beowulf's Armor." *English Literary History* 32 (1965): 409–41. The symbolism (or semiotics) of value, order, and violence in the poem.

Donahue, Charles. "Beowulf, Ireland and the Natural Good." *Traditio* 7 (1949–51):263–77. With the following item, the most congenial of the Christian readings of *Beowulf.*

―――. *"Beowulf* and Christian Tradition: A Reconsideration from a Celtic Stance." *Traditio* 21 (1965):55–116.

Frank, Roberta. "Old Norse Memorial Eulogies and the Ending of *Beowulf." Acta* 6 (1979):1–19. A valuable contribution to the study of the last word in *Beowulf.*

Halverson, John. "The World of *Beowulf." English Literary History* 36 (1969): 593–608. Reopened the discussion of the poem's social and political assumptions.

Kaske, Robert E. *"Sapientia et Fortitudo* as the Controlling Theme of *Beowulf." Studies in Philology* 55 (1958): 423–56. Overstates its case, but still a classic article much cited in later studies.

Kinney, Clare. "The Needs of the Moment: Poetic Foregrounding as a Narrative Device in *Beowulf." Studies in Philology* 82 (1985): 295–314. A new and intriguing perspective on the narrative art of the poem.

Lapidge, Michael. *"Beowulf,* Aldhelm, the *Liber Monstrorum* and Wessex." *Studi Medievali* 23 (1982): 151–92. A deeply learned and careful study urging that Wessex, Alfred's kingdom, may be the place of the poem's origin.

Leyerle, John. "Beowulf the Hero and the King." *Medium Ævum* 34 (1965): 89–102. Spells out the implications of Tolkien's brief remarks on *Beowulf* in "Homecoming" (see below).

Ringler, Richard N. *"Him seo wen geleah:* The Design for Irony in Grendel's Last Visit to Heorot." *Speculum* 41 (1966): 49–67. A brilliant study illuminating the poem and the age though directed to a single, brief passage.

Tolkien, J. R. R. *"Beowulf:* The Monsters and the Critics." *Proceedings of the British Academy* 22 (1936): 245–95. Established the modern critical paradigm.

———. "The Homecoming of Beorhtnoth, Beorhthelm's Son." *Essays and Studies,* n.s., 6 (1953):1–18. Includes brief but historically important comments on the ethos of the poem.

Whallon, William. "The Christianity of *Beowulf." Modern Philology* 60 (1962): 81–94. A hard look at the verbal evidence for the poem's religious perspective.

Subject Index

Æschere's Head, 96–97
Agnarr, as Grendel-analogue, 30
Alfred and traditional poetry, 39–40
Anglo-Saxon, early study of, 1–3, 145n11, 146n12
Audience of *Beowulf,* 16–17, 45–46, 72
Augury, practiced among the Geats, 53
Author, the, of *Beowulf,* 9, 11, 13; compared to the *Maldon poet,* 10–11
Author, the, of *Maldon,* 10
Author, the, of *Völuspá,* 11–12, 148n56

Battle in the mere, the: abrupt pace of, 99–100, 104; hero's isolation in, 104; realistic telling of, 99–101; supernatural elements in, 101–102, 103; warriors and weapons in, 101–104
Beowulf: altruism of, 134, 136, 142; and Christian ideals, 15, 16, 18; as avenger of Hygelac and Heardred, 132; as folktale hero, 29; as Hrothgar's heroic mentor, 107–108, as king and hero, 20, 134; moulded by society, 17, 20; as symbol of paganism, 14; battle with seamonsters, 64; compared to dragon, 126; to Old Norse saga heroes, 30; to Scyld, 47, 140; to Sigemund, 40–41; to Thor, 29; famous father of, 111; flaws of, 17, 20; future state of, 13, 17, 19, 149n80; in the Danish court, 54–56, 87, 105; melancholy at dragon's raids, 118; name of, 29, 48; note of triumph at funeral of, 141–42; plan for fighting the dragon, 119; pursuit of fame, 136, 141; victory over Grendel foreseen, 53–54; wisdom of, 84, 119; youthful memories of, 133. *See also,* Battle in the mere, the; Dragon-fight, the; Grendel-fight, the; Thorkell hákr

Beowulf: and Germanic paganism, 6, 14, 18; and traditional poetry, 37–42; as family history of the Wuffings, 152n26; as heroic narrative, 24–25; Biblical history in, 16; comic elements of, 67, 69; compared to Gothic art, 6; to *Maldon,* 10–11; early modern reception of, 7–8; excluded matters, 16, 45; folkloristic elements, 28–29, folktale and history in, 5, 7; influence of, 1, 2, 145n1; last word on the hero, 136–42; lyric structure of, 9, 23; modern critical paradigm for, 8–14; moral allegory in, 18–19; multiple sources of, 24; mythic elements of, 5, 6, 11, 24, 29; narrative movement of, 23–24, 51; recovery of, 3–7, 146n21; royalist bias of, 47–48; social realism of, 17, 25, 28, 49; unity of, 6, 13, 26–28, 33, 113, 122, 131; variable time-schemes of, 43, 44–46; variety in, 7, 28, 51, 133; theories of composite origin, 21–23
Beowulf I: as heroic comedy, 125; definable historical context, 114; social setting, 113–14, 115
Beowulf II: as epic tragedy, 125; composite narrative, 131; elemental setting, 114–16; indefinite historical context, 114; historical sweep of, 131–32
Beowulf-Manuscript: preservation of, 2–5
Black humor, 60, 76–77, 78
Breca story, 62–64, 155–56n38
Byrhtnoth and Beowulf compared, 12, 13, 20

Cain and popular Christianity in *Beowulf,* 46
Caedmon and traditional poetry, 39

Author Index